DATE DUE

MAR 3 1 1997	

1. DANTE GABRIEL ROSSETTI
by W. Holman Hunt

ROSALIE GLYNN GRYLLS

Portrait of Rossetti

SOUTHERN ILLINOIS UNIVERSITY PRESS
Carbondale and Edwardsville

FEFFER & SIMONS, INC.
London and Amsterdam

ARCT
URUS
BOOKS ®

AUTHOR'S NOTE

Rossetti presents more than one paradox in his character and in his career. He was an Italian who never went to Italy, a nature poet who hated the country, a mystic who became the symbol of the Fleshly School. And the movement he started as a hilarious lark—the Pre-Raphaelite Brotherhood—ended in greenery-yallery.

Some of his complexity came from his Anglo-Italian background, but it would be an over-simplification to attribute his sensuality to the Italian element and his uncomfortable conscience to English Victorian gentility, for his Tuscan ancestors were high-thinkers and plain-livers. His father was a Continental agnostic and his half-English mother an ardent church-woman of Tractarian persuasion.

Much has been written on the various aspects of Rossetti's character and of his work and, even more, about his contemporaries—and by them—in which he figures sometimes as a hero, sometimes as a villain, but always significantly: a man to be loved or hated. This book is an attempt to see the personality behind the painter and the poet, bearing in mind that last word on biography which he himself wrote on Blake:

"Any who can here find something to love will be the poet-painter's welcome guests . . . (who) can meet their host's eye with sympathy and with recognition even when he offers them the new strange fruits grown for himself in far-off gardens where he has dwelt alone . . ."

CONTENTS

ERRATA

Page 19, line 1: *For* Charlotteville *read* Charlottesville
Page 65, line 29: *For* Godstone *read* Godstow
Page 66, line 8: *For* William Jowett *read* Benjamin Jowett

ADDENDA

Page 170: "The Blessed Damozel" is now at the Fogg Museum, Cambridge, Mass.
Page 217: Mrs. Troxell's collection is now at Princeton University, Princeton, N.J.
Pages 245-47: Additional references
Hunt, Diana Holman, *Holman Hunt, His Wives and Loves*, 1969
Lutyens, Mary, *Millais and the Ruskins*, 1966

LIST OF PLATES

The author and publishers wish to thank the following for supplying illustrations: Mrs. Rossetti Angeli for 3, 13, 14, 17, 18; the Birmingham Art Gallery for 1; the British Museum for 2; the Henry E. Huntington Art Gallery and Library for 5; Mrs. Victor Kennett for 6; The Matron, The Lindens, Matlock, for 11; the late Mrs. Paul Nash for 12; the National Gallery of Scotland for 9; Mr. Kerriston Preston for 4; the Tate Gallery for 16; and the Warden of All Souls for 19. See also Acknowledgements.

PART ONE

YOUTH
1828–1856

I

He would walk along the London streets at a slow, almost slouching, pace that suddenly quickened when something aroused his interest. Then he would stop to look at it intently with his large dark eyes: hungrily, as if he wanted to devour what he saw and make it his own. "Stunner" was his word for anything that fascinated him—a beautiful woman, a striking man, or a fine view. An incongruous word, used, perhaps, like the slang of any generation, in order to hide what he felt. He wanted to put down his feelings, his reactions to life, in drawing or in verses, but often he was too impatient and would not take the trouble but hurried off to pour out what he felt in talk with his fellow-students at the Art School.

When he talked there was the same contrast in his voice between liveliness and languor as there was in his movements when he walked about the city streets, and it was this light and shade, the *chiaroscuro*, in his personality that his contemporaries found so magnetic.

The parents of Gabriel Rossetti were Anglo-Italian. His father had had his hour when a king shed tears over his verses and a mob chanted them on its revolutionary way. Now he was a refugee, harnessed to the jog-trot of language teaching at London University. The work was badly paid and exhausting, but he consoled himself with study for a *magnum opus*, which was to reveal a secret code in Dante. After him he had named his first-born son, Gabriel Charles Dante, born on 12th May, 1828.

> "And didst thou know indeed, when at the font
> Together with thy name thou gav'st me his,
> That also on thy son must Beatrice
> Decline her eyes according to her wont . . .
> Accepting me to be of those that haunt
> The vale of magical dark mysteries. . . ."

The "Charles" was for Sir Charles Lyell, an Italian scholar and father of the geologist—one of many distinguished Englishmen interested in Rossetti's studies who became his friends. Edward John Trelawny was another, introduced by Seymour Kirkup, who had been made a Barone for his services in discovering a portrait of Dante by Giotto under the whitewash in the Bargello in Florence.

When these admirers came to call at the small house in Charlotte Street (now Hallam Street) they would find themselves caught up into the foreign world of a little Italy, a cloak-and-dagger world in which talk of tyranny and liberation might refer as easily to the Florence of Dante or to their own day when King Bomba was the tyrant in Naples and the Carbonari were the red-shirted Resistance Movement. For patriots of all sorts, the *amici*, crowded into Rossetti's home, from their leader, the glamorous Mazzini, last of romantic refugees, to any passing organ-grinder welcomed in as a fellow-exile. English ladies, with the recurrent passion of the female islander for exiles from warmer climates, also came to call. One of them thrilled drawing-rooms with a tribute of her own composition:

> "Ausonia shall be free! Oh, not in vain
> Rossetti breathes his Heaven-inspired strain.
> Pindar of Italy! Thy strain shall wake
> A spirit that shall bid her tyrants shake.
> Pindar of Italy! My strain shall be
> Thy requiem of the foes of Italy."

Gabriele could draw a little, but he needed for his use sepia from the belly of the cuttle-fish or calamerello, an edible delicacy that he much missed in London.

Gabriel's mother, Frances Rossetti, was a daughter of Gaetano Polidori, who had been secretary to Count Alfieri in Paris at the time of the French Revolution. He actually saw the Bastille stormed and had a sword with blood on it thrust into his hands: "*Prenez, Citoyen, combattez pour la Patrie.*" Quickly passing it on to someone else, he made his plans to escape.

Once settled in London, Polidori did quite well by giving Italian lessons and married an English girl of genteel family, Anna Maria Pierce. One of their sons was John William, the young doctor who accompanied Byron to Switzerland on the visit when he met Shelley, and Eliza, the youngest daughter, went out to the Crimea as one of Florence Nightingale's nurses. The others, Charlotte and Maria Margaret, served terms as governesses in well-to-do aristocratic households, as did Frances Mary Lavinia before she married Gabriele Rossetti.

This training and the English blood of the Pierces developed in Mrs. Rossetti a strong sense of responsibility which strait-laced any southern exuberance into the pattern of Victorian middle-class conventionality. But she was not a rigid or a narrow woman and she kept a latin respect for intellect, which enabled her to extend to her children, equally with her husband, an intelligent understanding as well as affection.

Gabriel, always devoted to her, felt her serenity:

> "Our mother rose from where she sat:
> Her needles as she laid them down
> Met lightly, and her silken gown
> Settled: no other noise than that."

She believed in them all: they were to be scholars, painters, poets. Whether they made any money at it or not, did not matter. Together, in their shabby home, oppressed by grey skies and poverty, both Rossetti parents yet considered themselves blessed. "A hundred times," declared the old professor, "a hundred times do I thank God that my children are all studious and all good."

Gabriel, as he was usually called, enjoyed a happy childhood in spite of the straitened circumstances of his home and the emotional stresses of his own temperament. He had a younger brother, William Michael, and two sisters, Maria and Christina. William and Maria were the "calms", Gabriel and Christina the "storms"—the cyclothymic temperaments. From earliest childhood they all wrote verses or drew pictures: their greatest treat to fill in with colour the old theatrical prints that could be bought at bookshops for a halfpenny each. Gabriel, at six, composed a play, *The Slave*, for the rest of the family to act; at eleven he made drawings to illustrate Maria's copy of *The Iliad*; and at thirteen his narrative poem, *Sir Hugh the Heron*, was printed by grandfather Polidori on his private press. All four children put together a weekly paper, *Hodge-Podge*, succeeded by *The Illustrated Scrapbook*. As they shared the same tastes, no one was bored or left out, frustrated or under-privileged.

The girls kept up with the boys' interests when they went to school. Maria started Greek in order to read *The Iliad* with them, and when a prize was offered for a patriotic poem on China (it was the time of the Opium War) Christina composed one with the classic couplet:

> "Come, cheer up, my lads, 'tis to glory we steer,"
> As the soldier remarked whose post lay in the rear.

Great names in art and literature, both English and Italian, were as familiar to them as if they were elderly relations. As soon as they could look at pictures, they got to know the copies of Dante and the Bible and Shakespeare that lay about the shabby room, expurgated but lavishly illustrated.

A usual walk was over to the Zoological Gardens in Regent's Park, less well-stocked then and much less well-kept but still of absorbing interest to children. The favourites of the family were a singing antelope ("but he never sang"), the armadilloes and a sloth. Gabriel, always fond of out-of-the-way animals, was very pleased with himself when he managed to keep a dormouse alive through the winter in a drawer: less pleased were his parents when he gave his hedgehog some beer to drink and it reeled obscenely about the dining-room table.

His first letter to his mother, written when he was eight years old, is already characteristic.

> September 13th, 1836.
> "I am very glad to hear the news that you are so much better. A Tortoise puss yesterday, while our birds were in the garden, came in and, as I guess, to kill them. and we are going to hang them up in another part of the yard, where the wretch, as Fitch (man-of-all-work) terms that puss, cannot get at them. In the meantime we keep them in the back parlour . . . on Monday Pappa and myself dined at Mr. Sangiovannis. the sign of the Public house is changed into the Red Lion.
>
>   love to all and I
>   remain Your loving
>   Gabriel Charles Dante Rossetti."[1]

2

The boys first went daily to a small school in nearby Foley Street and then later to King's College School, to which their father as a professor had a right to send his sons at reduced fees. They walked to school along the side-streets of Tottenham Court Road and Cambridge Circus, so that from a small boy Gabriel learnt to know and to love the city streets. The school was an enlightened institution in advance of its time in its abolition of flogging and its teaching of other subjects besides the classics, but Gabriel was thoroughly bored there, finding nothing that he needed for mind or spirit to feed upon. Nor did he show any sign of the magnetism which was to make him a leader among his fellows. He and his brother, coming from such a different background, must have felt themselves outsiders among the other boys, and throughout life, where Gabriel could not shine, he would withdraw.

For Gabriel the real world was not at school nor in the London streets, but far away in the past with the Greeks of the Trojan War and the knights of the Middle Ages. He had soon found for himself an un-bowdlerized edition of Shakespeare and enlivened the classics with Monk Lewis and Scott. With Keats he thought poetry had ended, for there was no more to say; then he discovered Blake's *Songs of Innocence* and *Experience*, and then found two "stunners" of his own day, Tennyson and Browning. He devoured *Paracelsus* and *Sordello*, managing to digest their obscurity with a robust, youthful appetite. When he found *Pauline*, then anonymous, and recognised it for Browning's work, he wrote to the poet and received a friendly reply, admitting the authorship.

Staying in Boulogne, where he had been sent for his health, at fifteen, to the family of the Maenzas, Italian refugees, he wrote back home about the son: "I find that Peppino's tastes coincide in every respect with mine. He draws splendidly and is very fond of poetry, specially Byron."

But, as he grew up, perhaps because every young man must discover his own Father-figure, the poet whose work influenced him most immediately was the now forgotten Ebenezer Jones. His poems were to Rossetti what the sonnets of the Reverend William Lisle Bowles had been to Wordsworth and Coleridge.

Another enthusiasm was for *Joseph and His Brethren* by Charles Wells which persisted till he succeeded in securing its re-publication in 1877. He also bought eagerly the parts of *Vates* as they appeared; a romance by Dr. T. Gordon Hake afterwards entitled *Valdarno or the Ordeal of Art Worship*.

Following these "illustrious obscure" he came upon the work of an-other man who would be forgotten now if it were not for what he wrote of Rossetti in his autobiography—William Bell Scott.[2] His "Rosabell" so excited Gabriel that he wrote off to him to ask for more and enclosed some work of his own for criticism—a not unusual pattern of procedure for young poets, except that in this case the manuscripts included a first draft of *The Blessed Damozel*.

Scott, a north-countryman of thirty-five, was the younger brother of David Scott, whose disappointments in art rival those of Haydon. At this time he was in Newcastle as Master of one of the new Government Schools of Design on the recommendation of James Leathart, a cultured industrialist there. He was beginning also to establish himself with the Trevelyans at Wallington, but he was glad enough to accept the un-expected homage from Charlotte Street and called there when he came to London. William Michael thought him a "handsome, highly-impressive-looking man" and the Rossetti ladies also found him possessed of some personal charm, which certainly does not come through in his writings and letters, though conveyed in his brother's Byronic portrait of him. More will be heard of Scott later on, for he had a part to play at crucial stages in Rossetti's life.

But Gabriel drew more than he wrote and showed enough talent at it for the family to decide that he was to be the painter of the family and must therefore start training. He was not yet fifteen when he was sent to Sass's Art Academy in Bloomsbury, run by Francis Stephen Cary, a son of the translator of Dante. Every Saturday it was visited by Samuel Redgrave of *The Dictionary of Painters*' fame and enjoyed a high reputation for getting its pupils into the Academy.

But Rossetti found Sass's nearly as boring as school, for the teaching consisted solely in copying plaster casts. He would enliven his sheets of these with a frieze of grotesque figures in the margin, much upsetting Redgrave, who protested that "such liberties were hardly consistent with the dignity of the antique". Rossetti desisted when he felt more like writing sonnets anyway—and pasting them on bits of paper inside the tall hats of the other pupils. When he did not want to draw or to write he would throw back his dark head and sing "Alice Gray" at the top of his voice.

His attendance at Sass's was not very regular, but in July, 1846, he was sent on to the Royal Academy Schools. Here the teaching was no more imaginative, for First Year students were still confined to the Antique but, if the work was dull, the pupils' criticism of it and of the Academy tradition was lively (a perennial argument for conventional education) and in this Gabriel took a leading part. He was no longer the stranger that he had been among schoolboys: his Italian background was "romantic" and therefore an asset, and a rumour going round that he had had some poems published gave him added prestige. The warmth of the atmosphere brought him out. He found the others ready to listen to him and to wait on his pronouncements, to praise what he praised and mock what he mocked, so that the misfit became a leader. This late development of his charm meant that, even when Rossetti was fully conscious of his powers and put a high price on them, he remained always a little surprised at the attraction he had for other people. His loyalty to those to whom he owed gratitude and his generosity are his most endearing traits, but there was danger for the future in the development of so strong a personal mag-netism. Among his close friends of those days one whose name has survived was the handsome Walter Howell Deverell. He was born in

October, 1827, in Charlotteville, Virginia, where his father was a professor at the newly-founded University. When the family returned to England in 1829[3], Walter was articled to a solicitor but he managed to free himself and in December, 1846, was admitted to the Royal Academy Schools.

His mother sympathised enough with his artistic ambitions to make sure that other members of the family kept out of the way when Walter brought home fellow-students. It may well have been at his house, therefore, that Rossetti first proposed forming an association to circulate their drawings and their poems, for an early letter refers to "the old sketching club job" which one of their set called Compton wanted to revive. "For my part were there a prospect of its continuance I should feel disposed to join."[4] He then goes on to protest that his proposed translation of the *Nibelungen Lied* can hardly be expected to be now ready when there are forty Cantos of it. He is glad they agree on Leigh Hunt and ends by enquiring: "Are you doing anything in the literary way?"

He could be arbitrary, flinging in and out of his friends' "cribs", but he got away with it. Collinson wrote to Hunt: "I have seen Rossetti once since I came here; he came in one morning early about three months ago, turned over a portfolio, took liberties with everything in the room, gave a few vigorous shouts and said, 'I say, I shall cut' and so retired."[5]

Still eager for books, he used to go to the British Museum Reading Room, and one day an attendant in the Antique Gallery, William Palmer,[6] brother of Samuel, showed him a small manuscript book that had belonged to Blake. He offered to sell it for ten shillings. Gabriel rushed off to obtain the money from brother William.

The manuscript book is now one of the most precious of Blake relics, for it had originally belonged to his brother Robert and was, therefore, treasured by Blake who wrote and drew in it for over thirty years. The luck of Rossetti in being offered the book has suggested some mystical connection between the two painter-poets, for Rossetti was born exactly nine months after Blake's death and was to be connected with writing his biography years later.

But there were other experiences to be sought besides reading and drawing. He went further afield in London now, discovering Chelsea and, at the Pleasure Gardens of Cremorne, seeing a side of life from which he had been sheltered at home—those temptations and tragedies of the streets which were always to haunt him, as he was to show in his poem "Jenny" and the picture "Found".

> "Our learned London children know
> Poor Jenny, all your pride and woe."

When he walked about now and stopped to look at "stunners", he wanted to see them stripped and at one and the same time to see them attired in rich costumes accepting homage from knightly lovers. And if the *boulevardier* and the medievalist were in conflict with each other, so was the governess's son with both of them. He knew that he ought not to be talking or wandering the streets when he should be working at pictures that would bring in the money so badly needed at home, but the hours he spent walking about and talking and the books he read and the pictures he looked at were not wasted: he was not killing time but looking for something.

It was in this receptive mood that he went one day in March to the Free Exhibition, which let wall space to any artist who wanted to hire it. Here was showing a picture by Ford Madox Brown—"Wickliffe Reading his Translation of the Bible to John of Gaunt". Rossetti was struck by the full force of a new revelation. Here were colours bright and clear in contrast to the toneless, muddy shades used by fashionable contemporaries. This was what he had been waiting for. Here was a master. Full of enthusiasm, he went home and wrote off to Madox Brown—like another Shelley to Godwin—pouring out what he felt about the pictures and begging to be taken on as his pupil.

3

Ford Madox Brown, warm-tempered and prone to take offence, was not going to be insulted by some impertinent youth mocking him. Neglect and poverty and more than a fair share of troubles might have come his way in his twenty-six years, but they had not broken his spirit and anyone who tried to be clever or funny at his expense would soon find the laugh was on the other cheek. He seized a large knobbed walking-stick and strode over to Charlotte Street.

The sight of so indignant a figure on their doorstep must have astonished the mild Rossettis, but their mother was equal to the occasion and calmed him down. As soon as Gabriel himself appeared, his manner proved beyond a doubt that his letter had been written in entire sincerity. The encounter which began so inauspiciously was destined to bring nothing but good to both sides. Madox Brown agreed to accept Gabriel as a pupil in his studio, refusing to take any fee, for the shabbiness of the rooms must have shown him that the family would be hard put to it to pay, and perhaps from some presage of closer links to come, for in his relationship with the Rossetti household Madox Brown was to find exactly the balm that his spirit needed. It may not have been broken, but it had been severely bruised by the buffetings life had dealt it.

Only two years before his young wife had fallen into a decline and died on the way back from a visit to Italy (a recurrent fate from which nobody in the early nineteenth century ever drew the moral. Shelley could write of Rome:

> ". . . . at once the Paradise
> The Grave, the city and the wilderness"

but take no notice of his own warning). He was left with a baby daughter, Lucy, to care for.

Brown had been brought up on the Continent, trained in various Art schools in Belgium and Holland, and had sold a few pictures there. He had also worked in Paris, where his picture, "Parisina's Sleep", managed to shock the *Salon*, though afterwards innocuously exhibited in London at the British Institution. But for its future influence the most important outcome of his contacts abroad was his meeting in Rome with the German primitive painters, Overbeck and Cornelius; the "Nazarenes".

They had founded in 1810 a new school of Catholic Art in revolt against the accepted standards of the day. This aimed at putting some moral into the story that a picture told and in technique wanted a return to bright, primitive colours and firm outlines. With this had gone the intention to found a brotherhood of working artists and craftsmen, but all that was left of this ideal in 1845 was the long black-girdled habit in which Overbeck received visitors. The impression, however, made on the young Englishman by one of Cornelius's pictures standing on its easel was not to be effaced: "full of action and strange character . . . it was everything reverse of that dreadful commonplace into which art on the Continent seems to be hurrying back. "

When he started on his career in London, Brown found a studio in the backwater of Clipstone Street, and with a very small private income and no reputation from the Art Schools to back him, set to work. At this time he looked considerably older than his twenty-six years, with as marked an expression of deep-seated gloom as his emigrant in "The Last of England". That this lightened afterwards, although he remained "touchy", was due in large part to the influence of the Rossetti household, where serenity somehow overcame care and poverty, and to the encouragement of Gabriel with his tonic admiration.

Accepted as a pupil, Rossetti scribbled a note to Deverell that he was working "all day and every day. See you at Club on Saturday whither I hope this time to drag Hancock and Munro". Not that the pupillage went according to plan. Madox Brown believed in a discipline as dull as the schools and more rigorous. He was very much the music master who insists on the drudgery of scales before any "piece" can be attempted; in this case, the copying of a collection of pots and pickle-jars. This did not suit Gabriel at all and he was in an awkward position, for, having got his own way, he could no longer malinger as he had done at the Academy, and without other students there was no distraction in gossip and joking. Besides, the more he saw of Madox Brown, the more he liked and admired him, both as a man and as a painter. As was so often to happen, affection complicated the conflict in Gabriel's mind between duty and inclination.

In this case he was to resolve it easily enough by his flair for manipulating personal relationships. He became a friend rather than a pupil to the older painter: laughed at his malapropisms with people's names ("Bothwell" for "Boswell" was one of them); sat to him for the head of Chaucer in his picture, "Chaucer at the Court of Edward III", and read aloud his own poems for criticism and appreciation as he wrote them. Somehow Brown found himself proposing that Rossetti should vary his copying of the "pickle jars" by attending a Life Class at Heatherley's and raised no objection when he relinquished them altogether in favour of lessons in perspective from an Academy Schools contemporary, William Holman Hunt. Rossetti had seen his "Eve of St. Agnes" at the Academy and praised it in no uncertain terms—indeed so loudly and with such a foreign lack of restraint that Hunt had been considerably embarrassed.

He had not been able to refuse, however, when Rossetti begged for his advice—nor when he disregarded it and started on a definite picture long before he was really ready. Not nearly enough scales had prepared the way for the piece—and Rossetti was to regret it for the rest of his painting life. The personality of the man had scored a triumph at the expense of the artist.

But here now it was 1848; one *Annus Mirabilis* in Rossetti's life and the Year of Revolutions. Not that he bothered much about what was happening on the Continent nor with the Chartists at home, but left it to Hunt to take Millais as far as Kennington Common to see the Chartist petition, and to his father and his fellow exiles to rejoice at the defiance that the hated Austrians were meeting all round and to build castles in the air to which they would make a triumphant return. William was moved to write a sonnet on the Hungarian revolt called "The Evil under the Sun", to which his brother replied with "Not neath the altar, *only*", later entitled "Vox Ecclesiae, vox Christi", and also contributed to the cause "At the sun-rise in 1848" and "On the refusal of aid between nations". But on the whole Rossetti was typical of a second-generation refugee: he wanted to be regarded as an out-and-out Londoner, as his sometimes excessive use of Cockney slang shows. It must have been out of a loyal affection for his parents that it was the "Charles" he now dropped from his sonorous Christian names and not the "Dante".

Now, at twenty, the literary and the art worlds were his to conquer: he could paint and he could write, turning from one to the other as he felt like it or combining them in sonnets on his pictures. He knew other poets and painters of his own age and had made contact with some of his heroes: in literature Leigh Hunt (who, from sad experience, advised against a literary career), Browning and William Bell Scott; while in art, he had the freedom of Madox Brown's studio and of Holman Hunt's—a Father-figure and a Friend. What could any young man want more?

4

Holman Hunt, a few months older and shy, who had watched Rossetti, "centre of a clamorous throng", from a distance at the Schools, now found himself caught up in his train. He was dragged out by the gesticulating figure in an old dark overcoat gone brown in its shabbiness to take long walks on moonlight nights to spot "stunners", or to row in the afternoons on the river, which always attracted Rossetti, although he left it to others to do the work in the boat.

Once, like Shelley challenging the passengers in the coach to sit upon the floor and tell sad stories of the deaths of kings, Rossetti waiting for a penny-steamer vehemently addressed Southey's lines to a shoe-black:

"Shall the tyrant live for ever and the bloody priesthood reign?"

When the boy looked up speechless with astonishment, a young mechanic standing by called out: "What the hell's the use of asking him? You don't jolly well know yourself."

Rossetti's roar of laughter at this, said Val Prinsep, who told the story, "was a thing to hear".

They would go to the gallery at theatres and drop in at the "cribs" of friends. Several of them together would take a chop in cheap eating-houses or sit over cups of coffee in smoke-filled rooms, poring over the latest volume of engravings any one of them had contrived to buy or to borrow. They formed a Cyclographic Club to circulate their drawings for mutual criticism and at some point there was another club for cir-culating sonnets as well as drawings, as letters to Deverell and to Hunt show. To Hunt, whose criticism he much valued, he admitted there was a "hotness" in his verses, "a certain want of repose and straining after original modes of expression." [7] About meetings of the club he explains that when he suggested Christina should join, he did not mean that she should attend: that "would bring her to a pitch of nervousness infinitely beyond Collinson's". She will not even allow her brother to read out her poems for her: "under the impression that it would seem like display, I believe—a sort of thing she abhors".[7]

These societies soon broke up and were little more than excuses for getting together so that Rossetti could lead the talk into the small hours in his rich, beautiful voice. With fine embellishments from Blake—"Sir Sloshua" for Reynolds delighted them—they attacked the Academy tradition and made outrageous plans to overthrow it, shock the public and become famous themselves.

Among these friends were some whose names are still known, some now forgotten: Alexander Munro, James Smetham, Walter Deverell, Arthur Hughes, Charles Collins (brother of Wilkie), George Boyce, John Hancock, H. T. Wells, W. Cave Thomas, Robert Lowes Dickinson, and young writers like John Tupper (no relation to Martin), James Hannay, and Coventry Patmore, though he had already had work published. It is right to jumble them up like this, for any of them might have happened to be with Rossetti on the evening when the new movement was born.

Some club was already in existence in 1847, as a letter to Deverell shows:

"Have you managed to get hold of any other members? I vote that we organize a press-gang. You and I, you know, as originators of the scheme would form ourselves into a committee and eschew active service: so (between ourselves) should we avoid rebuffs and punches on the head."

Other associations that had been planned with Deverell might have "taken" but they didn't and it was this one which was to make history:

when chance brought together as its founders, Rossetti, Holman Hunt and Millais. Poles apart in everything, Hunt (poor, odd-looking and *gauche*) and Millais (the darling of the Schools, handsome and comfortably off) maintained their friendship despite vicissitudes. "If Rossetti will only work," wrote Madox Brown to Hunt, "you will form a trio which will play a great part in English art in spite of Egg's predictions."

The actual date of the formation of the Pre-Raphaelite Brotherhood cannot be positively given, but the occasion is known. It was sometime in September, 1848, when Rossetti and Hunt went to Millais' family home in Gower Street[8] to look at Lasinio's engravings of the Campo Santo frescoes in Pisa. Lasinio's work was called "execrable" by Ruskin, but enough came through of the original masterpiece to inspire those young men with enthusiasm for the medieval. This was greatly stimulated for Rossetti when he discovered Keats would have agreed. "He seems to have been a glorious fellow," he wrote, on reading Monckton Milnes' *Life of Keats*, "and says in one place (to my great delight) that having just looked over a folio of the first and second schools of Italian painting, he has come to the conclusion that some of the early men surpassed even Raphael himself."

Although, wise after the event, we know the movement was to have its place in history, it was at the time much like any other that is formed any term at any University. It was started as a lark, or whatever may be the current slang of the time, and kept going from some unacknowledged need to hold fast the unrelenting minute, to bank up the fires of mutual admiration against a colder world outside. And it followed the usual course: run with a fervour only equalled by casualness and inevitably breaking up as those who started it were the first to outgrow it, but keeping the loyalty of lesser spirits. Like a faded College photograph it was to represent for ever after a moment of communication achieved, a brush of eagle's feather. In this case there was no group photograph, but the eagle was Rossetti. As Madox Brown told the story in his old age: "Of course it was Rossetti who kept things going by his talking, or it wouldn't have lasted as long as it did, and he really talked them into founding it."

There were not enough Brothers to startle the world and in his exuberance Rossetti brought in William (who had attended Art School for a little and was not at all a bad draughtsman) and James Collinson, guaranteed to be a "born stunner" on the strength of his "Charity Boy". To these Hunt replied with a protégé of his own, Frederic James Stephens, not much of a painter but a talker, "the rhetorical cripple", and two sculptors, Alexander Munro and Thomas Woolner, who had been a pupil of Behnes and had already exhibited in public. Hunt then declared that the ranks must be closed. Poor Charles Collins was broken-hearted at his exclusion, which was indeed hard as he was to be one of those most savagely attacked by the critics. Walter Deverell, who was closer to Rossetti than any of the others, for he shared his literary interests, was also omitted, and so was Arthur Hughes, for long a faithful friend to them all.

The movement never clearly defined its aims. Mainly it was Anti: against the enervating influence of Raphael's followers down to contemporary Academicians with their trivial sentimentality and glossy surfaces; against the neglect of moral subject-matter and whatever obscured primary colours and definite outline on the canvas. Some strangely forward-looking ideas that were never developed appear in a statement by Stephens on what was lacking in contemporary art:

"There is something else we miss: there is the poetry of the things about us: our railways, factories, mines, roaring cities, steam vessels, and the endless novelties and wonders produced every day.... In reference to Painting, the public are taught to look with delight upon murky old masters, with dismally demoniac trees, and dull waters of lead, colourless and like ice, upon rocks that make geologists wonder, their angles are so impossible, their fractures so new."[9]

In technique they believed in painting with a bold free-hand sweep of the brush, at the same time demanding minute attention to detail. An older painter, like Dyce, was already doing much the same thing, but he can hardly be considered an influence, and Madox Brown, offered by Rossetti to the others as a ready-made *chef d'école*, was never accepted as such, nor wanted to be. It was his innovation of painting on to a prepared ground of white while still wet that was the movement's main contribution to British art, but no one bothered to stress this at the time or to formulate a theory about it.

In subject the two divergent streams were myth and social realism; the fantasies of medieval or Christian legends and contemporary scenes pointing a moral. Thus pictures as different as Millais' "Sir Isumbras at the Ford" and Brown's "Work", Burne-Jones' "King Cophetua and the Beggar Maid", Bell Scott's "Iron and Coal" are all of the company. The social realism was stressed by Holman Hunt, who had studied *Modern Painters* and under its influence declared that "Art should be a handmaid in the cause of Justice and Beauty"; and the nostalgic elements were largely contributed by Rossetti, from his enthusiasm for Malory and Dante, although he did not neglect the moral problems of the time.

Live issues vary from generation to generation: in our own day they may be said to be the Colour Bar and the Bomb. For the Pre-Raphaelites there were two others: poverty and prostitution. With poverty was bound up the attitude to work—its nobility—preached by Ruskin and, later with a varied emphasis, by William Morris. There was also a strong feeling for the pathos of middle-class poverty as shown in pictures like Martineau's "Last Day in the Old Home" or Madox Brown's "The Last of England". The falling-in of mortgages and the failure of banks is a favourite theme in novels of the time, hardly to be understood by a generation brought up on Hire Purchase and Limited Liability.

The other live issue was that of prostitution. Concern here was less for its social aspect than for the personal: regret for lost innocence and a belief that repentance was desirable and rescue possible. The classic Magdalen in modern dress is Hunt's "The Awakened Conscience", which he later accused Rossetti of plagiarising in "Found."* At the time Rossetti wrote openly to Hunt in Jerusalem in 1855 that anyone might well think this, "but not yourself, as you know I have long had in view subjects taking the same direction as my present one".[10] To which Hunt replied generously, if with some of the sanctimoniousness which was to grow upon him: "I could wish we were all employed about such subjects if there be any power in a simple representation by Art of such terrible incidents, wherein the guilty see the angels sorrowing for them to lead the unstained to guard their innocence."[10]

Rossetti felt strongly on the Magdalen theme; besides "Found", begun when he was twenty-five, but never finally completed throughout his life—a moral there in itself—there were also his Magdalens at the house of Simon, the "Gate of Memory" and "Hesterna Rosa".

The movement had a literary ancestry in the Romantic Revival. There was no Byronism in it, but Keats was an influence accepted by them all. There was also a Wordsworthian element in the attention to natural detail and to "homely" settings (the equivalent of his "everyday speech"), but this was unacknowledged, and Rossetti, for one, always "grudged him every vote he gets".

The Brothers went their way not unduly worried about their opposing aims—except perhaps Hunt, but that was later and from personal jealousy. At this time he wanted nothing better than to keep within Rossetti's orbit.

The only manifesto they issued was a haphazard list of Immortals—the names of those characters in history whom they considered to be both great and good. Christ and Shelley were included and, from con-

* See Appendix A, pp. 221–4.

temporaries, Haydon, Mrs. Browning and Thackeray, but not Dickens—
no doubt omitted, as was Ruskin, entirely from inadvertence.

Rossetti amused himself designing innumerable monograms of the
magic letters P.-R.B., and insisted that the pictures they were to send in
to next year's Academy must be signed with this and nothing else—a
heritage perhaps of his father's conspiratorial tendencies. He scribbled
off heaps of notes making dates to meet for "grub", to sit for each other,
to borrow "tin" or costumes or background drapes. "Be a good P.-R.B.
and . . ." do some job or other is a constant theme.

On one occasion six pieces of a monk's costume are to be found by
Stephens and sent off to him in the country: "The housekeeper would
get it all wrong." And on another Hunt asks "Stephie" to go to his
studio to set out pictures for the Brownings to see when Mrs. Patmore
brings them in his absence:

"I request that you will oblige me by marching over to Chelsea and
so arranging the pictures that they will not merely present a reflection
of the window panes and bars. With P.-R.B. thanks for your criticism
which determines me to repaint the Coptic's head."[11]

Later on this Brotherliness was very valuable, for W. M. Rossetti
and Stephens came to occupy strategic positions as critics and could be
relied upon for sympathetic notices. The secret society elements included help to friends who fell on evil days and Rossetti never ceased to
be generous in recommending the work of friends to his own patrons.

5

Rossetti enthusiastically introduced the Brothers and his family to each
other. When Hunt was brought to dinner, he was much embarrassed
at a background so different from his own English suburbia or the Millais'
gracious living in Gower Street. He found he had to tackle macaroni
and appear as unconcerned as the others who sat eating at their dinner-
table in the middle of the room while their father and his friends held
forth in Italian by the fireplace, jumping up in excitement or thumping
on the floor to make their points.

Amongst other of the students who went to Charlotte Street was
James Collinson. He became engaged to Christina, an event which is
only of interest now for her reactions to it, but there must have been
more to Collinson than is suggested by the jokes of the others about him

as a fat boy always falling asleep. His picture of "St. Elizabeth of Hungary" is so very derivative in its Early-Christian angularity that it provides little evidence of original talent, but two small portraits in oils of Maria and Christina indicate that his inclusion in the Brotherhood was not unjustified.

In order to paint, although he still slept at home, Rossetti made arrangements to share the studio that Hunt had taken at 7, Cleveland Street, Fitzroy Square. It was a first room of their own for both young painters and filled them with desire for better designs in furniture and materials. They railed against the fussy contorted patterns of the time and longed for a return to an epoch of plainer taste, when honest materials were hand-made and vegetable dyed and flowed in natural lines, whether in furnishings or women's clothes. But decoration was a secondary matter that could wait: their present job was to get on with the paintings that had to be sent in to the Academy Exhibition in May.

Rossetti's move into Hunt's studio to work on his "Girlhood of Mary Virgin" meant a considerable interference with Hunt's finishing of "Christian Missionaries pursued by Druids". The draping of the garments worn by the Virgin would not come right, nor would the child angel. The infant models naturally fidgeted after a few minutes' posing, and when Rossetti shouted at them, burst into tears. This threw him into an "Italian" passion of temper when he would storm about the room and throw his palette on the ground, making more noise than the child. Hunt would restore order but at the cost of much working time and nervous strain to himself.

Painting and writing and talk at the same time: such was the pattern of Rossetti's twenty-first year and he had energy for all of it. 1848 was for preparing the attack when the P.-R.B. paintings would burst upon an unsuspecting public and take the Academy by storm, which, oddly enough, they did.

But it was not to be at once. In 1849 Hunt and Millais received good notices for their pictures in the Academy, and so did Rossetti for "The Girlhood of Mary Virgin", all of them signed with the initials P.-R.B. Rossetti had decided to send in "The Girlhood" not to the Academy but to the Free Exhibition that opened a month earlier, no doubt influenced by Madox Brown's having shown there. He sold the picture to the Marchioness of Bath, his Aunt Charlotte's employer, for eighty guineas: she sent him sixty at first, but by tact and charm he raised it by twenty without giving offence.

On the proceeds of this and the one hundred and sixty guineas that

Hunt had been paid for "Rienzi", they went off to Paris, Holland and Belgium together—a visit mostly remarkable for the lack of any inspiration it provided and the banality of Rossetti's sonnets on his preference for England: "healthy wench".

> "A million Parisians:
> Cast up, they'll make an Englishman—perhaps."

In Paris they were home-sick for the Brothers:

> "Woolner and Stephens, Collinson, Millais,
> And my first brother, each and every one,
> What portion is theirs now beneath the sun
> Which even, as here, in England makes today.
>
> Meanwhile Hunt and myself race at full speed
> Along the Louvre, and yawn from school to school,
> Wishing worn-out those masters known as old,
> And no man asks of Browning: though indeed
> (As the book travels with me) any fool
> Who would might hear Sordello's story told."

When they returned, the idea was mooted of a communal studio in Cheyne Walk, at No. 16. "P.-R.B." on the door might be taken to mean "Please Ring Bell" said William Michael, but the idea fell through, and Rossetti installed himself at No. 72 Newman Street with Henry T. Wells and Lowes Dickinson. The studio had a Dancing Academy underneath which they called the "Hop Shop". All set to work on pictures for next year's exhibition. Models were still a difficulty and so were drapes, but in this case it would not matter, for, Gabriel told his brother, "the Virgin is to be in bed but without any bedclothes on, an arrangement which may be justified in consideration of the hot climate". A companion picture to it was to be "The Death of the Virgin", painted completely in white.

The tenancy came to a sudden end. One evening several of the Brothers had assembled to meet the visiting American poet-painter Buchanan Read, afterwards equally famous for his "Sheridan's Ride" as a poem and a picture. Read brought a friend with him and after frugal fare, but what Hunt calls "a lively and merry feast for the soul", the two Americans jumped to their feet and delivered set speeches of considerable solemnity on the importance of good Anglo-American relations.

"As I recall this unexpected outburst, I can see Walter Deverell—overcome with astonishment . . . Comparative silence followed, and the remark was made that the landlord and his people were singularly quiet; and Rossetti added that he had seen no one all day. Investigations proved that the house was deserted and that the terpsichorean hall was blank and drear." In a word, the landlord had flitted, which meant under the law of the day that his tenants' goods could be seized to pay his debts. "Even the transatlantic guests were converted into 'moon-lighters' as everyone seized some object of furniture to carry away to Madox Brown's studio; all between 1 and 2 in the morning!"[12]

But painting and writing poems were not enough for Rossetti's energies. He felt an overwhelming urge to express himself in action, to make the world listen to what he had to say. He suggested that the Brothers should launch a magazine to make their ideas known and hasten the revolution in art for which they stood. The authors among their friends were enlisted: Bell Scott, John Tupper, Christina, who was persuaded that there was no "display" in an anonymous appearance in print. There were two poems from Woolner (who to the end of his career went in for writing—and publishing—his verses), a sonnet by Madox Brown, and one from Deverell called "The Sight Beyond". Coventry Patmore, rather a scoop, contributed "The Seasons" in three stanzas but, disappointingly, insisted on being anonymous. Deverell was to approach Chapman and Hall to publish, but in the end they fell back on the Tuppers' father. Everything was to be orderly and efficient as Rossetti planned it. They "must always," he wrote to Stephens, "keep a no. in advance of the prints . . . for my part, it is my opinion that we may now make a very stunning thing indeed of this magazine, if we only like, and that it ought to be rightly stuck to . . . Now, do you not think that, just this time, the presence of a stray Tupper or so would be more than usually advisable? . . ." [13]

What was it to be called? Various titles were suggested, and "Thoughts towards Nature" decided upon when Cave Thomas had the idea of "The Germ". There was also a question whether to add "A publication conducted by artists". Rossetti wrote to Hunt on this: "I think this would be very useful myself as giving the thing a distinctive character and also acquiring to it the advantage of what celebrity our pictures may obtain. Stephens sides with me but Woolner is very much against it . . ."[13]

Like undergraduates of any other generation, they circularised famous people, in this case Lord John Russell and Peel, bombarded the press with copies, and themselves called on well-known bookshops with parcels of "The Germ" under their arms. They also stood outside the Academy to hand them out. What is unusual is the amount of notices they received: reviews appeared in "The Art Journal", "The Dispatch", "John Bull" (running under different colours then), "The Morning Chronicle", "The Spectator".

Also unusual is the amount of promise kept. In "The Germ" appeared Christina's poem "Dreamlands" and the poems of Rossetti's on which his general reputation is still based—from "The Blessed Damozel" to those runners-up as anthology pieces, "My Sister's Sleep" and "Sea Limits". His story, "Hand and Soul", also appeared there—an anecdote of an imaginary Italian painter from which much is quotable to point his own biography. He dashed it off one night between 2 a.m. and 7 a.m.: "in composition" he said of it later, "a sort of spiritual Turner among whose hills one ranges and in whose waters one strikes out at unknown liberty".[14]

To anticipate the fate of "The Germ"; the first issue appeared in January, 1850, and others in February, March and April with the name changed to "Art and Poetry", and the sub-title "Conducted principally by Artists" added; but it failed to cover expenses and was reluctantly dropped. The Brothers could laugh at its failure. Rossetti described the evening of its obsequies in a sonnet to Christina called "St. Wagnes Eve":

> "By eight the coffee was all drunk. At nine
> We gave the cat some milk. Our talk did shelve
> 'Ere ten to gasps and stupor. Helpless grief
> Made, towards eleven, my inmost spirit pine."

The Tuppers had to foot the immediate bill, though in the end William Michael paid a larger share than anyone else. George Tupper wrote to Stephens (10th May, 1850):

> "We are to meet to overhaul the accounts on Tuesday evening. I trust you will manage somehow or other to be present for without a staunch *backer* (Mind this is not a pun) in business matters like yourself, it will be impossible for me to prevent the meeting degenerating into a Poetico-spouting-railing-trolloping-mistifying-smoke-scandal . . . *ergo* be imperative-President—I beseech you . . ."[15]

This is signed *Princeps Juvenis*, some private P.-R.B. joke. And on 9th September, 1852, he had to write again that he was being pressed for payment by his father, "the Governor":

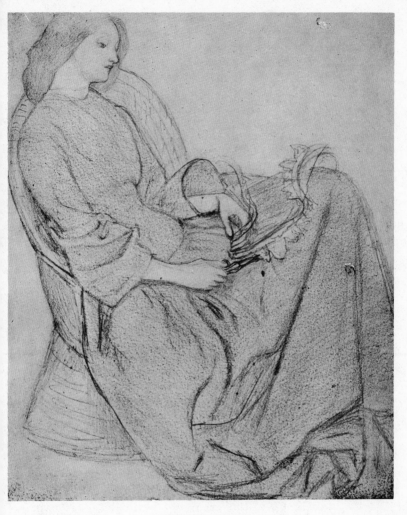

2. ELIZABETH SIDDAL
by D. G. Rossetti

3. CHRISTINA ROSSETTI
by James Collinson

4. ELIZABETH SIDDAL
by D. G. Rossetti
a study for "Regina Cordium"

"Jack having told me that Gabriel and William Rossetti are to be at your Crib this even. I have been endeavouring to contrive my presence, it being just the opportunity I wanted for arranging some scheme for settlement of the 'Gurm' . . . let it be determined who *will* and who *will not* pay at once, and let the amounts of the unfortunate 'wills' be settled, then if, at any future time, Tin can be extracted from the defaulters, it may always be divided between those who shall have paid for them."[15]

Amounts due were allotted. Hancock, who had never wanted the paper, refused to pay, therefore his share of £3 14s. 6d. had to be divided among the remaining six proprietors, which, according to George Tupper's letter to Deverell, meant that his share came to £2 6s. 11d., which was advanced to him by William Michael, "knowing that I wanted the tin".

"The Germ" overflows into 1850, and it was either late in 1849 or early in 1850—it would fit in more romantically to say it was in the spring—that Rossetti met Elizabeth Eleanor Siddal. She was first seen by Deverell when he accompanied his mother to a milliner's in Cranborne Alley off Leicester Square. Red-haired, willowy, pale, she was the perfect Pre-Raphaelite heroine. Deverell rushed to tell his friends about the "stunner" and then enlisted his mother's help in persuading her to sit for them. She consented and became the model for Viola in his own "Twelfth Night", for one of Hunt's Celts in "The Christians" and, later, for Millais' "Ophelia", lying in the water of a tin bath. Rossetti himself kept to Christina for his "Virgin" and the first known portrait he did of Lizzie, or "the Sid", as they called her, was "Rossovestita". Then she became his Beatrices from the "Marriage Feast" to "Beata Beatrix".

As May of 1850 drew near, the Brothers concentrated on getting their pictures finished for showing. Again Rossetti decided to send his "Ecce Ancilla Domini", with its two sonnets round the frame, to the Free Exhibition, now moved to Langham Street under the name of The National Institution and due to open late in April. Hunt sent his "Druids" to the Academy and so did Millais his "Christ in the House of His Parents", more often called "The Carpenter's Shop".

Last year's notices and sales had been satisfactory: and naturally they hoped that 1850 would improve on them. Then the unexpected happened: a storm of abuse broke over their heads.

6

The ostensible reason for the attacks suddenly heaped upon pictures not so different from those of a year before lay in the initials "P.-R.B." In the interval their meaning had been revealed by Alexander Munro to a journalist, Angus Reach, who wrote a gossip column note about them in "The Illustrated London News".[16] The painters were mocked as "ingenious gentlemen who profess themselves practitioners of 'Early Christian Art'," and who, "setting aside the medieval schools of Italy, the Raffaelles, Guidos and Titians, and all such small-beer daubers, devote their energies to the reproduction of saints squeezed out perfectly flat . . . their appearance being further improved by their limbs being stuck akimbo, so as to produce a most interesting series of angles and finely developed elbows . . ." An exact enough description of Collinson's "Saint Elizabeth" or Millais' "Lorenzo and Isabella"!

Rossetti was blamed by the others for the leakage and showed himself very upset: "a horrible and crushing thought", he wrote to Stephens. "The weather being too hot to work, this frightful news has weighed on me without possibility of liberation ever since I got your note. The first time we all come together some desperate means must be arrived at whereby to re-establish our mystery—even though it be done by the adoption of a new monogram."[17] The revelation cannot have been particularly breath-taking, since very few people would have heard of the painters or noticed the initials on their pictures anyway, but somehow it made a good story that could be exploited to suggest a subversive movement and a ridiculous one.

Hunt and Millais at the Academy bore the brunt of the attack. "The Times" called Hunt's "Fugitive Druids" "a deplorable example of perverted taste", and "The Athenaeum" declared both this and Millais' "Christ in the House of His Parents" to be "pictorial blasphemy". The absence of a bituminous background to give "a dim religious light" to a holy subject was thoroughly shocking; even more so would it have been to the Protestant public if they had suspected that originally the Infant was shown kissing his Mother. Dickens directed a leading article of abuse against the picture in his "Household Words": "In the foreground of that carpenter's shop is a hideous wry-necked blubbering boy in a night-gown who appears to have received a poke in the hand from the stick of another boy with whom he has been playing in an adjacent gutter and to be holding it up for the contemplation of a kneeling woman so horrible in her ugliness that (supposing it were possible for any human creature to exist for a moment with that dislocated throat) she would stand out from the rest of the company as a monster in the vilest cabaret in France or the lowest gin-shop in England."

No wonder the adoring Millais' parents wished that their infant prodigy had never taken up with that sly Italian, Rossetti.

By showing his "Ecce Ancilla Domini" (better known as "The Annunciation") at the Free Exhibition, Rossetti was out of the main path of the storm. Even so, Blackwood's critic called him "one of the high priests of this retrograde school . . . reverting for models not to art in its prime but to art in its uncultivated infancy. And a nice business they make of it! Regardless of anatomy and drawing, they delight in ugliness and revel in diseased aspects". "The Athenaeum", more in sorrow than in anger, referred to his "perversion of talent" and called it "a certain amount of talent distorted from its legitimate course by a prominent crochet".

The immediate reaction of the Brotherhood to the attack was one of despair: it meant that the Academy would not want to hang them again and that no buyers would be prepared to back their fancy against the disapproval and ridicule of the cultural Establishment. Each took the blow in his own way: Millais, who was in a position to be the least affected financially, was so wounded in his vanity that he decided for ever after to be on the winning side. Hunt, the worst hit, was hardened in his resolve to keep to his principles and to glory in a pious obstinacy, even when he had himself become a member of the Establishment. In both of them were sown the seeds of resentment against Rossetti: ostensibly because he had not exposed his pictures to the front-line fire but deeper down because he had been accorded the leadership. His own reaction was one of anger: he swore that he would never exhibit in public again.[18]

But things were not really so black and white. The leaders of the art world who were against the P.-R.B. were the President, Sir Charles Eastlake, and W. P. Frith, and what Madox Brown called "other disgusting muffs of influence like Stone and Hart". But among other older artists Dyce, Mulready and Maclise were far from hostile, while Linnell thought their paintings "the finest in the Academy".

Indeed, all was far from lost for the Brothers. This year, 1850, William Michael Rossetti became art critic on "The Spectator", and Woolner was well enough known for his medallion portraits to receive a summons

to the Lakes in order to make one of Tennyson, now Poet Laureate.
And while Augustus Egg offended Holman Hunt by securing for him
the chore of cleaning and restoring Rigaud's frescoes at Trinity House,
his youthful vanity was consoled by the hospitality at Oxford of Mr.
Thomas Combe of the Clarendon Press, who may claim to have been the
first of Pre-Raphaelite patrons.

Letters from Hunt to F. G. Stephens show him as a normal young man,
very different from the prig of later years. One has a sketch of a plain
girl with pimples at the top of the page:

"Imagine the above face on a young lady of 4.3/2 high and tell me if you ever
in all your life (and you *have had* your trials I know) had to walk out with
such an odious creature."[19]

And at Commem. Parties: "It is generally supposed that I am engaged to
the grinning, costive-looking virtue and I have no help but those arising from
stratagems calculated to risk my reputation in the eyes of good, angelic
Mrs. Combe. For instance, last night at Exeter Coll. I managed to fall in
love with a stunner in the company which fact I communicated to Mrs.
Combe as an apology for my lack of attention to Miss Costive and it answered
capitally. . . ."[19]

But he cannot get out of taking her to a Balliol breakfast, the Bishop's
sermon at St. Mary's and a balloon ascent!

Combe acted as Hunt's banker and adviser, and Hunt never ceased
to admire him and his wife as the best types of practising Christians he
had ever met. At this time he generously recommends Rossetti's work
to him, in particular the picture afterwards called "Dante drawing an
Angel" (30th December, 1852). "He [Rossetti] feels the most intense
interest in the event, regarding it as an embodiment of the whole character of Dante's youth, with whose works and life he is beyond doubt
better acquainted than *any man in the world* (I do not speak inconsiderately) therefore I believe that the proposed work will be a most beautiful
one . . . I must acquaint you that the characters of the design are Guido
Calvacanti and Cimabue with a procession of figures in addition to the
two principals."[20] It was to cost 40 guineas.

They planned to spend an autumn together in the country at Seven-
oaks: Millais, Stephens and Rossetti. Woolner and Hunt were to join
them later. Rossetti took a canvas with him on which he sketched in a
background afterwards used for "The Bower Maiden"; translated some
Italian, added to "Nineveh", but little else, for he was not at home in
the countryside and found no inspiration there. As he put it in a squib
to Jack Tupper:

"Though as to Nature, Jack,
   (Poor dear old hack)
   Touching sky, sun, stone, stick and stack,
   I guess I'm half a quack!
   For whom ten lines of Browning whack
   The whole of the Zodiac. . . ."

On another visit to the country, Edward Lear was much patronised by
Hunt, who wrote to Lowes Dickinson:

"I wish you were here painting. Lear is a very nice fellow but much too
old to live with always—he is about 40. I am being drilled in Italian by him
and in return I am letting him see me paint, which from his productions I
confess myself unable to feel is a very great advantage."[21]

It was concerning one of these occasions that a journalist friend of the
group, William Brough, wrote a satirical story called "Calmuck" for
"Household Words" and Hunt demanded an apology from Dickens as
editor on the grounds that he was ridiculed in it.

The name of the hero, Mildmay Strong, certainly scans like Holman
Hunt and he is described as "one of a turbulent and firebrand race of
young painters" who would go to any length to secure exact local colour.
Pompous as Hunt already showed himself, in his protests to Dickens he
certainly had a case and Dickens' denials are unconvincingly ingenuous.[22]

Rossetti was supported by small subsidies from his devoted aunts,
accepted, in the way of young men, as tributes very much his right. His
father had had to retire from King's College and the family had moved
to a smaller house, 38 Arlington Street, in Camden Town, where his
mother, with Christina and Maria, tried to run a school.

He was too honest to make fine speeches and delude himself that a
genius must go his own way—or, if he began, soon caught himself out
in the humbug of it—and at the same time he was too fond of his mother
and sisters to be indifferent to the hardships of their life. He would
have helped if he could, but he could not make himself into a practical
worker (he applied for a job as a railway telegraphist, but fled from the
sight of the apparatus) and he could not get more pictures painted. But
it was not any financial matter that was causing a strain in his relations
with his family, though he refused to acknowledge even to himself the
reserve in the welcome they gave to Elizabeth Siddal when he took her
to visit them.

It is not easy to account for this: was it possessiveness or a form of
snobbery? From William Michael's *Memoir* one suspects something of

the latter, for he protests too much that she was very "ladylike" and that "she knew how to look after herself". As insular as Holman Hunt and from the same background, Lizzie would be shy with the Rossettis, and when shy became at once off-hand and cocksure: "underbred" would have been the word for it in the idiom of a higher class at the time.

But Rossetti chose to be blind to that: he now completely monopolised her as a model and the others had to accept the position.

7

The Royal Academy Exhibition the next year—1851—must have been obscured by the more sensational opening of the Great Exhibition in the Crystal Palace. For the Pre-Raphaelite Brotherhood the two were connected: the Great Exhibition stood for all that they revolted against in design and its success encouraged the attacks of the Establishment upon themselves. Sir Charles Eastlake, P.R.A., was not able to stop the committee from hanging their pictures but saw to it that they had bad positions. Millais showed "Mariana", "The Return of the Dove to the Ark", and the "Woodman's Daughter". Hunt showed "The Two Gentlemen of Verona" (also called "Valentine receiving Proteus"). Associated with them, at least by the critics, were Collins with his "Convent Thoughts" and Madox Brown's "Chaucer".

If the attacks in 1850 had been a storm, in 1851, wrote Hunt, "they were a hurricane". But this time there was to be an answer. On Private View Day, Dyce had urged a certain visitor to look more closely at "The Dove", telling him that it exemplified what he was preaching in his books.

The visitor was John Ruskin. His reputation established by the publication of the second volume of *Stones of Venice*, he had raised the whole standard of art criticism. He was well-known in society also—a success that owed much to the charm of his pretty wife, the former Effie Gray, who was an inveterate party-goer in compensation for deficiencies in her married life at home.

Dyce's tact—if it were that—was as lucky for the Pre-Raphaelites as his generosity, for when "The Times" critic attacked Millais and Hunt and they asked Coventry Patmore if he could persuade Ruskin to say something on their behalf, it could not have come at a better moment.

Ruskin adopted these young painters as his protégés and wrote off his celebrated letter to The Times in their defence. He did not know them personally, he said, and indeed regretted their Romanist Tractarian tendencies, but they had shown high fidelity to "a certain order of truth and should be taken seriously". There was much else that was largely irrelevant. This letter, which appeared on the 13th May, was followed by another on the 20th clearing up the Tractarian misapprehension.

He also added a footnote to a new edition of *Modern Painters*, commending the high finish of their work; secured a buyer for Hunt's "Two Gentlemen" and made an offer for "The Dove" himself. It was already sold to Mr. Combe, but Ruskin took the opportunity to go with his wife to make a personal call on Millais in Gower Street.

The letters were published as a pamphlet in August and although there was much more in them about the Farnley collection of Turners and other matters, it was the reference to the P.-R.B. which caught the limelight. Critics set out to answer him. The Athenaeum declared that he had betaken himself "to satisfy that hot and cold are one, that licence and formality are alike to be reverenced and that with Turnerolatry as strongly professed by him as ever, the canonization of Millais and other Pre-Raphaelites is entirely compatible. . . ."

Such was a typical opinion of the world of professional art critics (cultural hacks as they were until Ruskin raised their status) but Ruskin had made for himself another audience to which he could speak over their heads. The Victorian self-made middle-class, outwardly smug, were inwardly unsure of themselves and longing to be told how to do the right thing by art. Ruskin was one of them himself by birth, but his genius had put him on the pedestal of a prophet whose castigation, like that of a popular preacher, the adoring public revelled in accepting. As he went on he soared so far above his station that he lost his balance, but that is another story.

At this time his influence confined to art and architecture was in the ascendant and, luckily for the Pre-Raphaelites, his admirers were prepared to back his fancy and to buy some of these revolutionary paintings that he recommended.

There is a time-lag in these things, however, and the Brothers were worried over their prospects. The first to repudiate his membership was James Collinson: he had reverted to Anglicanism in order to be considered in marriage by Christina, but now the attack on the P.-R.B. made him feel, so he said, that he must return to his faith and "cease consciously, as a Catholic, to assist in spreading the artistic opinions of those who are not". Deverell was put up in his place but the Brotherhood lapsed before he could be formally elected. Then Woolner, disappointed at his failure to win the prize for the Wordsworth Memorial, set out for Australia to prospect for gold with two friends, Bernhard Smith, another sculptor, and Edward Bateman, a decorative artist whose cousin, La Trobe, was Governor of Victoria. The others had considered emigration seriously too: even Rossetti, who blithely gave his views on agriculture to Deverell: "All I know of farming is that you can pop one turnip into the ground and up come two," and Hunt would have left, if he could have borne to be so far from Rossetti, for he wrote to Deverell: "I have only the few men of our circle to keep my thoughts homeward. I do not know what I should do away from Rossetti. It is true that I have not seen or heard from him for a long time, but I know him to be in the same land somewhere, and that at any time he can be found out and spoken with when necessary and this is enough . . ."

Rossetti, Hunt and Madox Brown were among the friends who went down to the docks to see them off: "all," wrote Rossetti, "plentifully stocked with corduroys, sou' westers, jerseys, fire-arms, and belts full of little bags to hold the expected nuggets." The occasion provided Madox Brown with the idea for "The Last of England".

The resignation of Collinson and the departure of Woolner provide less symbolic dates for the break-up of the Brotherhood than the election of Millais as an Associate of the Royal Academy in November, 1853. He was the "lost leader". Other friendships lingered on, and, as its founders deserted it, so the movement began to find its way into Art History. Painters not included in the original seven did work which could be called Pre-Raphaelite: for instance, Thomas Seddon, "The View of Jerusalem"; James Smetham, "Naboth's Vineyard"; William Lindsay Windus, "The Hunted Outlaw", and "The Stray Lamb"; Martineau, "The Last Day in the Old Home"; Arthur Hughes, "April Love" and "The Long Engagement"; Henry Wallis, "The Death of Chatterton", for which Meredith was the model; John Brett, "The Stone-Breakers"; and Edward Burne-Jones, of whom more hereafter.

The remaining Brothers continued to meet in still uproarious fellowship. Rossetti sent Deverell a sketch of some of them gathered together at Hannay's to hear Buchanan Read "spouting" Inez.* A welcome newcomer was William Allingham, a Customs Clerk from Ulster. His first volume of poems (1850), dedicated to Leigh Hunt, led to his meeting Tennyson; then, through Coventry Patmore, the P.-R.B. "Keen and

* See Appendix A.1, p. 220.

cutting," Madox Brown described him, though Carlyle seems nearer the mark when he turned on him in the Embankment Gardens: "Have a care now, have a care, for ye have a tur-r-rable faculty for developing into a bore." To a later generation he looks both a tuft-hunter and fey, forever seeing little Bridgets at the bottom of the garden as he trotted after Tennyson round the Island.

Until now, Rossetti had continued to live at home with his family, although he rented studios outside, but in November 1852 he moved to 14 Chatham Place—an unsalubrious spot overlooking the river at Blackfriars. But he would hear nothing against it. He enormously admired the view of Benjamin Woodward's recently built Crown Insurance Office—"the most perfect piece of civil architecture that I have seen in London: I never cease to look at it with delight". Inside, his furniture was an odd mixture of cast-offs that he had been given by his family and pieces picked up in junk shops—sometimes valuable, sometimes worthless. Tables with unmended legs were propped up with the books which overflowed their shelves on to the floor everywhere.

But he was thoroughly happy with it all. "You cannot imagine what delightful rooms these are for a party, regularly built out into the river and with windows on all sides; also a large balcony over the water, large enough to sit there with a model and paint—a feat I actually accomplished the other day for several hours in the teeth of the elements," he wrote to Woolner in one of the circular letters that the group had promised to send illustrated with sketches of each other.

He added characteristically enthusiastic reports of their friends' work: "Hunt sent in three pictures to the R.A. . . . all glorious." Millais' "Release" and "The Proscribed Royalists" were "both very remarkable works indeed. Deverell has sent in, I think, five pictures of various merit, but some really excellent. Munro has got several groups and sketches . . . very beautiful, I think. Hughes, always behindhand, like myself, began something but did not finish. . . ."

An evening at No. 14 is described by George Boyce, the watercolourist, who had known Rossetti at the Academy Schools, and saw him with increasing frequency from now on:

"December 30th. 1852 . . . Met there Wells, J. P. Seddon, Clayton, and Mr. Munro, Mr. Stephens and Mr. Hughes. Rossetti showed me his studio but none of his works (which is his way). He had a quantity of Gavarni's works, and a grand and most striking mask of Dante taken from a caste of his face in death: a tracing of his head from Giotto's fresco with the eye imperfect: a pen and ink sketch by Millais from Keats' Isabella. In the physical way, roast chestnuts and coffee, honey and hot spirits. . . ."[23]

8

At Chatham Place Rossetti came into his own as a king with a court. Admirers came to listen to that deep rich voice as he talked or read aloud, improvised limericks or exchanged badinage. Refreshments were frugal, but laughter lavish, as the host lolled on a sofa or stood stockily pointing out the beauties of the river scene from the balcony.

He revelled in his independence. Although he remained devoted to his family and retained all kinds of pet names for his mother—variations on the "Antique", which included "Teak", "Teaksicum"—throughout his life, he could no longer accept regular hours nor any restriction of the company he kept.

In these first years at Chatham Place he was not tied by worse restrictions of his own making. He saw Lizzie how and when he wanted. She would come to sit as a model or simply to sit, lethargic in an armchair, or suddenly darting up to seize pencil and paper and dash off sketches or verses. She lived in rooms in Weymouth Street—an arrangement which suited her respectability and Rossetti's freedom of movement.

He pursued stunners light-heartedly. A letter to Allingham talks about one familiar to them both who "came in on purpose in a lilac walking costume", and he had no compunction in running after any girl with red or blonde hair to ask her to sit to him. How he got away with it can be seen in a rather coy letter from Mrs. Gaskell (of all people!) to Charles Eliot Norton, when she talks of meeting Rossetti at parties: "where I had a good deal of talk with him, always excepting the times when ladies with beautiful hair came in when he was like the cat turned into a lady who jumped out of bed and ran after a mouse. It did not signify what we were talking about or how agreeable I was, if a particular kind of reddish brown, crepe-wavy hair came in, he was away in a moment. . . . He is not mad as a March hare, but hair-mad".

There was a ready market with good prices paid for the watercolours that he started upon in these years, but he was always at pains to protest that his work was not confined to them. In order to prove his seriousness he made a determined effort in the autumn of 1854 to get on with "Found". Conscientiously Pre-Raphaelite he searched for a suitable brick wall and found one at Chiswick which "consists chiefly, as I ought to have remembered, of that material". He was entertained there by friends called Keightley, but he came over to Finchley to draw the symbolically white calf found at a farm opposite to the Madox Browns'.

The calf proved as recalcitrant as the child-angels in Hunt's studio. Indeed, Rossetti wrote out to him in Palestine: "I am far from having painted him as well as I hoped to do—perhaps through my having performed the feat, an open-air one, in the time just preceding Christmas, and also through the great difficulty of the net drawn over him—the motion constantly throwing one out—me especially, quite new as I was to any animal painting."[24]

Rossetti borrowed things from Brown and upset his domestic arrangements by refusing to leave. Brown grumbled in his diary: "March 27th. Endless emendations, no perceptible progress from day to day and all the time he wearing my great coat, which I want, and a pair of my breeches, besides food and an unlimited supply of turpentine . . ."[25]

It was certainly awkward for him. When he wanted to paint in the woman's shawl[26] in "The Last of England"—which had to be done *en plein air*—he dressed himself in "blanket round feet, two coats, shawl and gloves. Very cold in spite".

The long talks into the night were too much for him. On 13th December he recorded that they discussed suicide until 5 a.m. And, three days later, when his guest coolly announced that the cart would not be finished for several days more, Brown put his foot down. His wife was due to be confined in a week and they would need the parlour where Rossetti had put up his bed. If he had work to finish he must do it by coming up every day: he could get the 'bus one way and walk back the other.

This didn't suit Rossetti at all and he went back to the wall at Chiswick. But how little this contretemps affected the relationship between the two men is shown in Rossetti's letter:

"I shall turn up there (in an increased ratio of seediness) one of these days, and make you crusty, and get crusty myself, about Art as usual. Meanwhile believe me

Your affectionate
Rossetti."

This same year he was invited with Millais and Hunt to contribute to an illustrated edition of Allingham's *Day and Night Songs*.

In the event he only completed one, "The Maids of Elfenmere". With this, as with those he did later (1856) for Moxon's *Tennyson*, there was continual trouble with the engraver, Dalziel. He wrote to Bell Scott:

"After a fortnight's work my block goes to the engraver; like Agag, delicately, and is hewn to pieces before the Lord Harry. Address to the Dalziel Brothers.

> O Woodman, spare that block,
> O gash not any how!
> It took ten days by clock
> I'd fain protect it now.
> Chorus: Wild laughter from Dalziel's workshop."

Woolner kept the Tennysons (or at least Mrs. Tennyson, who had taken him up) *au fait* with the progress of such of the illustrations as were to be carried out by his friends:

"I saw one of the engravings of Rossetti's design for 'Mariana' and think it perfectly lovely. I know you will be charmed with it. Saw another of Millais' on the block—as good as possible—some of Hunt's are remarkably fine, two most splendid, one was badly cut I fancy."

The frontispiece was to be from his own medallion, but Tennyson had insisted on Maclise, Mulready and Stanfield as ballast to the moderns.

Tennyson approved of Millais' interpretations, but shook his head over the others—as well he might. He had only meant there to be one or two steps down in "The Beggar Maid", not a whole flight, and over Hunt's "Lady of Shallot" he protested that he "never said her hair was flying about all over the shop like this!" As to Rossetti's "St. Cecilia", he might blame the Dalziels' for the way the angel looks as if he were going to peck the saint on the forehead, but he is responsible for the musical instrument being placed on a city wall and the conception of Cecilia swooning. It appears from a collection of Lizzie's drawings that these ideas were hers:[27] Rossetti evidently threw out the suggestion that she should try her hand at the illustrations and the saint's death-wish starts with her.

9

From the late 1850's Rossetti found himself welcome in the houses of well-known people who had only been names to him a few years before. He had been introduced to the Brownings by Buchanan Read and was invited to be present on an evening when Tennyson was coming.* He asked if he might bring William Michael with him and together the brothers watched Tennyson reading *Maud* aloud in a sing-song voice with tears running down his face. The reading was interrupted, Rossetti told Allingham, by the poet's "groanings and horrors over the reviews of *Maud*. His conversation was really one perpetual groan. All this to the intense wonder of Browning who, as you know, treats reviewers in the way they deserve".[28]

He made a sketch of him and also one of Browning reading aloud *Fra Lippo Lippi* which he admired much more. His first impression of Mrs. Browning was of her extreme delicacy: "so worn out with illness and speaks in the tone of an invalid!"[29] His friendship with them both became close—Browning always sent him presentation copies of his poems—and he could offer introductions to them to friends going to Italy. To Allingham he wrote:

"(18 December, 1856) The Brownings are long gone back now and with them one of my delights—an evening resort where I never feel unhappy. How large a part of the real world, I wonder, are those two small people? taking meanwhile so little room in any railway carriage and hardly needing a double bed at the Inn. . . ."[30]

He attended the Thursday evening Tobacco Parliaments at Alexander Macmillan's, the publisher; was taken up by Mrs. Julia Cameron, who brought him into the Little Holland House circle though he never cultivated it; also by William and Mary Howitt, "culture-vultures" of the time, who edited various periodicals and collected lions to roar in them and in their Hampstead drawing-room. It was they who got Rossetti's "Sister Helen" published in a Düsseldorf magazine. He also made a loyal friend in the rather unexpected person of Barbara Leigh-Smith, the future Madame Bodichon. At this time her considerable energies were devoted not to feminism but to art, and Rossetti described her as "blessed with large rations of tin, fat, enthusiasm and golden hair, who thinks nothing of climbing up a mountain in breeches or wading through a stream in none, in the sacred name of pigment".

And there was despoiling of the Philistines, as he so openly regarded his patrons that none of them resented it and some of them had the good nature—and the good sense—to invest in the friends he recommended. He would look round to see who most needed a commission and what was the best line to take to persuade the right person to provide it and then

* See Appendix B, p. 224.

make him or her feel that he was lucky to be put on to a good thing. He told Miss Ellen Heaton, for instance, that to admire Hughes "is a proof of *great* discernment".[31] Later, when both he and Ruskin pressed Burne-Jones on her attention they were not successful—in fact Ruskin had to keep for himself the sketch he ordered on her behalf: "You have nothing, I think," Rossetti wrote, "by Edward Burne-Jones—one of the greatest painters we have ever had, though as yet young and not fully known. I saw the other day a most inexpressibly lovely work of his . . . 'Cupid and Psyche sharpening arrows'. It is 45 guineas."[31]

But it was Madox Brown he was particularly concerned to push. When Thomas Plint, the Leeds stockbroker, was interested, Rossetti used this to warn Miss Heaton of Brown's coming scarcity value. "Of smaller things he has but few left by him at present . . . anything by Madox Brown will be sure to increase yearly in value now, and no one's work, except those of Hunt and Millais, will ultimately be so highly esteemed or stand so high in the market as his. The tide of justice is beginning to set in towards him."[31]

Plint made his conditions. He only bought "Work" on condition that Carlyle and Kingsley were introduced into it (which explains why they look so out of place) and that one of the original fashionable young ladies should be changed into a "*quiet-earnest*, holy-looking one, with a book or two and tracts".

Brown, grumbling, complied—he had a family to keep: but Rossetti himself had been so angry at the request for a "sunset flush" to be washed over "The Annunciation" that he refused to sell it to Plint at all.

"Nobbut, Mr. Rossetti," Plint had begged in the Yorkshire accent he never ironed out. "Couldn't you put a soonset floosh over the whole thing?"

Plint might have qualified with another patron, Francis MacCracken of Belfast, for Rossetti's squib, in parody of Tennyson's "The Kraken".

". . . while the P.-R.B.
Must keep the shady side, he walks a swell
Through spungings of perennial growth and height."

MacCracken had a tiresome habit of expecting painters to take somebody else's pictures in part exchange. He had offered a Danby to Deverell and now to Madox Brown who exploded to Hunt:

"His cheek in again offering me his Danby after getting it abused by every fool in London is something superhuman—I will take no pictures in exchange again either my own or other people's nor will I abate any of the price."[32]

But more tiresome than any Philistine patron was Ruskin with his chatter about painting. What artist could be expected to put up with much of this from an art critic:

"I forgot to say also that I really do covet your drawings as much as I covet Turner's. . . . Only I won't have them after they have been more than nine times rubbed entirely out—remember that."

and

"Please oblige me in two matters, or you will make me ill again. Take all the pure green out of the flesh in 'The Nativity' I send and try to make it a little less like worsted-work by Wednesday."

Ruskin seems to have been at his nervous worst with Rossetti, for his scolding bossiness sounds quite different when he writes to Miss Heaton of one drawing: "it wasn't entirely scratched out—only a hole about a quarter of an inch deep in the cheek of one of the principal figures. When I last wrote to you it had just come to the scratch point";[33] or of another that had had the principal head scratched out three times "and then cut out boldly—and put in a patch—and so he added a bit here and there till he said he would charge 50 gns for it instead of 40". It did not occur to him that Rossetti might be a perfectionist too, under his banter as serious about Art as Ruskin himself.

But either perceptiveness or some glimpse of what lay ahead for both of them may be read into his complaint that Rossetti lacked cheerfulness in his subjects. He wrote to Miss Heaton: "You did quite right in your other commission to forbid melancholy. It is as bad for Rossetti as disagreeable for others." Yet with all this he could testify to Rossetti's deep understanding of what he drew. Of "Paulo and Francesca", which he offered to take over as unfit for the walls of an unmarried lady, he says, "The common pretty-timid-mistletoe-bough kind of kiss was not what Dante meant. Rossetti has thoroughly understood this passage throughout." Again, over the allegorical figures of Leah and Rachel and Matilda and Beatrice, he goes to a lot of trouble to explain their symbolism and Rossetti's just appreciation of it.

But somehow they could not meet on this ground. Rossetti saw Ruskin much as Blake saw Hayley. He was useful as a buyer and as a booster. "As he is only half-informed about art," Rossetti wrote to Woolner, "anything he says in favour of one's work is, of course, sure to prove invaluable in a professional way, and, I only hope, for the sake of my rubbish, that he may have the honesty to say publicly in his new book what he has said privately, but I doubt this."

Rossetti reacted strongly against the preaching element in Ruskin; it brought out an unaccustomed harshness in his usual sardonic self-mockery, so that his tenderness and humour were denied to Ruskin in later years as well as now. In 1869 he reported to Bell Scott: "Ruskin called the other day & seemed to tend towards a grand proposal of banding together for the regeneration of the world. I told him at once that any individual *I* came near was sure to be the worse for it. You should have seen him wring his hand and soul towards his forlorn species, while the wombat burrowed between his coat and waistcoat."[34]

Rossetti and Lizzie must have come as a providential boon to Ruskin, for it was in April, 1854, that his wife filed her nullity suit against him and retired to her parents' home in Scotland to allow a decent interval to elapse before she married Millais. Ruskin tried to fill this vacuum in his life with Rossetti and, what seemed to promise greater satisfaction, Lizzie—"Ida", he called her, after Tennyson's "Princess". He considered her sketches showed real promise: "By-the-bye there is one of Rossetti's pupils—a good girl—dying I am afraid—of ineffable genius—to whom something or other—a commission may by encouragement & sympathy be charity—but there is no hurry as she dont work *well* enough yet, & Rossetti and I will take care of her till she does, if she lives."[33]

His praise of her work genuinely pleased Rossetti and made it easier to accept the offer of a regular income to enable her to seek health in a warmer climate and to repay it by pictures of what she saw. "I have given her the means of going to Nice for the winter: she being sanguine of being able to paint there and send me home beautiful drawings of blue sea and orange groves . . ."[33] Ruskin lavished a generosity on Lizzie meant for someone else: if only Effie had been like this, as beautiful and as undemanding sexually!

The upshot was less happy: Lizzie went to France with a woman friend, but lingered in Paris, where Rossetti joined her. Munro met them there when he went over to see the Great Exhibition and wrote to Bell Scott: "We enjoyed Paris immensely, in different ways, of course, for Rossetti was every day with his sweetheart, of whom he is more foolishly fond than ever I saw lover." But she took refuge in illness and remained at home when Rossetti went out to call on the Brownings, staying in the Rue de Grenelle, *en route* for Florence. He had wanted to paint Mrs. Browning for some time but the poetess was determined to evade him: in a letter to her sister, Arabella, she said that she demurred at being

5. Rossetti with a group of friends: a sketch from a letter to Deverell.

6. ANNIE MILLER
by D. G. Rossetti

7. From a drawing on a zinc plate by D. G. Rossetti intended for the title page of *The Early Italian Poets*, 1861.

"perpetuated in sublime ugliness by the head of the Pre-Raphaelite school".[35]

Both spent too much money and shamelessly applied to Ruskin for more, which strained their relations but did not yet cause a break. Ruskin could not afford to confess to himself that yet another personal friendship had failed. He persisted in trying to get to the bottom of Lizzie's ill-health. Not discouraged by the outcome of the French trip, he proposed that Lizzie should be seen by his Oxford friend from undergraduate days, Dr. Henry Acland. He came to the conclusion that she was suffering from "mental power long spent up and lately over-taxed", a diagnosis about as much use therapeutically as that of Keats's doctor, Robert Bree, who declared there was no organic complaint, only "anxiety of mind". Psychosomatic medicine must sometimes attend to the "soma".

At least Dr. Acland made the useful suggestion that Lizzie should relax in some secluded cottage on his family's Devon estates as treatment, but she would no more consent to this than she would to Barbara Bodichon's plan for her to enter Florence Nightingale's new nursing home in Harley Street for poor gentlewomen. The most she would agree to do was to stay in rooms at Hastings, near Barbara's country house, Scalands, and here Rossetti joined her. On a visit to the house they all scratched their initials on a pane of one of the windows. "Everyone adores and reveres Lizzie," wrote Rossetti, on the defensive, to his family.

To repay Ruskin's kindness—or interference—Rossetti let himself be persuaded into taking some Art classes at the Working Men's College in Red Lion Square, newly founded by F. D. Maurice.[36] He had gone to watch Ruskin teaching there, reporting to Bell Scott: "The enthusiasm of the pupils with their heads all clustered round the master and his diagram quite affected me, as well as Woolner, who was with me, though we refrained from tears." At first he and Lowes Dickinson shared a class with Ruskin on Thursdays, but the next term he was responsible for Monday evenings on his own: "The Figure and Animals—colour." Apparently all classes were open to visitors, as he advises Aunt Charlotte that Lady Bath and Lord Ashburton could "drive to the College any time between half past seven till ten . . . to see the system of teaching in full force".

He enjoyed it more than he expected and was very successful at it. His methods were unorthodox: "None of your Freehand drawing-books used," he said in a letter to Bell Scott. "The British mind is brought to bear on the British mug at once, and with results that would astonish you."

What a breath of fresh air to blow away the stuffiness of Ruskin and of Maurice! Rossetti, who hated to be patronised himself, did not patronise other people. He respected any approach to art which was made with sincere humility and, equally, he detested snobbish pretensions. When a pupil anxious to show off asked him for advice on the best class of colour shop, he replied: "I don't know: I generally use the halfpenny colours from the oilshop myself."

IO

When the first excitement of his new freedom had worn off—and of his new success; pictures selling well and famous people seeking him out—the other side of Rossetti's nature began to assert itself; the side born to haunt "the vale of magical, dark mysteries", or, if you like, the depressive. As early as 1853, when all seemed set fair and he had gone with Bell Scott on a walking tour in the north, based on Newcastle, he had had a premonition of melancholy which shows itself in the poem written then, "The Hill Summit". Did he feel that in returning to Chatham Place he was going downhill into the dark?

> "And now that I have climbed and seen this height
> I must tread downward through the sloping shade
> And travel the bewildered tracks till night. . . ."

A year later, in April, 1854, his father had died.[37] It was a happy release, for poor Gabriele had become totally blind and was a burden to the women of the family who had to nurse him while they were struggling to maintain a small day-school. He may have wished that his son had been able to help the family finances more, but probably he had enough in common with him to feel it was more important that he had come round to appreciation of Dante.

He addressed him with satisfaction enough in his verse *Autobiography*, translated from the Italian by William Michael:

> "An able poet I hear you already hailed,
> Already as able painter see you admired.
> Now onward, and the double race-course win.
> You will be doing what I could not do."

No doubt his Mother's love towards him was strong also to forgive and somehow understand when after the funeral he did not stay to comfort her, but hurried off to Hastings to join Lizzie.

In that same year two deaths among contemporaries had bewildered the tracks where first youth was disappearing. The handsome Deverell, only twenty-seven, had aggravated a fatal disease by overwork to support his mother and sisters. Rossetti invited him to stay at Chatham Place for a change and rest-cure and took much trouble to see his "Twelfth Night" packed off to MacCracken. His last pictures were "The Doctor's Last Visit" and "Young Children watching a Funeral" and a self-portrait. When he had to give up work and was forced to remain in bed, Millais used to go and read the Bible to him. Stephens was another who called regularly, and Ruskin also visited him. On his death Rossetti wrote to Hunt now in Palestine (20th March, 1824): "I am glad I insisted on seeing him (just a week before his death) against his doctor's orders and cannot help wishing that I had been with him at the last, and thinking that he might perhaps have wished so too. . . . He is buried in the churchyard of the Holy Trinity at Brompton whither I followed his funeral."[38]

Rossetti went to call on the family the next day and made a sketch of the head of the young brother, Wykeham Deverell.[39] "I have never yet had to bear a loss so great to me as that of your brother . . ." he wrote to one of the sisters. The depressive side of his character shows itself in a further passage in the letter to Hunt when he goes on to say that his earliest remembrances of decay in nature was when, as a child, he had taken dead pods to his Mother to ask her what they were. Deverell's death made him wonder how long his own days may be, but practical common-sense pulled him up and he admits, "probably this is owing chiefly to botherations & constant sleeplessness which has troubled me of late", adding also, "you know I scarcely see anyone . . ."[40]

In the same year Thomas Seddon died at Cairo, whither he had accompanied Hunt on the way to Jerusalem. The Brothers had a whip-round among themselves and other friends to try to help his family. Millais sent a picture to Gambart, the dealer, to raffle and Rossetti approached Miller of Liverpool and MacCracken to buy.

But, as a brotherhood in art, Rossetti was bored with the P-.R.B., and showed only a short-lived enthusiasm for "The Folio", last of the cyclographic ventures, for which Millais was persuaded to invest in a green portfolio with a lock. The Hogarth Club was another unsuccessful successor, whose failure Bell Scott blamed on Rossetti and on Madox Brown who "quarrelled it out of existence". Rossetti had already made fun of P.-R.B. titles ("Gil Blas about to assume an air of unconcern while waiting on the robbers in their cave"), but this was characteristic of him when his feelings were deeply engaged. In a letter to Hunt he had refused to attend a meeting because he felt himself unworthy. This is very revealing of an ambivalence that persisted throughout his career. He has often been accused of getting tired of things (or people), of slackness in finishing work and of displaying a form of vanity in his refusal to exhibit his pictures, but this passage shows how much there existed of genuine diffidence in his withdrawals. It wasn't that he feared criticism or felt "too proud to show", but that he held himself not good enough:

> "14 Chatham Place.   Thursday evening.
>   Much as I desire to set eyes on you again, I shall not come tomorrow evening to the meeting at your place. What between remissness and disappointments in my painting, it has come to that pass with me, that until I have done something decisive and got again into the field, I should feel like a pretender at any meeting connected with the artistic interests of the brotherhood. I say this to you which, of course, I should not care to say to another."[40]

At a deeper level he began to mock his own medievalism: although he persisted in it for some time yet, it no more satisfied him than had the religious symbolism of his Christian pictures, for there was a side to him too acutely aware of the Here-Now ever to permit him to be an exoticist. He needed food for the spirit more sustaining than asphodel. And Here-Now was disappointing. What he did in poetry or painting left his energies unsatisfied and he recovered with less resilience from each successive bout of idleness, or failure to act upon a decision. "My devil of delay", as he called this incapacity, prevented him from going out to Italy to see the Brownings. What he had written of the painter in "Hand and Soul" applied to himself: "When at his work, he was blind and deaf to all else, but he feared sloth: for then his stealthy thoughts would begin, as it were, to beat round and round him, seeking a point for attack."

A new point for attack, an emotional fifth column, was provided by his obsession with Lizzie. It was not a passion that he could satisfy physically nor sublimate in his work. He began to see in her an image of his own creation: no longer an ordinary girl with lovely red hair willing to sit quietly for hours as a model or amuse herself with his pencils but a medieval *Dame Lointaine*.

In all his close relationships with women the opposing sides of his nature come into conflict and form a fatal pattern. The initial happy-go-lucky companionship changes as he begins to see the woman under a literary light—a Beatrice or a Magdalen or a Proserpine—and then develops a sense of responsibility towards the image. Inevitably the women did not live up to it—nor did he. He doted on the beauty of women, but he could not enjoy it without relating it to spiritual values:

> "Thy soul I know not from thy body, nor
> Thee from myself, neither our love from God."

But this Dantesque statement did not really come naturally to him. He was not living in the Middle Ages and for him Shelley's rueful remark rang truer: "the error consists in seeking in a mortal image the likeness of what is perhaps eternal."

Lizzie had the golden hair whose thread had run through his poems since boyhood: ". . . and round his heart one strangling, golden hair". Again, in "Eden Bower":

> "And the threads of my hair are golden
> And there in a net his heart was holden,"

and in "Hand and Soul": "He knew her hair to be the golden veil through which he beheld his dreams."

"The Sid" was aloof: chaste as the maidens of medieval legend, yet compliant and talented. "Stunning" he called her pictures, insisted they were much better than his own and hung them, and only them, round the walls of the sitting-room at Chatham Place. Indeed, strangely good they are—not copies of his own nor under his influence by any hypnotism of love or of propinquity, for they look much more like Blake—or Fuseli —than anything of Rossetti's done at the same time.

If Lizzie was Beatrice, she was also *La Belle Dame sans Merci*, who took —and did not give—her kisses four. But when we deck her out in these literary allusions, sentimental or sinister, we must remember that she and Gabriel used to call each other "Gug" and "Guggums" and that to other people the golden hair was "carrots". Frederick Stephens got into trouble for saying she had freckles.

Her personality was compounded of several paradoxes: if she seemed quiet and withdrawn, she could also be perky and flippant, given to facetious and rather silly sharp retorts. "Of a chaffing nature," declared the puzzled William, feeling that flightiness did not become her. She would seldom talk seriously and yet she had a morbid preoccupation with death. Her flippancy may have been a defence or a guard against the blows of the unsympathetic. Her spirit, like her surprising talents— shown in verse as well as drawing—must have been driven underground by her upbringing. Starved on a diet of shabby gentility and shocked by the talk of other girls at the milliners', some emotional wound had festered as physically had been sown the seeds of some disease.

If Gabriel was complicated, Lizzie was complex; the elements of her personality inextricably tangled.

The golden girl, something of a slattern, moving lazily about the shabby rooms with their pervasive river smells, was a Lilith, never the abundant Eve.

> "Adam's first damosel,
>   Be on thy guard against her lovely hair."

Lizzie's was not a creative quietude like Catherine Blake's, whose husband "free, found he could only love his wife", but a lethargy that was a poison infiltrating a blood stream already allergic to it. She was the spirit of *accidie* under whose spell he was only too ready to fall, as in sketch after sketch he catches her lilied languor. With a true instinct the Rossetti family saw this and could not like her: other people might find her talented and good, but his mother and sisters knew that all that mattered was that she was not good for Dante Gabriel. They sensed that his consuming—and it was that—passion for Lizzie was an insidious cancer in his spirit; its effects not immediately observable but deadly for the future.

It is usually considered that the root of their trouble was that Rossetti could not bring himself to the point of marriage with Lizzie, but is it not possible that at the outset it was she who would not consent to marry him? With marriage she could no longer have retained the virginity that tantalised him, for that she was sexually cold is suggested by the fact that the two men with whom she got on best were Ruskin and Swinburne. As the years went by her natural conventionality came to demand a wedding-ring. When others of their circle wore it, she would not be left out and traded her ill-health to get one.

Rossetti's obsession was summed up in a sonnet of Christina's called "In the Artist's Studio", though the convenience of using his sister's poems as biographical material for Dante Gabriel must not be exploited. She had her own troubles and she was a poet, not a reporter.

> "One face looks out from all his canvasses,
>   One selfsame figure sits or walks or leans:
>   We found her hidden just behind those screens,
>   That mirror gave back all her loveliness."

Note the word "leans" and the element of withdrawal so characteristic of her in "behind those screens", and, following on the unconvincing convention of "kind eyes" and "joyful lights" there comes the sudden penetrating truth of the two final lines: his love for his image of her.

"He feeds upon her face by day and night
    And she with true kind eyes looks back on him,
Fair as the moon and joyful as the light:
    Not wan with waiting, nor with sorrow dim:
Not as she is, but was when hope shone bright:
    Not as she is, but as she fills his dream."

PART TWO

OXFORD RENAISSANCE
1857–1862

II

In Rossetti's life there was more than one *Annus Mirabilis*. When he was getting bored with things as they were, with his Here-Now, something would happen to change it. Events, like people, waited on him, responding to his need, or he can be said to have experienced the spiritual periodicity, the ebb and flow of creativity, common to all men of genius: their "ups and downs", in fact.

1856 was one of these operative years for him. The first period at Chatham Place comes conveniently to an end and a fresh epoch begins, marked by new endeavour and by new encounters. First, there was the commission to undertake the painting of the triptych for the high altar in the newly-restored Llandaff cathedral.[41] This was secured for him by the architect, J. H. Seddon, brother of Thomas. Rossetti chose for subject "The Seed of David" which he wanted to make more dramatic in subject than anything he had done before, and he wanted it to have direct appeal to those who would see it. "I do not care in the least to be wiser than the most ordinary spectator of my picture, & for that reason should be perfectly indifferent to elaborate orientalism in Bible subjects; but I do not want people to refuse to look at what I do because they are 'not so green'." Although he regretted that he had had no training in decorative art, it remains one of his most satisfying works. He must somehow have kept Lord Aberdare (then the Honourable Henry Austin Bruce) and his Committee sweet in spite of his delays, for he was able to persuade them to employ Woolner on the bas reliefs.

Then there was a new encounter—with Fanny Cornforth, whom he may have met cracking nuts with her teeth in the Strand and throwing the husks at him as he stared at her, or whose golden hair he may have loosed "accidentally on purpose" in a restaurant, or he may have met her, as she said that he did, when he was strolling with friends at a firework display in Cremorne. Whichever way it was, he took her back with him to put her head against his canvas for the girl in "Found". She was the exact model he wanted for the seduced country girl and the story she told him of her life fitted in too. Whether it was true or not, she was no innocent now but, more amusing to deal with, an unshockable cockney. Her real name was Cox and she afterwards married men called Hughes and Schott, but it is as Fanny Cornforth that she is known in Rossetti's pictures and in his life—the name Cornforth "assumed by her in a spirit of girlish caprice".[42]

But what mattered even more than the recognition he received in the Llandaff commission and in coming across at last the right model for "Found" was the introduction by an old friend, Vernon Lushington, of a shy and gangling undergraduate just down from Oxford. The new interest needed at this point to revitalise his inspiration were to be provided in the person of Edward Coley Burne-Jones.

At Oxford in January, 1853, two undergraduates of Exeter College had discovered each other: William Morris and Edward Burne-Jones. It was a meeting that was to have far-reaching repercussions, much like that other encounter years before, when Hogg and Shelley had sat next to each other in Hall at University College.

Burne-Jones took Morris to join the Birmingham set at Pembroke, who had been his school-fellows at King Edward's School there. Richard Watson Dixon was the leader among them, a minor poet who took Orders and became a Canon, but who is mostly remembered now for his correspondence with Gerard Manley Hopkins. Of the others, William Fulford also went into the Church, Cormell Price became the Headmaster of Kipling's *Stalky and Co.*, and Charles J. Faulkner,[43] a mathematician, became a Fellow of University College and a business associate of William Morris.

The group were serious-minded young men who wanted to better the world and had thought that the Church would offer them the best opportunity of service—sentiments based on a hereditary nonconformity steeped in the backwash of Tractarianism. But, as they talked together in Oxford, the aesthetic side of religion began to predominate in its appeal to them. Morris and Burne-Jones particularly went on Church-crawls together, admiring a medievalism in architecture which they were beginning to question in dogma, and Morris showed himself already ahead of his time in his indignation at the vandalistic restoration of old buildings or their destruction (the Broad Street front of his own College a few years later was to be one of the worst). At the same time they approved the traditional decoration that a Fellow of Merton, Hungerford Pollen, had just carried out on the chapel there, recently restored by Butterfield.

They probably first heard the name of the Pre-Raphaelites through Ruskin, either in his *Pre-Raphaelitism*, which came out in August, 1851, or in the fifth edition of *Modern Painters* and the third volume of *Stones of Venice*. They had also seen Millais' "Return of the Dove" at Wyatt's, the Oxford print dealer's, and when Mr. Combe invited them to the Clarendon Press they enormously admired Hunt's "Christians Fleeing" and Rossetti's water-colour of "Dante drawing Beatrice". This was what they were looking for and Rossetti became their ideal.

So that when the first number of their inevitable magazine came out on 1st January, 1856, the most significant contribution was an article by Burne-Jones on "The Newcomes", in which a digression on book-illustration extolled Rossetti's "Maids of Elfenmere".

"The Oxford and Cambridge Magazine", as it was called, was planned in Dixon's rooms and had for joint editors Fulford and another of the Birmingham school-fellows, William Heeley, who had gone up to Cambridge. Its aims were to propagate the ideas of the group, social and aesthetic, in that order. More ambitious than "The Germ" it aimed at a national circulation—and a longer life. Morris tried his hand as verse for it, working at "The Willow and the Red Cliff" in Dixon's room despite the talk and arguments going on. When the others admired the composition he declared:

"Well, if this is poetry, it is very easy to write"—an attitude that he sustained all his life.

Heeley went one better than the Oxford side when he secured contributions from Rossetti himself: "The Burden of Nineveh", "The Staff and the Scrip" and a new rendering of "The Blessed Damozel". But "The Oxford and Cambridge Magazine" petered out by the end of the year. In compensation during the Christmas vacation, Godfrey, Lushington, offered to introduce Burne-Jones to Rossetti in London. He was much too shy to accept but declared he would be content if he could attend some meeting at the Working Men's College just to listen to him and see him.

"I was two and twenty and had never met, or even seen, a painter in my life. I knew no one who had ever seen one, or had been in a studio, and of all men who lived on earth, the one that I wanted to see was Rossetti. . . . I was told that there was to be a monthly meeting that very evening . . . and that anyone could get admittance by paying threepence, including tea. . . . So I waited a good half-hour or two . . . and then Lushington whispered to me that Rossetti had come in, so I saw him for the first time, his face satisfying all my worship. . . ."

A few nights later Vernon, brother of Godfrey Lushington, prevailed on Burne-Jones to come to his rooms to meet Rossetti. He was not disappointed. Immediately Rossetti came in he captured the room; putting in his place someone who spoke disrespectfully of Browning's *Men and*

Women, just published: "I saw my hero could be a tyrant and I thought it sat finely upon him." Someone else ventured to praise metaphysics and was told that there was no other occupation for man than painting, though he conceded later that those who couldn't paint could be saved by buying. So it went on: with exaggeration and laughter and teasing and, best of all, at the end, Burne-Jones was bidden to call at Chatham Place the next day.

On his side Rossetti was naturally not unmoved at the adoration of this new undergraduate brotherhood so similar to the Pre-Raphaelites. But, only six years older anyway, he could laugh at himself as a *Maître* and, as he was never inclined to pomposity or patronage, he accepted Burne-Jones on an equality and invited him to bring any of his friends to call also. The first to come was William Morris. As he is one of those characters in literary history who are always shown as they were in late middle age, it is as well to remember that in his early twenties he was strikingly handsome. There was no beard left long and matted to cover the absence of a tie and the grizzled hair on his massive head was then dark and curling, "like exquisite wrought metal", wrote Mackail, and, "so strong that he afterwards used to amuse his children by letting them take hold of it to lift them off the ground". His friends called him Topsy because of this great mop. He was clumsy in his movements, walking with a sailor's rolling gait (as, oddly enough, did Rossetti), "brash", perhaps, and given to violent outbursts of temper, but fundamentally good-natured and entirely without malice. He was a little slow in response so that Rossetti could not resist running rings round him and encouraging the others to do the same. At this time those who met him (in common, indeed, with many of his admirers since) were too dazzled by his energy and enthusiasm to notice a certain lack of sensitivity, or to wonder if the smallness of the eyes in that fine head hinted at limitations unsuspected in the Samson-Jason he looked at first sight.

It was Rossetti's influence that started William Morris on his life work. Without it he might have remained in the transitional stage of being a church architect, for he entered Street's office as an articled pupil and found himself working, ironically enough, on the restoration of churches in Oxford. But "paint, paint" was Rossetti's creed, and if this for Morris eventually meant devotion to craftsmanship rather than to art, it was nevertheless a revelation to him of his job in life.[44] In these early days he acknowledged the debt fully. When Burne-Jones once remonstrated with him for following a Rossetti design instead of his own, he replied: "I have got beyond that; I want to imitate Gabriel as much as I can."

When they came down from Oxford in 1856, Burne-Jones and Morris set up house together in the rooms Rossetti had shared with Deverell at 17 Red Lion Square. "It was the quaintest room in all London, hung with brasses of old knights and drawings of Albert Dürer"—and with contemporary pictures, for Rossetti persuaded Morris to buy when he found that he was rich. Hughes' "April Love" was among them and a landscape by Madox Brown, who entered in his Diary: "Yesterday Rossetti brought his ardent admirer Morriss (sic) of Oxford, who bought my little hay field for 40 gnas—this was kind of Gubby. He has also brought Browning here lately who is, it turns out, a great admirer of me."

They were waited on by a Dickensian character, Red Lion Mary. She reserved the most comfortable mattress for Rossetti when he chose to stay the night and prepared her best dishes for him and for Burne-Jones, even if it was always rabbit. Morris she did not care for: "He had always the worst bed and the coldest water!" Burne-Jones recalled: "and the end of the puddings with no currants in".

"Ned", who a year before had never set eyes on a painter in the flesh, now moved freely among the Pre-Raphaelite group. Hunt he described as "a tallish slim man with a beautiful red beard, something of a turn-up nose and deep-set dark eyes: a beautiful man". He could write home to Birmingham:

> "We know Rossetti now as a daily friend, and we know Browning too, who is the greatest poet alive, and we know Arthur Hughes and Woolner and Madox Brown. Madox Brown is a lark. I asked him the other day if I wasn't very old to begin painting and he said 'O, no, there was a man I knew who began older: by-the-by, he cut his throat the other day'."

Rossetti, always a *boulevardier* ("usual Captain on such occasions and notorious night-bird" as Allingham called him), walked over to them when they did not come to him and dragged them out, humming through closed teeth as he walked, "a *sotto voce* note of defiance to the universe". He took them off to theatres and out again before a performance ended, if he thought it too boring to sit through, or took them back to Chatham Place and "tired the sun with talking" over the coffee.

Lizzie was away much of this time, taking various holidays for her health (was it worse because she felt neglected?) and each time she returned, her irritability told the tale of her condition. Rossetti made efforts to be patient with her, but she no longer filled his horizon, nor did Fanny. If he satisfied his sexual needs with her from time to time or in chance encounters at Cremorne Gardens, what mattered to him more was the tonic his spirits received from this new "movement".

He was proud of his pupils: "They have turned artists instead of taking up any other career to which the University generally leads," he wrote to Bell Scott, and, "both are men of real genius. Jones' designs are unequalled by anything unless perhaps Albert Dürer's finest works and Morris, though without practice as yet, has no less power, I fancy. He has written some really wonderful poetry too, and as I happen to have a song of his in my pocket I enclose it to you."

Poems by admiring younger men, letters recommending the work of his friends to his own patrons, notes raising money for other painters or writers who had fallen on hard times; such were the things that "happened" to fill Rossetti's pockets in the late 1850's when he was in his thirtieth year.

12

The first outcome of Rossetti's connection with this new Pre-Raphaelite movement was the decoration of the Oxford Union. But this is to over-simplify; as always in Rossetti's life the canvas is so crowded that in picking out what seem the salient features it is easy to overlook the equally important background. If these new young men, Burne-Jones and Morris, loomed large among his friendships, it must not be forgotten that at the same time he was keeping up with many others: with his family, with his old P.-R.B. associates, with Allingham and Bell Scott, or friends like the Tuppers and James Hannay, a journalist. Other names, now forgotten, appear spasmodically in his wide correspondence.

Among an outer circle of acquaintances was Benjamin Woodward, the architect, "a good thirteenth-century man", and he now—in July, 1857—invited Rossetti to undertake some of the mural decorations for the Science Museum in Parks Road, Oxford, a building for which Henry Acland had fought a hard and lone campaign in the University—opening the way for the ruination of the Parks a hundred years later. Woolner had already been commissioned to do a statue of Bacon and Munro one of Galileo. But the subject suggested to Rossetti, "Newton gathering pebbles on the shores of the Ocean of Truth", did not appeal to him. With Blake he felt:

"May God us keep
From single vision and Newton's sleep."

However, he went up to Oxford one afternoon and with Morris was shown the Museum by Woodward, and must have shared the enthusiasm for it shown by an undergraduate who wrote: "The lovely Museum rose before us like an exhalation; its every detail, down to panels and foot-boards, gas-burners and door handles, an object lesson in art." They went on to the Debating Hall (now the Library) which Woodward was adding to the Union buildings in St. Michael's Street. It was a curious shape: a rectangle with an apse at each end and a roof of open beams resting on a drum divided into ten bays. In this were twenty-six windows like port holes.

At once Rossetti exclaimed that it needed frescoes—and of his own choice of subject. Morris, remembering Merton Chapel, backed him up. Together they persuaded not only Woodward but the Union Building Committee to allow them a free hand in exchange for their materials and the expenses of board and lodging.

The subjects must come from the *Morte D'Arthur* and ten painters be found to share the work. When they got back to London, friends were mobilised at once: of course "Ned", as they called Burne-Jones, and Arthur Hughes, and Spencer Stanhope, and the young Val Prinsep, dragged away from the dedicated shrine of Watts at Little Holland House, and, to provide the ballast of experience—though he did not have much chance—John Hungerford Pollen.

They could not wait to find others and, as it was all to be finished before the next term began, they took undergraduate digs in The High. It would be a glorious summer lark; with painting all day, sculling on the river for recreation, talking all night in their rooms. "Topsy-baiting" was a favourite sport, for Morris's discomfiture and his violent rages caused great amusement to the others. He was sent off to make a sketch of the Innkeeper's daughter at Godstone—"stunner *Lipscombe*"—but was put to rout by the girl's mother.[45] In his absence someone, probably Rossetti, wrote on a placard over his bedroom door:

"Poor Topsy has gone to make a sketch of Miss Lipscombe,
　But he cant draw the head, and dont know where the hips come."

He was not only made to paint but to write poems ("grinds") and to read them aloud.

"I say, Top," said Rossetti, who had been humming to himself on the sofa, "read us one of your grinds."
"But Gabriel," growled Morris, "you've heard them all!"
"Never mind, old fellow; here's Val"—he had already taken to calling me

by my Christian name, but he generally called me "Wal"—"does not know them. Besides, they're devilish good."

Often they were joined by undergraduates who were presented with brushes and paint and made to climb up the ladders and get on with it. One who was introduced and soon made friends was a young man with high voice and flaming red hair who Rossetti wanted as a model. He was Algernon Charles Swinburne, already a poet and somewhat eccentric.[46] But the Master of Balliol, William Jowett, was determined not to let his college make itself ridiculous by treating him as University had treated Shelley. He encouraged a tactful withdrawal from Oxford in Swinburne's last year and remained a life-long friend.

What fun it was to shock the bourgeoisie—and the dons! Swinburne described one occasion as they watched the painting: he and Burne-Jones, Stanhope and someone called Swan:

> "We defended our idea of Heaven: vis., a rose-garden full of stunners. Atrocities of an appalling nature were uttered on the other side.
> "We became so fierce that two respectable members of the University—entering to see the pictures—stood mute and looked at us . . . and after listening five minutes to our language, they literally fled from the room! Conceive our mutual ecstacy of delight."

But there were other Oxford residents willing to provide appreciation: picture-buyers like Wyatt and Combe, and Dr. Acland and his wife in The Broad, all too ready with offers of hospitality which bored the young men. There was also a theatre where, of all things lucky, Rossetti discovered his favourite stunner of an actress was to appear—Ruth Herbert. He made sketches of her and threw them on to the stage, and, later, through Tom Taylor persuaded her to sit to him. "She's coming at $\frac{1}{2}$ past 11," he wrote ecstatically to Bell Scott. "She has the most varied and highest expression I ever saw in a woman's face besides abundant beauty, golden hair, etc. Did you ever see her? O my eye."

An undergraduate of the time, staying up to work, wrote:[47]

> "A merry, rollicking set they were: I was working daily in the Library . . . and heard their laughter, and songs, and jokes, and the volleys of their soda-water corks, for this innutrient fluid was furnished to them without stint at the Society's expense."

Morris took medievalism literally and set out to have some armour made to measure. Burne-Jones described what happened to the

". . . designs for an ancient kind of helmet called a basinet and for a great surcoat of ringed mail with a hood of mail and the skirt coming below the knees . . . made for him by a stout little smith who had a forge near the castle. . . . One afternoon when I was working high at my picture I heard a strange bellowing in the building and turning round to find a cause, saw an unwonted sight. The basinet was being tried on but the visor for some reason would not lift and I saw Morris embedded in iron, dancing with rage and roaring inside."

No wonder Val Prinsep was to remember "What fun we had in that Union! What jokes! What roars of laughter!" Too much fun, thought Little Holland House, and asked Ruskin to rescue Val from it all. He agreed:

"I see well enough there's plenty of stuff in him—but the worst of it is that all the fun of these fellows goes straight into their work—one can't get them to be quiet at it—or resist a fancy if it strikes them over so little a stroke on the bells of their soul—away they go jingle-jangle without ever caring what o'clock it is."

Away they went, "jingle-jangle": too medieval by half when they slipped in little paintings of wombats among the figures or caricatured Morris straddling the beams, or let paint drop on the heads of the stone-masons below. Another swig at the soda-water and on they went again, filling in the outlined figures with small brushes only fit for water-colour and finding it hard work on the damp walls.

It would all come out right in the end: but in practice it did not. The paint flaked off the unprepared surfaces and such pictures as remained became streaked with smoke from the gas-jets that flared up on to them from below. Despite the quip: "O tempora, O Morris," the design that remained the longest was Morris's luxuriant clamour of sunflowers all over the beams; a trailer for his later wallpapers.

The two Brothers, Millais and Hunt, who considered they had staked an earlier claim to Oxford, did not care for the proceedings. Hunt wrote disapprovingly: "Every time I visited Oxford I heard more and more of the sensation Rossetti was making there. It was in character with Rossetti's sanguine enthusiasm that he induced many undergraduates with little or no previous training to cover certain spaces. . . ."

On another night at the theatre when Rossetti was with Morris, "Ned" and Arthur Hughes, or, some say, when they were looking out of a window in the King's Arms—or in church, which they sometimes attended on Sundays in their search for models—a chance encounter occurred which was to change their lives. They saw two sisters; one of them a "stunner". She had a head of thick black hair set on a column of a neck and eyes so deep-set that she seemed to come from a different race—a throw-back to some ancient British stock in the Cotswolds. They found her father, Robert Burden, was a groom living over the livery stables at No. 65 Holywell (now a garage). They managed to get introduced and persuaded her to sit for them—two phrases that go together when Rossetti exercised his charm. From then onwards she was regularly with them: a model for the Union pictures, or a companion at the theatre or on river expeditions. She must have been surprised at the admiration she aroused, for she and her sister would have been considered frightening by boys of their own age in the town and by undergraduates who came to hire horses—too big and too dark-skinned at a time when pink-and-white complexions were admired.

But these artists, young and high-spirited, let Jane know that they thought she was beautiful. They made her pose as a Queen and called her a "stunner". She responded: the gypsy from the Cotswolds broke through Victorian Holywell and, no longer shy, enjoyed the horse-play and the laughter: her vitality in strong contrast to Lizzie's lassitude.

The few records that exist of Jane's character are of much later date, when it had changed. She became, according to Henry James and Bernard Shaw, exceptionally silent, but there is also other evidence which points to her retaining a strong, even broad, sense of humour when in congenial company.

> ". . . Of that face
> What shall be said,—which, like a governing star,
> Gathers and garners from all things that are
> Their silent, penetrative loveliness?"
>
> (Silent Noon).

Jane's may have been a world-face but it was also a misfit.[48] She was one of those goddesses in whom there is imprisoned a little woman signalling to escape: in her case, a tomboy. She wanted to be like other girls, wearing the same clothes and invited to the same sort of parties and free to laugh loudly or play practical jokes if she felt like it. Now, at eighteen, she was offered something of this by the group of unusual young men who had taken her up and shown her that she was both beautiful and good company. The price she had to pay was not exacted for some time.

She stepped into the outline of Queen Guinevere, her black hair taking the place of golden. In the design for the vision of the San Graal: "Lancelot has fallen asleep before the shrine full of angels, and between

him and it rises in his dreams the image of Queen Guinevere, the cause
of it all. She stands gazing at him with her arms extended in the branches
of an apple tree!"

For Rossetti the Jovial Campaign had enabled him to enjoy again
something of the first fine careless rapture of the P.-R.B. He won a holiday, a respite from life, such as is granted to few, as he sat once again
with a chosen company about an enchanted Round Table—not Round,
perhaps, as he himself was so obviously at its head. But there was a
difference, and, when the laughter died down and he was left alone,
he knew it. He was no longer a free man but tied "by a strand of golden
hair" to the ailing Lizzie, seeking health in various parts of the country.
He tried to keep the laughter loud enough to drown the echo of her
sighs: and usually it did.

The frescoes were by no means finished by the end of the Long
Vacation that summer, but Jane Burden became engaged to William
Morris. In the interval of two years before they were married, perhaps
Jane went away to be educated, for her later reading is unexpectedly
wide for the daughter of a groom, who can then barely have been
literate. As Morris had ample private means there seems no other reason
for the delay. The wedding took place in St. Michael's Church, Oxford,
on 26th April, 1859.[49] Richard Dixon, by then ordained, officiated. He
had been so thoroughly warned by the members of the Pembroke set
in their old teasing way against making any slip that he pronounced
them man and wife under the names of "William" and "Mary".

13

The Union paintings dragged on long past the appointed time and two
years later some of them were still unfinished. Since then they have been
more than once restored. It is remarkable that Woodward and the Building Committee, severely disappointed by the delays and the cost (for
"expenses" came heavy) as they must have been, were still willing to
commission a bas-relief by Munro from a design of Rossetti's and, on
his suggestions, statues from Woolner and Tupper.

Rossetti had had to leave Oxford sometime in the autumn of 1857
in order to join Lizzie in Matlock, where they stayed at Lime Tree View,
a Temperance Hotel high up above the town.[50] They went for walks

in the neighbouring fields and on expeditions to show places, but the magnificence of the scenery is nowhere reflected in Rossetti's work. He must have looked back nostalgically to Oxford and to the London he had begun to conquer. That he was not forgotten there, a letter to Mrs. Julia Cameron shows. Written on 29th December it thanks her for a vellum volume of *Edwin the Fair*, illustrated by Watts, and praises Val Prinsep's contribution to the Union: "Your nephew's work—already promised to rank with the best 'first pictures' within my experience", and he wishes all at Little Holland House a happy New Year.[51] There is no mention of Lizzie. Matlock did not help Lizzie any more than Bath so that in May it was decided that she might as well return to London, particularly as "tin" was short.

As her physical condition deteriorated, so did her behaviour. She was not helped by the unwise sympathy she received from Madox Brown's young second wife, Emma, who compensated her own sense of inferiority by encouraging Lizzie to protest and to run off to their house whenever she felt neglected. Poor Bruno was much interrupted in his work by the scenes that took place when Rossetti would arrive to fetch her back. On one occasion Rossetti refused to speak to Emma because she had encouraged Lizzie in her tantrums and this involved the two men in letters of protest and apology. The scenes she made only drove Rossetti out, and, besides amusing himself with casual encounters, at this time he became involved more seriously with Annie Miller.

It all began with Holman Hunt, who had used her as a model for "The Awakened Conscience", and then decided that she was an innocent in danger of corruption whom it was his duty to save. To this end he undertook to pay for her education and to improve her health under a good doctor. One was found who pronounced that her lungs were "weak but not diseased".[52] (To be tubercular was undoubtedly romantic.) When she had been cured and educated, she was to be rewarded with a wedding ring.

The Pre-Raphaelite group were particularly addicted to this form of matrimony: there was Madox Brown and his Emma; Stephens and Clara (whom he taught to write in school copybooks); Frederick Shields, a later friend, who was about as unsuccessful in his marriage with the sixteen-year-old Matilda Booth as the better-known "classic" cases of Watts and Ellen Terry, Ruskin and Effie Gray.

It was part of the Victorian ethos, a passion for improvement that went with faith in progress. If a woman were succoured she would be grateful and become good and devoted to the man responsible. Then she would fulfil the Tennysonian ideal:

> "In laws of marriage charactered in gold
> Upon the blanched tablets of her heart."

Or, as it was expressed by that poetic associate of the P.-R.B., Coventry Patmore:

> "A rapture of submission lifts
> Her life into celestial rest . . .
> And all the wisdom that she has
> Is to love him for being wise."

During the interval when Hunt went off to Palestine, he left a restricted list of artists to whom Annie might sit and amusements in which she might indulge. On his return he found her life had been anything but retired: she had been seen walking down Regent Street with a "swell whore", and in St. James' with a notorious rake, Lord Ranelagh. Hunt blamed this on Rossetti's influence, for he had encouraged her to sit to artists not on the list and had taken her to forbidden places of entertainment. Rossetti was not alone in being attracted to the girl, for if he and Boyce took her to dine at Bertolini's and to dance at Cremorne, William had also taken her out "boating; forgetful, it seems, of Miss R. [Rentoul] as Gabriel, sad dog, is of Guggums. They all seem mad about Annie", commented Brown in his Diary. Imperious as he was, Rossetti seems to have kept his sense of humour, at least where Boyce was concerned, in rivalry over her posing. (18th February, 1860) "Dear Boyce, Blow *you*, Annie is coming to *me* tomorrow (Wednesday). I'm sure you wont mind, like a good chap. Will you write to her for another day? She would hardly consent to ill-using you in this style, but I bored her till she did."[53]

To Stephens, his main confidant in the business, Hunt wrote: "If she cannot be preached to from the facts of her own bitter experience then she cannot be awakened at all. Do not omit to say that in rejecting my advice to avoid going to Rossetti and Boyce to sit she sacrificed my interest in her welfare to a very great extent."[52]

Later, when he was planning to marry someone else, Hunt asked Stephens to get back some of his letters to Annie, giving detailed instructions about placing a £5 note and a sovereign temptingly on the table in front of her. He was also to go to Boyce: "I suggest a more doubtful tone in talking to B. and a good scenting of his letter-table to see whether certain handwriting is there; lead him on with show of confidence . . . then add as a feeler that another cause of disagreement is that she will not give up a certain letter which she received from Brussels."

W. M. Rossetti, in his *Memoir*, admits that over Annie Miller his brother "was guilty of an offence", and that "it behoves me to add that Mr. Hunt was wholly blameless in the matter". It had all blown over by September according to Madox Brown. "Hunt and he seem all right again: Gabriel has forsworn flirting with Annie Miller it seems. Guggums having rebelled against it and he and Guggums seem on the best of terms now. She is painting at her picture."

In the conventional sense, Lizzie undoubtedly had cause for jealousy. Rossetti's casual encounters were frequent, if not serious (not even with Annie Miller), but in Fanny there were elements dangerous indeed to her hold over him. Fanny was healthy and abounding: she had "large, lovely arms and a neck like a Tower", no damozel but a sensuous woman. Even William Michael had to admire her: "a pre-eminently fine woman, with regular and sweet features, and a mass of the most lovely blonde hair". George Boyce records going off with him to dinner and "afterwards adjourned to 24, Dean Street, Soho, to see 'Fanny'. Interesting face and jolly hair and engaging disposition". He employed her himself at times as a model and once bought her a meal: "Went into Argyle Rooms. There met Fanny and took her to supper at Quinn's. She was in considerable trepidation lest Rossetti should come in—and lo! he did so." They must have all laughed it off together.

But it was a turning-point in Rossetti's life, as in his art, when he painted Fanny as "Bocca Baciata", a study in golds: Fanny's hair, her jewellery, the apple and the marigolds that she called "Them be'inds merrygoes". It took on "a rather Venetian aspect", Rossetti told Boyce, but friends like Hunt and Bell Scott disapproved of the picture's coarseness of conception. In a sense they were right: but he had to move out of mysticism into sensuality if he was to achieve a synthesis of them later.

At this time Rossetti was in the prime of his vigour as a man and as an artist, showing the "magnificent animality" that Ruskin praised aesthetically but disapproved in practice, and Fanny was a woman who could provide the satisfaction that Lizzie could not, would not, give.

The marvel is that it did not happen earlier and that he should have been satisfied for so long with such a literary love. In the words of that later parody of the P.-R.B. movement, Gilbert and Sullivan's *Patience*:

"If he's content with a vegetable love which would certainly not suit me,
    Why, what a most particularly pure young man this pure young man must be!"

Rossetti's friends were high-spirited; they enjoyed boisterous jokes and, except for Hunt, were not inclined to be pompous or puritanical, but there was no one among them in tune with the latin cast of his mind. The others had no natural irony or scepticism to question their enthusiasms. And William Michael was too nice to be of help.

In the matter of breaking with Lizzie Siddal a more ruthless and single-minded man would have cut his losses: would have killed his love.

> "The kind man does it with a sword,
> The coward with a kiss."

But Rossetti was not single-minded. His English-governess side believed that he had a duty to Lizzie; in short that with misplaced chivalry he ought to make an honest woman of her. The side of him that was superstitious dreaded the remorse he would feel if he were to fail in his duty and have her physical death on his conscience. He took her to Hastings and from there wrote to William about their marriage licence:

> "I still trust to God we may be able to use it. If not I shall have so much to grieve for, and (what is worse) so much to reproach myself with, and I do not know how it might end for me . . ."

Although, on the surface, he hastens to agree with the friends who advised that marriage might prove a cure for her illness more effective than medicines or changes of air, deep down may be suspected a subconscious desire for his freedom.

They were married in Hastings at St. Clement's Church on 23rd May, 1860.[54] After the ceremony, which was attended only by the necessary witnesses, he wrote to his mother:

> "Lizzie and I are just back from church. We are going to Folkestone today, hoping to get on to Paris if possible: but you will be grieved to hear her health is no better at all. Love to all."

Strange that the invalid at death's door could stand the journey to France! But no miracle rewarded him for doing his duty, and the painting he chose to work upon was ominous enough—another rendering of the legend "How They Met Themselves", which he had started before. In it a young couple come face to face with their own ghosts in a wood: the four stand enclosed in their own group and beyond them is an entanglement of menacing trees.

"The trees wave their heads with an omen to tell." When Lizzie and Gabriel faced the ghosts of their earlier selves, the double image gave them no encouragement in the way they had to take together through the wood.

14

Rossetti, who had been bored with Paris when he went there as a young man with Hunt, was not less so on his honeymoon. The newly-married Burne-Jones had hoped to join them there.[55] "I want to see you so badly, I hope Lizzie will stand me," Ned had written. "I'll do anything to be agreeable—so will Georgie," but the plan fell through. A Cockney abroad, Rossetti read Pepys aloud and completed his unlikely water-colour, "Dr. Johnson at the Mitre". He continued in his line of duty by remaining there for three weeks as the air seemed to do Lizzie good, but for once in his life he cannot have been sorry when "tin" gave out and return to England was essential.

London always cheered him: the miasma of the Thames was a tonic and for a moment it seemed they had come right back to the mood of their first meetings. On arrival at Chatham Place they heard of the death of Brough, whose family was left destitute. They dashed into a cab, kept it waiting while they pawned Lizzie's little bits and pieces of jewellery and hurried off to press on the widow what money they had raised. Back in Chatham Place together they must have felt a glow of satisfaction which promised harmony and happiness ahead.

There was plenty to do: pictures to be painted that had been already commissioned and paid for, and translations of Italian poems to be completed for a volume that he projected. It was tiresome to have to take time off to wander round Hampstead looking for some house where the air would be better for Lizzie, but as a dutiful husband he did it and found rooms in Downshire Hill where he installed her and returned there nightly from working all day in Blackfriars. Both were relieved when the landlord of Chatham Place proposed to extend their sitting-room into the next-door house. This did nothing to improve the con-dition of the riverside air, but they snatched at the scheme as an excuse not to move.

Like any other newly-married couple, they were left to themselves in the first weeks of their return. Friends accepted the convention of not interrupting them in the business of settling-in, in this case perhaps a little more uncertain than usual as to their welcome. Rossetti wrote with rather strained coyness to Alexander Munro:[56] "I have been wondering about you, whether you were yet 'one of us'—to wit, the respectables, but supposing not as I did not hear of it, & hoping most sincerely that what you told me of the lady & illness when last I saw you does not continue to be the case to the extent of deferring your marriage, as I have seen by the great change in cheerfulness which has been evident in you since the day was fixed, how far greater your prospect of happiness will be by this than any other means. . . ."

Gradually this changed—as it would with any other couple. First there were old friends in the same boat to be seen: William and Janey Morris at Red House, Upton—"The Towers of Topsy", built specially for them by their young architect friend, Philip Webb, and furnished and decorated with things Morris had made for himself when he was disgusted with the ugliness of those he found in the shops.

Then there was Ned himself, whose wife, Georgiana, had been one of the beautiful and talented Macdonald sisters, who each made interesting marriages. Wedded on "Dante's own day", 9th June, 1860, they were now living, rather hard up, in Russell Place, and were to meet, together with the Madox Browns, in the Zoological Gardens, "by the wombats' lair". "Georgie", now and for some years the confidante and comforter of the other women of the P.-R.B., became in later life a stormy petrel herself. Suffragette and pro-Boer, she had to be rescued from an angry crowd at Rottingdean by her nephew, Rudyard Kipling.

Ruskin was a belated visitor. No doubt allergic to newly-wed households, he was touchy about their reception of him. Were they not fond enough of him to receive him at any time with open arms?

> "I wish Lizzie and you liked me enough to—say—put on a dressing-gown and run in for a minute rather than not see me: or paint on a picture in an unsightly state, rather than not amuse me when I was ill. But you can't *make* yourselves like me, and you would only like me less if you tried."

This querulous-pathetic note was to be sounded throughout the year in complaints that Rossetti was procrastinating in painting his portrait, intended for Charles Eliot Norton, the American professor and collector. However dilatory Rossetti could be in fulfilling commissions, in this case it was the sitter's vagaries that were to blame, for his *odi et amo* regard for himself shows nowhere so clearly as in his neurotic attitude to having his likeness taken, as even Burne-Jones was to find.

Other newer friends came to call at Chatham Place; Swinburne, following up his hero-worship of Rossetti at Oxford with an intense admiration—a *schwärmerei*—for Lizzie. "We lived," he wrote, "on terms of affectionate kindness and exuberant generosity." Rossetti's encouragement led to the writing of some of his best poetry and in return he himself enjoyed intellectual stimulation from the younger man. In sheer brain power Rossetti was far ahead of his early friends; probably only in Swinburne did he find the same quality, and Swinburne was a better scholar and much more widely read.

Swinburne brought George Meredith, who had published *Richard Feverel* but enjoyed so little success from it that he had to earn a sparse living from journalism. At this time he was at the height of his Greek God handsomeness and strength: when he laughed, "it was of short duration but it was a roar".

Simeon Solomon was also introduced by Swinburne. A promising young painter, who had made a corner in the Jewish pictures inspired by his Hebraic upbringing, he wanted nothing so much as to sit at the feet of Rossetti. This extended to the framing of his pictures, for Holman Hunt meeting him in Italy wrote to Stephens: "Little Solomon who came here a short time since was horrified at seeing the glitter of the burnish, and burnishing, you know, having been consistently denounced by Rossetti for the last twenty years, is considered quite a crime."[57] At this time Solomon had charm and good looks and was a long way from the physical and moral wreck who died in a Workhouse Infirmary. He provides in his career a sorry link between pre-Raphaelitism and the 'Nineties, paying a price for decadence that those who led him to it avoided for themselves.

Solomon brought the eminently respectable Henry Holliday, who was mainly working on stained glass at this time. His picture "The Meeting of Dante and Beatrice", painted in the 1880's, rivalled Millais' "Bubbles" in popularity as a print and brought to a wide public the story that Rossetti was the first to re-tell to the Victorian age. Frederic Sandys, whose caricature of "Sir Isumbras at the Ford" had amused them at the Union, also became a regular visitor. Looking like Don Quixote and, however hard up, always managing to wear a spotless white waistcoat, he stayed at home when it had to go to the wash. He was a wit but an unstable character and in later years bit the hands that fed him, notably Rossetti's. And, very important for the outcome, there also called Alexander Gilchrist, who was embarking on his biography of Blake and wanted to see the note-book that Rossetti had bought from Palmer. He generously allowed this but, he told Bell Scott, "on condition of his printing the whole of the printable contents, as I have always meant to do something with it, and should not like its effect as a whole to be weakened".[58]

When Rossetti and Lizzie went to stay at Red House, they took a hand in the decoration as if it were another Union lark. Rossetti painted panels for a cabinet and a door, and Ned contributed to the walls some murals of "Chaldeans in Extract Vermilion".

They had mock-battles with the apples from the trees in the garden and played hide-and-seek over the great settle indoors. "Topsy-baiting" went on in his own house much as it had done in the Union days, and Janey, as a hostess, was much more the groom's daughter than Guinevere. There is a story of Morris sitting on a stool in front of the fire and someone—probably the large Val Prinsep—coming up and slapping him hard behind. "Don't do it, Janey!" called out Morris, without looking round.

And once, when they all went for a walk together, they overheard the village children singing a hymn in their schoolroom. "Amen," shouted Rossetti loudly outside the window and ran away.

On one of these visits the idea of The Firm was started. These fine things that Morris was making, why not sell them to the public, make money and encourage better taste? Other good fellows among their friends could be roped in. Burne-Jones had already designed the St. Frideswide's window in Christ Church, Oxford; Webb often made the tables and chairs for his houses; Arthur Hughes had tried his hand at jewellery as well as at stained glass; and Madox Brown was something of a cabinet-maker and had built himself several pieces of furniture. Faulkner was brought in to keep the books because he was a Mathematics don, and Paul Marshall for no reason at all.

The times were ripe for The Firm, with the expansion in Victorian prestige house-building and with the new interest in church decoration, due to the Tractarian movement. Rossetti drafted most of the first prospectus—applying his literary ability to his latin turn for haggling —and made some optimistic claims in it. The artists concerned were "men of varied experience" and undertook that decorative work of all classes would be "estimated for, and executed in a business-like manner". But, although successful beyond their expectations, The Firm hardly confirmed the idealistic belief that "good decoration involving rather the luxury of taste than the luxury of costliness will be found to be much less expensive than is generally supposed."*

If The Firm was the third of the movements which owed their inspiration to Rossetti—another conspiracy of the P.-R.B. to influence public taste and despoil the Philistines—it was also the last of them. In craftsmanship William Morris found his vocation and gone for ever

* See Appendix C, p. 225.

was the time when he looked to Rossetti as his master. He did not try his hand at painting again and his poetry was to be at the opposite pole from Rossetti's.

15

A conventional chapter of friendships and enterprises with other newly-married young couples cannot be the whole story when the husband is Rossetti. He was a painter and a poet and a complicated personality. He had formed habits which he did not want to give up and only the English-governess side of him thought it necessary that he should. "Marriage was not a tie he had become able to bear," wrote Bell Scott later, and, in a passage suppressed by his editor: "Marriage by the colour of the hair is rather a precarious way of dealing with the most momentous action of life." Paradoxically, Rossetti was more prepared than Lizzie to settle down. He could have done with a background as emotionally stable and sympathetic as the home of his parents, if his wife could have provided it—if she had been willing to tend the house for him, for, although he was untidy, Rossetti was also house-proud. He liked to collect antiques and junk and, with increasing enthusiasm, strange animals, which needed someone to care for them, as much as he did himself. Inspired by "the house that Top built", Rossetti even tried his hand at designing wall-paper on "common brown packing paper and on blue grocer's paper, to try which is best", as he described the operation with a sketch to Allingham.

Their life together is sometimes called Bohemian but it was not so in the sense of being disorderly from heavy drinking or having wild parties. Certainly both of them were feckless, rushing out to small cheap restaurants for their meals; often hard up, lending and borrowing freely, and Lizzie was inclined to be slatternly, but in the way in which she might conveniently have been Bohemian she was all too middle-class, at once suspicious and resentful of her husband's relations with other women. How gladly would Gabriel have come back to her as a wife if she had been a mother-figure ready to forgive and to comfort—and to cook.

His relations with his family after his marriage were guarded, which was not a comfortable situation for a son particularly devoted to his mother. Neither side wanted a breach and he was at pains to keep her informed of the state of Lizzie's health—which always prevented her from accepting the invitations from Albany Street. Rossetti kept closely in touch with his family on literary matters, seeking help with his translations of Italian poems from William, whose accuracy was invaluable in collating his versions with the originals, and also exchanging criticisms with Christina. He had interested Macmillan in her "Up Hill" which first appeared in Macmillan's "Magazine" in 1860, and he had sent "Goblin Market" to Ruskin, but was much annoyed when he received the reply: "Your sister should exercise herself in the severest commonplace of metre until she can write as the public like. Then if she puts in her observation and passion all will become precious."

"Most senseless," Rossetti wrote to William Michael. "I have told him something of the sort in my letter."

Between his marriage in 1860 till the end of 1861, Rossetti worked on completing the "Cassandra" for which Annie Miller had posed, and started on "Fair Rosamund" from Fanny. That his association with her continued, although she had now married a man called Hughes, is shown by her husband's appearance as the young David in the left panel of the Llandaff triptych. Morris is the crowned king on the right.

"I am not so despairingly dilatory quite now, I think, as I used to be in those former old days." He also had his translations put into print in the spring of 1861, as this made it easier to correct and revise them. A few of these trial-books were sent to friends, although not primarily intended for private circulation. One went to Bell Scott in April: "I am sending you my book of translations by Book Post—printed but not yet fathered by a publisher—which work I am now about."

The poems came out later in the year, 1861, from Smith, Elder under the title *The Early Italian Poets, together with Dante's Vita Nuova*.[59] Ruskin had guaranteed expenses which, when repaid eight years later, meant a new profit of £9 to Rossetti. The volume was, in a sense, a trailer for original verse to follow—indeed, this was advertised at the time so that when asking Allingham for advice he could add: "it is therefore not time wasted to advise me". He also showed considerable anxiety for the manuscripts he sent round to friends to be returned promptly as he had made no copies. On "Jenny" he asked Allingham whether he saw any objection in the treatment, "or any side of the subject left untouched which ought to be included".

He was very annoyed with Ruskin's strictures when, with other poems, he sent it to him to put before Thackeray, then editing "The Cornhill". "Jenny" did not rhyme with "guinea" he complained, and "the character of the speaker himself is too doubtful . . . no affection for the girl shows itself—his throwing the money into her hair is disorderly—he is alto-gether a disorderly person. My chief reason for not sending it to Thack-eray is this discordance and too great boldness for common readers".

Rossetti could hardly expect Ruskin to be treated solely as a literary agent and from his experience over Christina's poems should have been forewarned. This time there was an additional bitterness in his suspicion that Ruskin now saw Rossetti himself as something of a "disorderly person".

It was sometime this year that Rossetti found Fitzgerald's *Omar Khay-yam*. The story must be discarded that he came across a copy in the penny-box outside a bookshop in Leicester Square, for he was given it on 10th July, 1861, by a friend, Whitley Stokes.* Nevertheless, it was Rossetti's excitement over the poem communicated to Swinburne which "put it on the market", and the story of their return to the bookstall for more and their indignation that the price had risen to twopence is still *ben trovato*.

"You should have heard, you can imagine," wrote Swinburne, "the eloquent and impressive severity of Gabriel's humorous expostulations with the stall-keeper on behalf of a defrauded if limited public."

Another story can be substituted of Rossetti and Swinburne taking the precious book with them on a Saturday afternoon's excursion to Meredith at Copsham and declaiming it with him on a mound in his garden. Afterwards, indoors, Swinburne took up a quill pen and wrote off the first thirteen stanzas of "Laus Veneris" in red ink.

Another writer discovered by the Rossettis about this time was Walt Whitman, a copy of whose *Leaves of Grass* had been sent to William Michael by Bell Scott. "Obliterate utterly," Bell Scott wrote, "with the blackest ink half-a-dozen lines and half-a-dozen words, ignore the author altogether, and read as one does the books that express human life like the Bible—books that have aggregated rather than been written—and one finds these *Leaves of Grass* grow up in a wonderful manner. The book is very like an opening into a quite new poetic condition . . ."

The brothers never quite agreed on Whitman. W.M. at once thought him "glorious", but Gabriel would not go further than to declare him-self "not without appreciation of his fine qualities". His first reaction to the new poetic condition was expressed to Allingham: "I have not been so happy in loathing anything for a long while—except, I think, *Leaves of Grass* by that Orson of yours." Another thing loathed was Longfellow's *Wishi-washi*, as he called *The Golden Legend*.

The literary activity of most importance to Rossetti at this time was

* See Appendix D, p. 226.

the help he gave to Gilchrist in the work on Blake. With his usual enthusiasm for bringing in friends, he suggested that Georgie Burne-Jones, supervised by Ned, might make blocks for the illustrations, but this fell through. He and Gilchrist used to dine together at the Cheshire Cheese, and he admired the capable and sympathetic Anne Gilchrist. It is a pity that he and her husband did not listen to her protests at their methods of editing! Not only did they alter punctuation and actual lines—"my rather unceremonious shaking up of Blake's rhymes", Rossetti shamelessly called it—but they made a bonfire of scraps that they thought valueless.

There is an affinity between Blake and Rossetti closer than simply that of both being painter-poets, even if the view of a mystical relation between the death of one and the birth of the other is not accepted. Rossetti, who had the superstitiousness of the non-religious, as he had the hard-headedness of the romantic south, would probably have been prepared to agree to something of it, for he was one who did not deny curious links in the universe.

> "The angels most heedful
> Receive each mild spirit
> New worlds to inherit. . . ."

That he shared a sense of such continuity is shown in his own:

> "I have been here before
> But when or how I cannot tell . . ."

and of some other than mortal heritage again in "The Birth-Bond":

> "That among souls allied to mine as yet
> One nearer kindred than life hinted of.
> O born with me somewhere that men forget,
> And though in years of sight and sound unmet,
> Known for my soul's birth-partner well enough."

Rossetti's poetry is much more akin to that of Blake than to any of his own contemporaries. There is a similar economy of language. Simple words are used by both to express complex thoughts: indeed, with Rossetti, his style could be summed up in a snap judgment as "sentiments lush, statement stark". There is no doubt that they had an outlook in common, albeit Blake's independence was more robust, or, simply, he was luckier in the age into which he was born, when there was more to revolt against: there was no Reynolds for the Pre-Raphaelites to attack. And Blake was luckier in his love-life in the possession of his Catherine. When Rossetti wrote on Blake, he showed himself completely at home. He understood him so well that he could praise or criticise justly with no temptation to fall into the biographer's besetting sin of patronage. Anything beyond his knowledge or experience he accepts as something to be respected—a "new strange fruit" that belonged to his subject alone. There is no sense of strain in Rossetti's prose whether he is explaining a difficult passage or picture, or, with characteristic generosity, bringing in references to his own contemporaries; his clarity is inspired. In the last words of his Introduction he provides a text that should be written large over every biographer's desk: "Any who can find here anything to love will be the poet-painter's welcome guests . . . (who) can meet their host's eye with sympathy and recognition even when he offers them the new strange fruits grown for himself in far-off gardens where he has dwelt alone, or pours for them the wines which he has learned to love in lands they never travelled."

It was a severe blow to Rossetti when Gilchrist died suddenly in November from scarlatina, caught from his children. Rossetti has been criticised for absenting himself from the funeral; "it would hardly be safe" —how he hated illness!—but he was to render the best service possible to his memory in helping his widow to finish the book on Blake.

It has been said that Rossetti's friends moved away from him as they "saw through him" or outgrew his influence and that on his side he was a leader greedy for followers, dependent on them to boost his ego. There is less than half a truth in this. It is the common fate of pioneers—like parents—to have their offspring outgrow them, but the further they go and the sooner, the greater should be the credit to those who begot them. As Rossetti wrote in a note-book: "In early life the affinities of men are uppermost to draw them together: later their individualities become tyrannous & sunder them." Under Rossetti's influence Burne-Jones and Morris found themselves—as both admitted. Holman Hunt, jealous and resentful as he was later, owed everything to the early fertilising inspiration of the P.-R.B., and Madox Brown, their master, declared that from the moment Rossetti had been his pupil he himself never painted without his approbation in mind.

What is extraordinary in the Pre-Raphaelite Brotherhood is not its break-up, but how many friendships survived and for how long. 1848–1861, thirteen years, would be a record for most comrades in Club photographs. Naturally there was some regrouping as the years went on.

After 1860 Hunt and Woolner saw less of Rossetti and drew closer together, moving in the same set (that of Lord Leighton and Little Holland House), and becoming brothers-in-law through marriage to the Waugh sisters, Woolner to Alice in 1864, Hunt to Fanny in 1865 and to Edith in 1873, though this led to a complete break between them, as Edith was a deceased wife's sister and Woolner disapproved. Hunt wrote to Stephens, evidently on the principle that it is better to marry than to burn: "My passions still burn within me and the fear that those—having no lawful hope—should burst out by contact with unlawful tender into an unholy flame."[60] But he could not face the ordeals of a long engagement: "The sort of thing that Woolner is going through now, a long examination, a dreary series of courtship before second persons and introductions."

The trouble over Annie Miller had aggravated Hunt's disapproval of Rossetti, and, anxious to be free of his influence, he picked a quarrel over their pictures, "Found" and "The Soul's Awakening", accusing Rossetti of stealing his subject. Anything less alike it is difficult to imagine but at this period the question of exclusive subjects and also titles was a burning one. Rossetti considered that Millais, for instance, was a "sneak" capable of stealing from his contemporaries.* The root of the trouble with Hunt was his jealousy and may be summed up in the garbled version of a young grand-daughter fed on his widow's propaganda against Rossetti:

"He was Grandpa's pupil and never paid the rent and sent his picture—Grandpa painted most of it—to an Exhibition without telling him and Johnnie Millais although he had said he wouldn't until theirs was ready too ... It was Grandpa and Millais who started it all and it was Pre-Raphaelitism with a T."

Oddly enough, the one Brother to whom Hunt remained loyal to the end, was the one who moved the farthest away from their first ideals—Millais. His popularity established by "The Black Brunswicker" and deliberately maintained by sentimental pot-boilers, he had come to terms with all their early enemies from Dickens to the Royal Academy and Society. He and Effie now graced every assembly and departed from London at the correct times of year for the grouse moors and for Scotland. Hunt was not jealous of success in a field so different from his own: if anything, it heightened by contrast his own loyalty to their early principles. He could forgive deviation but not competition. What

* See Appendix AII, p. 221.

rankled was the leadership of the P.-R.B., accorded to that "sly Italian", whose ghost was to haunt the Olympian heights of Melbury Road.

The Brother who became most conceited and over-bearing was Woolner. When he won "the honour, tip-top" of being commissioned to do Palmerston's statue for Palace Yard in 1867, he wrote to Stephens: "It opens the ball of my Metropolitan career and you might give a hint to an able editor as to the propriety of recognising the advance of a hastening and inevitable fact."[61] He may be suspected of some duplicity when he secured the commission for the sculptures at Wallington over Munro's head—Bell Scott had introduced both of them to the Trevelyans —and he was involved in the scandal about the Catalogue to the International Exhibition of 1862 when Palgrave "puffed" Woolner while abusing Marochetti, Adam and Munro. Exception was taken to this and, when it was discovered that Palgrave and Woolner shared the same house, the Catalogue had to be re-written.

Munro, who paired-off with Arthur Hughes, kept up his friendship with Rossetti to the end, and so did F. G. Stephens, although, for all his loyalty, one suspects that Rossetti found him rather a bore. He survived as art critic to "The Athenaeum" until 1905, when he was displaced by Roger Fry.

In a later generation, Rossetti's influence inspired Swinburne to his best work, as he readily admitted, and he "discovered" not only *Omar Khayyam* and Blake, but also Walt Whitman, even if he disliked much of him. He was one of the first to appreciate *Richard Feverel* and later he was to suggest the theme of *The Deemster* to the young Hall Caine. Sometimes he thrust his enthusiasms down unwilling throats: *Joseph and his Brethren*, a poetic drama by Charles Jeremiah Wells, was one which Meredith refused to recommend to Chapman and Hall, though Swinburne was ready to listen "devoutly" to it read aloud for hours on end and tried to emulate Rossetti's rendering on visits to the Trevelyans at Wallington.

The succession of new admirers displacing the old, one literary discovery following another, is evidence of Rossetti's intense vitality. His personal magnetism held beyond first youth, for his exuberant and generous enthusiasm was backed by a strong intellect. He insisted on the need for "fundamental brainwork" in painting and in poetry and was capable of applying it, but too often he did not do so for complexity of character hamstrung his will and personal charm let him "get by". That was his weakness.

16

At the opening of 1861 it seemed as if Rossetti's marriage might be entering upon a new phase, for Lizzie was pregnant. The ordinary young wife in her should have gained confidence from an event that put her in the same condition as such settled and respectable matrons as Janey Morris and Georgie Burne-Jones. She was to be a mother now and no longer an elf-girl. It might be a straw to clutch at for her salvation. But in May she was brought to bed of a dead child, a girl who had been lifeless in her womb for the past three weeks. Rossetti's thoughts were all for her, relieved of the guilt he would have felt if it had been his wife who had died for his child. "She herself is so far the most important that I can feel nothing but thankfulness."

But at a party at Red House for the christening of the infant daughter of Top and Janey, Rossetti was very depressed. He sat gloomy and silent, eating raisins from a large bowl and refusing to touch any wine to raise his spirits. Georgie asked him to pass her the water: "I beg your pardon, Georgie: I had forgotten that you, like myself, are a temperate person." Rossetti priggish!

Perhaps he knew that they were not only celebrating the birth of Morris' child but also the death of their old way of life. No more Jovial Campaigns: no more splashing paint on the panels of Red House doors or hilarious games of hide-and-seek round the great settle. "At eight, the coffee was all drunk," but this time it was not a joke.

When Lizzie went to stay next at Red House, while Rossetti was in Yorkshire painting a commissioned portrait of Mrs. Aldam Heaton,[62] she fled the new atmosphere. Inconsiderately she left no word as to her intentions and Rossetti had to appeal to his mother in the absence of William Michael:

> "My dear Mama,
>   I am out here painting a portrait and left Lizzie staying with the Morrises. Now she writes that she had left them in a hurry, making me very uneasy, as I know there was not a halfpenny of money at Chatham Place. If at all possible, would you go there, and take her some few pounds. . . ."

Again Lizzie was out of things: there was the inevitable change at "the house that Top built" and back in London, in October, the Burne-Joneses also had a baby. She had offered her layette to Georgie but

Rossetti intervened: "Lizzie had been talking to me of parting with a certain small wardrobe to you. But don't let her, please. It looks such a bad omen for us."

Courageously she went with Janey Morris to pay a call on the new-comer. Presumably she was pregnant again, for Georgie prefaces her description of the two "Goddesses" by saying "neither of them was under the cloud of ill-health, so that, as an Oriental might say, the purpose of the creator was manifest in them".

"They were as unlike as possible and quite perfect as a contrast to each other . . . the difference between the two women may be typified broadly as that between sculpture and painting, Mrs. Morris being the statue and Mrs. Rossetti the picture: the grave nobility and colourless perfection of feature in the one was made human by kindness that looked from 'her great eyes standing far apart', while a wistfulness that often accompanies the brilliant loveliness and grace of the other gave an unearthly character to her beauty."

But Lizzie did not always bother to keep up appearances. Even to the Madox Browns, the most understanding and loyal of friends, Rossetti had to apologise for one of her sudden departures; particularly embarrassing when he had brought along a patron to interest him in Brown's work:

"I could not mention about Lizzie's leaving before Mr. Rae . . . I hope if she comes again she may be better and give you less trouble. I write this word, since her departure must have surprised you, as her return did me."

Someone meeting her at Red House described her as "appearing without a word at dinner, rising—gliding away silent and unobserved as she had come—a ghost in the house of the living". Her Eurydice vanishings became more frequent as fits of depression deepened, re-acting on her physical health.

She no longer had the energy to paint: "Unhappily," wrote Rossetti to Charles E. Norton, "she is too confirmed an invalid to leave a hope now that she will ever be able to make the most of her genius." But she could still write those plaintive verses in the old ballad form that have real tenderness and poignancy, and, alas, prophecy.

> "And, Mother dear, take a sapling twig
> And green grass newly mown,
> And lay them on my empty bed
> That my sorrow be not known.

> And, Mother dear, when the sun has set,
> And the pale church grass waves,
> Then carry me through the dim twilight
> And hide me among the graves."

The suggestion that she was pregnant again is supported by the account of a visit paid to her by Bessie Parkes on February 9th, when she seemed unusually cheerful as she sat sewing at baby garments. If it were so, it must have been with more apprehension than hope that she and Gabriel looked forward to the outcome. Was she not now already a confirmed invalid?

The lovely Guggums "a confirmed invalid": the very phrase, so bourgeois, so Victorian, spells disillusion and reflects the strain the situation was putting on her artist husband. He had been very "good" to her, performing all the offices of a nurse on those Cures and at Hastings before their marriage—and they were not pretty. To Madox Brown he had written in April, 1860: "Lizzie, I find, prefers being alone with me, and indeed it would be too painful for anyone to witness." She had a sister, Clara, who occasionally visited them, and a brother, James,[63] afterwards claimed, "during the latter years of the fifties, I saw much of my sister", but the Rossetti family had been too often rebuffed to offer their services. She only wanted Gabriel; his vitality was all that kept her alive.

Rossetti tried, too, to be patient with her moods, realising that she was under the influence of the drugs she had taken for neuralgia since the still-birth, but he must have found it less and less easy, for he was not a placid man—he and Christina had been the "storms" of the family as children—and he had work to do. After a quarrel what more likely and understandable than that he would fling out of the house along to Cremorne Gardens, or to Fanny, ready with comfort and no questions asked? She might provide sexual satisfaction and, more important, relaxation; some jokes, coarse but at least good-tempered, and a meal, for Fanny knew how "to feed the beast" and would quickly prepare for him some favourite dish.

Sometimes he would try to pretend that all was well and invite a party of men friends to "oysters and obloquy" in the studio. It had worked all right when their wives could talk together, but now Janey and Georgie were too occupied with their babies, and Emma Brown—little as he cared for her influence anyway—could not leave Oliver, the infant prodigy, or risk again the younger child, whose health she had endangered already by going backwards and forwards to attend Lizzie while she was feeding him.

Lizzie had repulsed other acquaintances and now she simply retired to bed while the men talked into the small hours in the studio; some of them insisting—fussily, thought Rossetti—on keeping the balcony window shut because of the smell from the river. Only Swinburne was always welcome. With him Lizzie became her old, lively, chaffing self or would lie quite still on her chaise-longue listening while he read to her from the Elizabethan dramatists, as carefully bowdlerised for her ears as were his own poems. Their two red heads made them look like brother and sister together—a relationship that suited both.

It was with pleasure, therefore, that Lizzie must have looked forward to the Monday evening (February 10th) when they were to try out his latest discovery in restaurants—the Sablonière in Leicester Square—which excited him because it was the haunt of Continental conspirators. Later Rimbaud was to feel at home there, enjoying in its nostalgic atmosphere of distant revolution, *réunions ardentes et combatives*.[64]

She had a new mantle for the occasion and was particularly gay during the meal, which was early, at 6.30 or so. By eight o'clock they were back at the door of Chatham Place. Swinburne went off alone and Rossetti saw Lizzie upstairs before going to the Working Men's College. A neighbour, Ellen McIntyre, dropped in for a few minutes.

So much is known, but there are possible differences of emphasis and interpretation. Was her gaiety hysterical—reaction from some quarrel during the afternoon—or the effect of too much brandy taken after the laudanum? Did Rossetti linger on his way back home from the College? And with what thoughts did Lizzie prepare for sleep?

> I can but give a sinking heart
>   And weary eyes of pain;
> A faded mouth that cannot smile
>   And may not laugh again.
>
> Yet keep thine arms around me, love,
>   Until I drop to sleep;
> Then leave me—saying no good bye
>   Lest I might fall asleep.

Rossetti returned about half-past eleven to find the house strangely still. He called out but there was no response. He mounted the stairs to their bedroom, and when he turned up the light saw her lying on the bed unconscious, her breath coming in strangled gasps. Distraught, he rushed to call Miss McIntyre and the caretaker in the flat below, then went out himself for the doctor, Francis Hutchinson. The doctor came at once and tried every remedy he knew. To be there while the stomach pump was being used was too much for Rossetti, who set off to walk up to Madox Brown's. This good friend, awakened at what was now five in the morning, did not hesitate but dressed and accompanied him back to Chatham Place where Dr. Hutchinson had to tell them that there was nothing he could do. Lizzie was dead. Not believing it, Rossetti set out for Dr. John Marshall, a personal friend, and made him come himself and bring two other doctors with him.

So lovely she looked, lying peacefully as he had so often drawn her, with her bright hair undimmed, that when the undertakers came to close the coffin lid, Rossetti left Brown and William for a moment and going into the room alone placed his book of poems under the hair he had loved. "I have often been working at these poems when she was ill and suffering and I might have been attending to her and now they shall go."

There was a poem she had written and possibly copied out that evening which William Michael found and treasured. It is a last flicker of the talent that had been brought to life under the warmth of her lover's influence. Blake-like wraiths hover about the gold bar of heaven with the name of God for a Pre-Raphaelite prop.

> "How is it in the unknown land?
>   Do the dead wander hand in hand?
>   Do we clasp dead hands, and quiver
>   With an endless joy for ever?
>   Is the air filled with sound
>   Of spirits circling round and round?
>   Are there lakes of endless song
>   To rest our tired eyes upon?
>   Do tall white angels gaze and wend
>   Along the banks where lilies bend?
>   Lord, we know not how this may be:
>   Good Lord we put our faith in thee—
>   O God, remember me."

At the inquest held on 12th February, 1862, the verdict was returned that Elizabeth Eleanor Rossetti had "by means aforesaid accidentally and casually and by misfortune come to her death". It was kindly meant so that the young woman should escape the indignity of burial outside the churchyard walls. Lizzie, who had no dogmatic faith, would hardly have minded one way or the other. Would she not have given a wry smile and perhaps made a tart remark if she had known she was to be honoured by burial in the Rossetti grave at Highgate, where the old Professor already lay?

Since then other inquests have been held and other verdicts offered: intentional suicide and, in Violet Hunt's innuendo, murder. Much depends on the piece of paper found in the room and not mentioned at the official inquest. According to one version it was pinned to her nightgown: according to another it was lying on the floor. Whichever way it was, Rossetti thrust it into his pocket and showed it to Madox Brown, who destroyed it—foolishly, no doubt, but not criminally. Rumour had it that the message on the paper ran, "Perhaps you'll be sorry now," or "My life is so miserable I wish for no more of it." On these versions Violet Hunt based two stories: one that Lizzie could bear no more of her husband's infidelities: the other that they had quarrelled violently on returning from the restaurant and Rossetti had pushed the laudanum bottle over to her, telling her to take as much as she liked of it—then flung out to Fanny at Wapping.

But there has been definite evidence since that what the note[65] said was "Take care of Harry", Harry being one of her brothers who was feeble-minded. The destruction of the note was unfortunate and so has been suppression of entries in Allingham's *Diary* and Bell Scott's *Autobiographical Notes*, though the latter do not throw any new light on the matter.[66] In times of crisis people do not act sensibly and later on may go on covering up until something that needs to be covered up is created. That there was a note at all proves deliberate suicide, but what was the motive? The drug within reach would have offered eternal relief from the nagging pain that was wearing her out and making fatal inroads on the beauty so precious to her husband, or it might have provided the means of revenge by which she could punish him for reproaches or moments of neglect. Or, perhaps, by the early years of their delight together, she may have been freely granting Rossetti his release from bondage to the ghost of her youth and her beauty.

PART THREE

SUCCESS IN CHEYNE WALK
1863–1870

17

Mrs. Rossetti took her son back to the family home, for he could not bear to stay on in his once-beloved Chatham Place, and friends rallied round. Georgie and Ned Burne-Jones heard the news from Red Lion Mary, who arrived in hysterics exclaiming, "O, Mrs. Rissetti, Mrs. Rissetti." When they calmed her down and found out what had happened, Georgie at once went to see if she could be of any help, begging Ned "not to go out in such weather". Ruskin presumably heard from the Burne-Joneses for he called soon after and was seen by William Michael, with whom he had an unexpectedly sympathetic talk, glad, perhaps, to discuss his growing religious doubts with an enlightened agnostic—one of those he now regarded as a possibly "higher class of thinker", since he himself had now reached a critical point "on the very edge of infidelity".

As Rossetti made periodical bonfires of all papers except bills, there is no direct evidence of the reactions of his friends to the tragedy, but from their comments in books or in correspondence with each other there comes through a strong feeling that Lizzie's death was a happy release. Despite the shock of it, the tragedy had been in her suffering, not in the finish to it. For many of those who had known her it must have seemed as if this was just one more of her disappearances. She had faded away for the last time—Eurydice returned to the shades from which she had been reclaimed by her lover.

Except for Swinburne's account of finding the widower "sobbing and unmanned", there is a consensus of opinion in support of William's evidence that "he was not prostrated in that kind of way which makes a man incapable of self-regulation".[67] This restraint shows itself in a letter to Anne Gilchrist whose sympathy was among the most understanding that he received: "Of my dear wife," he wrote, "I do not dare to speak now, nor to attempt any vain conjecture whether it may ever be possible for me, or I be found worthy, to meet her again." There is an echo here of a phrase he had used to Gilchrist himself on the occasion of the death of Woodward, which shows his desire for belief in some form of immortality in order that friends might be met again: "If I am ever

found worthy to meet him again, it will be where the dejection is un-
needed which I cannot but feel at this moment."

But he could not accept orthodox Christianity. If he went back to his
mother's house, he did not go back to her faith. In breaking free from
it, however, he could not as easily rid himself of the conscience that he
had inherited, although neither his first emotional reaction when he put
the poems in Lizzie's coffin nor his later remorse necessarily prove that
he had any reason to blame himself for her death. There is bound to be
self-reproach for the mourner at any death-bed, and Rossetti would not
be immune from it. He had given her cause for jealousy as a lover, and
he had neglected her when he left her side for his work or his friends,
but these are infidelities which do not demand retribution out of measure.
This is borne out with simple common-sense by Lizzie's brother James,
who wrote years afterwards to W. M. Rossetti:

> "It was well-known in the family that my sister was given to fits of melan-
> choly and on those occasions there would be nothing extraordinary in a man
> like Rossetti—the poet and painter—withdrawing himself for the moment
> from his wife's side. Nothing beyond the common misunderstandings
> between married people to the knowledge of my sister's family ever occurred
> between my sister and her husband."[68]

If they had quarrelled on returning from the restaurant, it is possible
that Rossetti rushed out of the house, either without bothering to measure
out her dose for her or doing it carelessly.[69] This could provide a basis
for Violet Hunt's garbled versions and, indeed, for the neurotic remorse
that Rossetti exhibited later.

At the time, his period of mourning for the dead Lizzie was not
morbidly prolonged. Free from the burden of nursing an invalid, he
soon found himself in better health than he had known for years and
was able to take up his work again. The obligation he felt under to help
finish Gilchrist's *Life of Blake* started him on a new train of writing—a
play, *The Wife's Tragedy*, which is unfortunately lost. On a visit to
Madox Brown's he executed a small painting, "A Girl at a Lattice",
which broke any spell he might have imagined cast upon his brush. It
was appropriate it should be at Bruno's, for he had been his first master
and was to remain a friend to whom he turned in trouble, serious or
trivial. Between them was no need of gratitude or kindness: their help
to each other came from deep mutual affection and respect.

The support of the Burne-Joneses was also precious to him, but
in May they were swept away to Italy by Ruskin as companions to himself
and for the sake of Ned's health. From Venice he wrote (June 19)

that they had left Ruskin behind in Milan, "rather seedy. He has been so stunning all the time in every kind way he could think of. Whenever he talked of you it was in the most affectionate manner and in other ways that did one good to hear."[70]

Ned was always a *malade imaginaire*, but there seems no adequate reason why he should have felt quite so sorry for himself with the company of Ruskin and of a delightful wife in Georgie and a growing reputation. He writes: "I'm afraid I'm horribly nervous about myself and keep contrasting the little I can do now with the heaps I could do before when Val was with me: in 3 weeks we shall be moving homewards: if I must go to pot let that pot be among the blokes is my only prayer."

There was a break with Holman Hunt at this time over a curious affair called by William Michael "The Imbroglio".[71] Hunt reported that at a party of Monckton Milnes's Swinburne had made damaging references to Rossetti. Swinburne denied the charges emphatically to Brown, who was much alarmed by his "excited and distressed state". Hunt then wrote to Brown from the Lushingtons at Ockham Park on October 12th, blandly stating that "Swinburne is perfectly correct in saying that he never spoke to me of Rossetti at Monckton Milnes's . . . and I am quite perplexed to find how it could have got into your head that I mentioned him as my authority for the story."

The incident is mainly of interest for Rossetti's reaction to it: he passed it off with a shrug of his shoulders, writing to Brown on paper that has a thick black border: (7 October)

> "My dear Brown, I meant to come but being prevented I write. I suppose it is better you should write to Hunt (though I am sorry for your trouble) as Swinburne wishes it & lest I should seem to want the matter suppressed. But as for doing any material good in making me less the subject of foolish scandal & tattle, that I perceive would be vain to attempt."

He then goes on to speak about settling in to his new house in Chelsea.

The natural resilience with which Rossetti picked up the threads of his life again is shown in the interest he took in finding somewhere to live. Too much water had flowed under the bridges for him to be able to settle permanently again *en famille* with his mother and sisters and William Michael and the aunts. He tried living for a time in rooms in 77 Newman Street and then took a studio in Lincoln's Inn Fields, but he was always drawn to the river. He thought again of taking The Retreat, Upper Mall, Hammersmith, but by October had decided on Tudor House, 16 Cheyne

Walk, Chelsea. At this time the Embankment had not been built and river life went on much nearer to the houses so that Rossetti could find some literal satisfaction for his *nostalgie de la boue* in its noises and its smells.

While the house was being prepared and to get away from the embarrassment of a family Christmas, he went up in December to Bell Scott in Newcastle again. On this visit he made drawings of Scott's Egeria, Miss Alice Boyd, the owner of Penkill Castle in Ayrshire, where Scott and his wife hung up their hats for the rest of their lives. She had restored her health and spirits, broken after attending on family illnesses, by taking drawing lessons from Bell Scott. Though stalwart in face and figure, she was of a gentle and kindly disposition and quite a good water-colourist herself.

On the same occasion Rossetti painted Mrs. James Leathart, a very beautiful woman of considerable culture. The trouble he took with the details of the picture—her brooch, for instance, and the crimson ribbons lining the brim of her hat—shows he must have enjoyed the commission. He seems to have spent Christmas with the Leatharts and their young family in their house at Low Fell, called Bracken Dene, already well-stocked with some of the best-known P.-R.B. pictures[72]—Millais' "Autumn Leaves", Madox Brown's "Pretty Baa-Lambs" and a smaller version of "Work", Hunt's "Hireling Shepherd", and Arthur Hughes' two delightful group portraits of the family. His own "Salutation of Beatrice" was to join them. Never ungenerous to a brother-artist, he replied tactfully when Leathart asked his opinion of Albert Moore, whom he considered a "dull dog": (22nd April, 1868) "there can be no doubt that he possesses certain gifts of drawing and of design (in its artistic relation) in an admirable degree. I have not seen anything of his done lately."[73]

Back in London, Rossetti found a presentation copy from Browning of his latest publication.

"Many thanks indeed," he wrote in reply (5th January), "for the Selections which have not long reached me on my return from a working trip to Newcastle-on-Tyne. But, indeed, concerning this book, all your lieges of oldest standing will feel some pangs of selfishness: Had I, each one will say, but had the doing of it! For not even the poking of one's own fire, perhaps, is so peculiar and unapproachable a privilege, as the insight into one's own Poet."[74]

It was at first decided that William Michael and Swinburne should share the rent at Tudor House in exchange for the right to spend certain

8. CHRISTINA IN A RAGE

by D. G. Rossetti

This is a skit on "The Times" review of her poems which had used the phrase:
"Miss Rossetti can point to work which could not easily be mended."

9. FANNY CORNFORTH
by D. G. Rossetti

nights of each week there. Boyce was invited to make a third and, in-deed, urged to do so when at one point Ruskin suggested joining the ménage. In the end Boyce took over 14 Chatham Place and Meredith became the third co-tenant.

The house, which is still there, complete with L.C.C. plaque and a memorial bust[75] by Brown and Seddon in the gardens in front, has often been described. It is said to have been "the cheerful new house" of Thackeray's *Esmond* and had earlier traditions of housing Catherine Parr in her retirement, though the initials "C.R." entwined in the beautiful ironwork of the gates stand not for "Catherine Regina" but, less roman-tically, for the owner, "Richard Chapman", who had them put up. It is sometimes called "Tudor House" and sometimes "Queen's House" in the memoirs of the time, but Rossetti always uses the former name. Meredith described it as "a strange quaint old place with an immense garden, magnificent panelled staircase and rooms, a palace".

It is usually said that Meredith did not stay there long because he disapproved of the disorder of the household.* As a methodical man, an early riser and a believer in fresh air, he may well have thought Rossetti's habits slack, even if the story is untrue that he could not endure morning after morning seeing Rossetti's fried eggs bleed to death on his plate. Another story has it that Rossetti and some friends noticing the shabbi-ness of the shoes put outside his door for cleaning exchanged them for a new pair, and that Meredith put them on but walked away for ever; or, according to Scawen Blunt, via Wilfred Meynell, that Rossetti resented some remark of Meredith's, said he would throw a cup of tea in his face if he repeated it, and did so; or, again, that Meredith made disparaging comments on Rossetti's work at the dinner party on 30th April, when Leathart was present. In later life Meredith denied all these stories and spoke most generously of Rossetti, saying of his poetry to a friend: "It is not wild and bluff and coarse, but rich, refined, royal-robed. He would please you more than I do." As late as 1871, when he sent a copy of *Harry Richmond* ("I wish it were poetry")[76], he added how delightful it would be to stroll and have talks together once again.

But there was undoubtedly incompatibility of temperament, par-ticularly of sense of humour. Rossetti's teasing of friends was high-spirited, sometimes rather adolescent but never bitter, whereas Meredith mocked with a sarcastic tongue, acid from deep-rooted grievances.

* See Appendix E, p. 227.

18

Rossetti set about filling Tudor House with the pieces of old furniture he enjoyed picking up. He had an eye for what was good as well as what was curious—genuine pieces as well as junk—and now could afford to back his fancy. He began to fill the large garden, too, with statuary and with the strange animals that became such a feature of the place: indeed, it was due to Rossetti that there remains a clause in the leases of the Cadogan estates forbidding tenants to keep peacocks.

Wombats were always favourites with him and one of them was the original of the dormouse in *Alice in Wonderland*. Its sudden decease much grieved him: "I had gone to the expense of a magnificent glazed mansion for him, picked up at a broker's shop." The characteristic mixture in Rossetti of a whimsical but practical affection for his pets comes out also in a later letter to Madame Bodichon from Scalands:[77]

"My joys here have been overshadowed at intervals by the sight of darling little moles lying murdered. I mean to get two and keep them in a large glass case, so as to see them sometimes."

And referring to some dormice he had sent her for a child in London:

"They eat apples, nuts, corn, etc., and require no drink—indeed ought not to have water as a rule but may be allowed a little milksop which they like. Their bed should be of hay rather than of wool. Will you give the young lady my love with them?"

Ellen Terry had a story of Rossetti giving a party to celebrate the waking-up of some white dormice in the spring. "'They are awake now,' he said, 'but how quiet they are! How full of repose!'

"One of the guests went to inspect the bodies and Rossetti followed. 'Wake up,' he said, prodding them.

"'They'll never do that,' said the guest. 'They're *dead*. I believe they've been dead some days.' Do you think Rossetti gave up livestock after this? Not a bit of it; he tried armadillos and tortoises!"

In that upstairs drawing-room running the full length of the house, Rossetti collected people as miscellaneous as the animals in the garden. George Boyce, who had taken over Chatham Place, provides lively descriptions of his visits.

The first was on 13th November: "Called on D.G.R. . . . Found Fanny there. He has furnished his house most picturesquely, mostly with fine old Renaissance furniture bought of a man at 8 Buckingham Street."

In other entries the constant presence of Fanny is noticeable, but other friends as well as Boyce accepted her as part of a bachelor-artist's establishment, like Kiomo, the gypsy girl who lived with Sandys (she is the dusky attendant in "The Beloved") or Whistler's Jo. At this time she was willing to be unobtrusive, leaving visitors to themselves and tolerating other models who came to sit, but there are signs, even if humorous, that she was not entirely submissive. Rossetti, writing in April, 1863, to Red Lion Mary about mending some tapestry and embroidering a bell-pull for the house, adds: "Fanny says she would like to know what I am saying to you as I am writing such a lot, so I had better leave off before I am scratched about the nose and eyes."[78]

Boyce often went in to watch the models sitting: "Miss Ford was there (she was looking very lovely: stayed and dined). Swinburne came in later. He lent me the *Liaisons Dangereuses*." Boyce enjoyed as much as any of them, Meredith included, Swinburne's skit on a French novel, *La Fille du Policeman*, in which Queen Victoria has a twin sister who goes on the streets, is ravished by the *Bishop de Londres* "dans un cab-safety" and "consumed by an ill-requited attachment to Lord John Russell charcoals herself to death".[79] But they all began to be apprehensive that Swinburne might go too far in his excitement and have an epileptic fit. The "frantic delight" that his audience took in his readings from *Justine* (a gift from Monckton Milnes) was apt to be too much for the disciple of the Marquis, particularly if he had had a little to drink. "I read out [the scene between M. de Verneuil and Mme d'Estuval] and the auditors rolled and roared," reported Swinburne to Monckton Milnes. "Then Rossetti read out the dissection of the interesting Rosalie and her infant, and the rest of that refreshing episode: and I wonder to this minute that we did not raise the whole house by our screams of laughter."

But Rossetti also held entirely respectable gatherings at Tudor House. One of them is described at length by Georgie Burne-Jones, who remembered the date, April 12th, because early that morning she and Aggie had seen their sister, Alice, and John Kipling off to India.

It was to have been a dinner, but because of the extra Macdonalds, it had to be an after-dinner party. William Michael was there but Christina and Mrs. Bell Scott had excused themselves as it was Passion Week. William Morris and Jane dined first with the Burne-Joneses (now in Kensington Square) and when they went on together found assembled, Arthur Hughes and his wife; Munro and his wife; the Warrington Taylors (he was a partner in The Firm) and Alphonse Legros (who looked so much less French than Whistler. He was to succeed Sir Edward Poynter as Principal of the Slade school); F. G. Stephens, and Philip Webb. Late arrivals were the Madox Browns with daughters Cathy and Lucy, who had taken a round-about-way via Kew and Clapham to get there.

A contretemps is noted by the sharp eyes of Aggie Macdonald in her letter home: "Mrs. Brown who was otherwise very nice spilled a cup of coffee down Georgie's chinese blue silk dress like our bonnets [bought for the Kipling wedding] and for this we don't thank her as time can ne'er restore that dress or another like it. You wouldn't think that Providence, while Georgie was leaving the room to dabble her dress, permitted a waiter to upset a milk jug on her, but so it did."

The impression made by Tudor House can be seen through the eyes of the young Agnes Macdonald. She wrote back home to the Manse in Wolverhampton:

"It's beautiful till it makes one ache nearly and I kept sorrowfully thinking of its lost mistress. Just fancy, large panelled rooms, narrow tall windows with seats, a large garden at the back, at the front a paved court, with tall iron gates to the narrow road and lastly the Thames in a flood of moonlight. . . ."

In the letters of this sister, who was to marry Edward Poynter, Rossetti is regarded as a king to condescend. He is kind enough to come and see them: "He spent the evening here yesterday, for the first time for nearly two years, so it was a great treat." And when Alice Kipling had paid him a farewell visit: "He was very kind to them, shewed them all there was to be seen and said many gracious things to them."

It is unending the list of people who came to Tudor House. The names of many of them have not survived: some were genuinely congenial friends, others claimed to know the poet-painter better than they did. Munro introduced Lady Ashburton, and she was allowed on another day to bring Mrs. Carlyle with her from round the corner in Cheyne Row; Mr. and Mrs. Cowper Temple called and were taken off to see Burne-Jones' studio, and sketches of Lizzie made at Chatham Place were shown to George Eliot,[80] whose appreciation he continued to seek and who remained a loyal friend.

A visitor who was to become more than an acquaintance, was Charles Augustus Howell, a "card" if ever there was one. He had approached W. M. Rossetti as early as 1857 to solicit a Ruskin autograph and then disappeared to the Continent in 1858, just in time for the Orsini outrage in which he may have been involved. He may also have been a Portuguese, as he said he was (he looked a dark and dashing Mediterranean type) and possibly some of the other things he claimed: chief engineer of the Badajos Railroad; gold-diver, painter, horse-dealer, a page to the Pope. Not the least odd feature in his career was becoming secretary to Ruskin with the assignment to take a house near to the Burne-Jones' in order to keep an eye on the precious Ned, who at first liked him immensely, though Georgie seems always to have had her reservations. But soon both ceased to be amused at his bravado and flamboyance. "He was a stranger to all our life meant," wrote Georgie severely, and indeed his correspondence with Swinburne shows that this could easily be the case.

Rossetti accepted Howell as good company and employed him as an agent, for he had an undoubted flair as a middle-man, bringing together people and things to be bought and sold, sometimes to be lent and stolen. He was kind-hearted, always ready to initiate or to support schemes for helping friends who had fallen on evil days. Rossetti, asking him to find employment for the husband of Red Lion Mary, ends: "As you are one of those exceptional fools who take an interest in people according to their need of it, I write you a line to ask if it would be any use for poor Nicholson to call on you . . ." He never minded what he did to oblige a friend. Rossetti asks him to be a model for him in an emergency: "Can you sit to me for legs on Tuesday—1 or 2 or so? That bloke with the wig has only shanks."[81]

Even Rossetti endeavoured to check his exuberant exhibitionism when he put fifteen initials after his name on a School Board circular (for, oddly enough, he became a Governor and a successful one). "I assure you they are likely to produce an injurious impression."

It was through Howell that there was a lively traffic in "blue pots" between Rossetti and Whistler. They were friendly rivals in collecting Nankin blue and white porcelain. Rossetti gave the name "Hawthorn" to the honey jars, and "Long Eliza" was Whistler's variant on *langes leises*. Friends caught the enthusiasm. To Anderson Rose, his solicitor, Rossetti scribbles a black border on a page of a letter recommending an "undertaker" to mend broken specimens. (3rd March, 1865) "The name of the sad undertaker in question is Neill and his dark abode is in Eccleston Street South . . . where he dwells amid shattered hopes and pots in the shadow, as it were, of the weeping willow pattern. What more can I say? *Hodie tibi, cras mihi!* Your brother potsherd."[82]

The larks of the early Brotherhood days and the romps of Red House were carried on under Howell's influence in more sophisticated forms.

On one occasion, when he had picked up a perfect specimen of a blue Nankin dish, he summoned his rival collectors to a dinner to feast their eyes upon it as it lay under a cloth as the centre-piece of the table. When the meal was over the host rose to uncover his treasure and was rewarded with their admiring and envious exclamations. Later, when farewells were being said in the hall, Rossetti made an excuse to return to the dining-room. Finding it fortunately empty, he took the dish and hid it under the folds of his Inverness cape. Back in the hall he expressed thanks for the dinner and appreciation of the latest find and went out into the street to hail a hansom cab. At home he hid the parcel in the large cupboard downstairs which housed the drapes and the robes that his models wore, and then sat down to write notes to invite the same company to dinner with him later in the week.

Most of them were able to accept, and Howell came earlier in the afternoon for a chat in the studio about the disposal of some pictures and then excused himself to go back to change. That evening Rossetti lifted out his parcel, still wrapped in its cloth, and placed it in the centre of his long dining-table. When the meal was finished, he rose to uncover the treasure he had summoned friends to see. But when he lifted the cloth he found underneath it a blue dish, cracked and burnt from many an oven roasting. "Confound it! See what the spirits have done!" he exclaimed, while the others burst out laughing, only Howell keeping a straight face. With one look at him Rossetti saw what had happened and joined in the joke against himself.

19

It was through Swinburne that Rossetti became friendly with Whistler, living at 7 Lindsey Row, further down Cheyne Walk. Boyce knew him too: (May 17th)

> "To Hampton Court with Wm. Rossetti. Back by rail to Waterloo, whence in cab to Cheyne Walk and on to Whistler, Lindsey Row, where found him and 'Jo'. Gabriel Rossetti and Fanny came in later."

There were two kings in Chelsea. Both of them accustomed to exacting tribute: Whistler physically with blows if it were not forthcoming— "the springs in him prompt for the challenge", as Meredith characteristically put it—or, in Rossetti's limerick:

"There is a young artist called Whistler
Who in every respect is a bristler:
   A tube of white lead
   Or a punch on the head
Come equally handy to Whistler."

But Rossetti and Whistler enjoyed each other's company and had a deep-rooted respect for each other. Whistler wrote: "The only pleasant moments in one's life of dissatisfaction are those in which sympathy of such men as yourself is won by one's work."[83]

Each was independent-minded. Rossetti was more widely-read but much more restricted in knowledge and appreciation of Art. Whistler had a man-of-the-world attitude to sexual morals that would have dispelled much of the governess-guilt from which Rossetti suffered. With his gallic turn of mind fostered by French training, he was really more akin to Rossetti than many older and closer friends and if they could have met at an earlier age when friendships take root in deeper soil would have had a healthy influence on him. At the same time, the "chaffing" of the early P.-R.B. days would have been good for Whistler. As it was, he enlarged Rossetti's artistic taste, and his scepticism was valuable in preventing him from taking seriously the spiritualistic experiments that were sometimes tried at Tudor House. These were fashionable at the time like some new party game. Charles Kingsley, in a muscular attack on Shelley, wrote of those who admired him as "a mesmerizing, table-turning, spirit-rapping, spiritualizing, Romanizing generation . . ." But in the respectable Methodist household of the Macdonalds, for instance, there was a table-turning session when the Minister himself leapt on the table which continued to spin: "We ran round and round with it, laughing at our amazed father." There was not necessarily anything superstitious or morbid about the experiments, even if Home's influence on Mrs. Browning had given them a bad name in "Mr. Sludge, the medium":

"One does see somewhat when one shuts one's eyes
   If only spots and streaks: tables do tip
   In the oddest way of themselves: and pens, good Lord
Who knows if you drive them, or they drive you?"

When Rossetti went over to Paris, Whistler gave him an introduction to Fantin Latour, but he proved himself as *borné* as Whistler had observed. Of the "Homage to Delacroix" picture, in which he had been offered a place, he wrote home to William: "It has a great deal of very able painting in parts; but it is a great slovenly scrawl after all, like the rest of this incredible new French school—people painted with two eyes in one socket through merely being too lazy to efface the first, and what not."

And to "my dear Mamma", after telling her about a Japanese shop whose owner laughs at his rivalry with Whistler in china-collecting, he went on: "There is a man named Manet (to whose studio I was taken by Fantin) whose pictures are for the most part mere scrawls, and who seems to be one of the lights of the school. Courbet, the head of it, is not much better." To Bell Scott, however, he protested, "Courbet, you know, is a fine fellow & should not be snubbed."[84]

Rossetti, very successful at this time when Whistler was still struggling, gladly included him in his expansive salesmanship. He took "La Princesse du Pays de la Porcelaine" into his own studio and sold it for a hundred pounds in spite of the buyer's objection to Whistler's signature scrawled across the canvas. From the monogram that Rossetti designed for him instead grew the famous butterfly he afterwards used. The model for "La Princesse" was Christine Spartali, one of the daughters of the Greek Consul-General: her even more beautiful sister, Marie, discovered by Madox Brown, was much sought-after as a model. She was described by Graham Robertson as "Mrs. Morris for beginners. Study of her trained the eye to understand the more esoteric beauty of Mrs. Morris." She is certainly easier to appreciate. "The two marvels had many points in common: the same lofty structure, the same long sweep of limb, the 'neck like a tower', the night-dark tresses and the eyes of mystery . . ."

Another family in the Greek colony with whom they all became intimate were the Ionides, "which name," wrote Rossetti to Madox Brown, "and not Jonydese please fix in your mind". Constantine Ionides was the most important patron, but his brothers, Luke and Alexander (Alecco), were not far behind. One of their sisters, Aglaia Coronio, became a tender friend to Morris and to Burne-Jones, with both of whom she was on Christian-name terms. Rossetti also corresponded with her until a late date but always as "Mrs. Coronio".

Designing a monogram for Whistler, marketing his pictures and resigning from the Burlington in protest when he was expelled—after giving him some very sensible advice which was not appreciated—were some of those services Rossetti was always willing to render a friend.* During the spring months he carried on daily correspondence with Christina, convalescing at Hastings, over her new book of poems, *The Prince's Progress*, suggesting alterations (he wanted a tournament intro-

* See Appendix F, p. 228.

duced as a narrative device) and, to make up bulk, resurrecting juvenilia printed by their uncle, Polidori. To this Christina replied: "I have but to launch forth into the rag-and-bone store; thence, by main force, something must emerge."

His talent for haggling was applied for the benefit of others as much as for himself. The whole Pre-Raphaelite Brotherhood profited by it. I. W. Inchbold (once called "Raphael's great disciple") summed it up for others in a letter to Stephens: [85]

> "I meant to have thanked you for your kind and quick notice . . . I do not know that it has power to sell—this seems to be effected by cramming a picture down the throat of a supposed lover of Art—he resisting all the time. I once *saw* Millais and Leech strangle, nearly, a man in this way with a picture of mine, and I know Rossetti effected the same feat with or without strangulation. . . . As for the painter himself, it is unfitting work."

Other letters show Rossetti raising funds for the widow and ten children of Edward Davis[86], who had died in Rome. He asks Madame Bodichon to contribute one of his landscapes to be raffled: "though unequal he belonged to the rarest order of men in his own walk, deserving at his best to be named with Crome and Constable". He offered to house Deverell's pictures to help his sister—"Any trouble will I gladly take for the sake of my old friend"; asks Stephens to give a good notice to Smetham's "Last Supper"; answers the importunities of Coventry Patmore's blacksheep brother, Gurney.[87] Each friend's form of aid was characteristic: William Michael, with plenty of other responsibilities, managed to put together some old clothes: Woolner grudgingly contributed a parcel of "traps" but said: "He has a rich brother who is the natural sustainer of the poor fellow's misfortunes. . . . If the pressure is not rightly adjusted now, when is it to be done?" Rossetti sent money but drew the line at correspondence: "His handwriting is something monstrous in carelessness and I have received two postcards from him, both so filthy as even to excite remark from the servants and to suggest a previous use only negatived by the thickness of the tissue."

Rossetti's helpfulness was invaluable to Madox Brown in organising the then unusual experiment of a One-Man Show. As Brown did not send in to the Academy he was not qualified to exhibit in the latest *Salon des Refusés*, the Cosmopolitan Club organised by Hunt. Although his work had appeared with others in a few provincial exhibitions, the pictures which represented a lifetime's work had never been shown in their entirety to the public. An habitually modest man, Brown decided for once to assert himself.

The show was to be held at 196 Piccadilly in March, 1865. The whole idea stimulated Rossetti's sense of salesmanship and he showed a flair for advertising ahead of his time: he had the germ of the matter in him.

"You should begin by enormous placards with the one word Work, thus W and go on with this for a week or two. Then another week of *Mr.*
   O
   R
   K
F. M. Brown's Work and then condescend to further particulars. If, in addition to this, you put up a sign over your door representing a Brown Mad Ox crossing a Ford marked *British Art*, with you holding on to his horns with a palette and brushes, and R.A. and *Public Press* waving red flags to frighten him on either bank, the success could no longer be dubious."

To John Skelton, the Scottish barrister, who contributed to various journals, he wrote an omnibus appeal: (13th March, 1865)

"Do write something concerning Swinburne. You will find his *Atalanta* a most noble thing, never surpassed to my thinking. I hope you will be in town during Madox Brown's admirable exhibition—— My sister Christina will soon have a new volume out."

The success of the show enabled Madox Brown to move nearer into London—to Fitzroy Square, where he held successful fortnightly At Homes at which "everyone" was to be met. Awkward as Brown could be, he proved a genial host and managed to keep Emma decorously in the background. His eldest daughter, Lucy, was to marry William Michael in March, 1874, and Catharine in 1872 married Franz Hueffer, a music critic of German origin, who became editor of the first Tauchnitz editions in English. But the apple of his father's eye was Oliver, "Nolly"; a boy prodigy who was producing poems and pictures at the age of eleven and was allowed to appear at Pre-Raphaelite gatherings with white rats clinging to his arms. Rossetti's appreciation of him and his ready invitations to visit the private zoo of Cheyne Walk was something that Madox Brown never forgot.

Another friend for whom loyalty and affection demanded support was Swinburne when he had trouble with his publisher, Moxon. After the adverse reviews of *Poems and Ballads* in April, 1866, Rossetti went with Sandys to make a protest at what he considered unfair treatment "as a friendly duty . . . though not certainly, as you know, because we think the genius displayed in his work benefits by its association with certain accessory tendencies".

He was by no means happy at what was happening to Swinburne. Acquaintance with Monckton Milnes had over-stimulated his perversive tendencies and the measure of success he enjoyed in a limited but important influential circle after the publication of *Atalanta in Calydon* had gone to his head. Some people were inclined to blame Rossetti for his "corruption"—even Arthur Hughes considered "the praise he got from such as yourself inflated and misled him to think that his metal was all without alloy, or the alloy was fit for publicity".[88]

To Tennyson, in a letter of great dignity and clarity, Rossetti protested: "As no one delights more keenly in his genius than I do, I also have a right to say that no one has more strenuously combatted its wayward exercise in certain instances, to the extent of having repeatedly begged him not to read me such portions of his writings when in MS."

That Rossetti was one of those who exercised as far as he could a restraining influence on Swinburne, is shown by the letters of appreciation he received from Admiral and Lady Jane Swinburne. The formal gratitude in these notes stands out pathetically among the exuberant smut of their son's correspondence with Monckton Milnes, George Powell (co-editor of the *Icelandic Sagas*, with Magnússen, a friend of Morris's) and Howell. He evidently tried it on with both Rossettis but met with little response. Although he exchanged Rabelaisian doggerel with Gabriel, he never dared ask him to supply the lubricious drawings that he demanded from Howell.

Rossetti encouraged him in his love-affair with the circus rider, Adah Menken, to whom he was himself attracted, hoping the normality of it would be a cure for his other tendencies, but probably without result. Another cure and a more effective one was to sublimate Swinburne's emotions in work for the Italian *risorgimento*. To this end the magnetism of Mazzini was enlisted through the agency of Karl Blind, the refugee German liberal scholar. When Swinburne met Mazzini, he fell on his knees before his hero and launched into a recitation of his "Song of Italy". It was fully appreciated. "Dedicate your glorious powers to the service of the Republic, my son," said Mazzini.

Over this question of Italian unity Rossetti was a disappointment. When Swinburne raved about it, the English-born Italian became bored. He wrote to Scott: "I was very glad to hear of his [Swinburne] having done something not in the liberty-flibberty-gibbety style of which I confess myself weary, though he puts such wonderful things into it."

Aware of this, Swinburne retorted that he had only been able to feel the pure passion of patriotism (for some other nation) when he broke away from Rossetti's doctrine of "Art for Art's sake"; an over-simplification that was to contribute to later misconceptions. *"Malgré ce cher Marquis et ces foutus journaux*, it is *nice* to have something to love and believe in as I do in Italy."

This lack of political sympathy was one element that contributed to the break-up of their friendship some years later. At the moment it continued, although Rossetti made some excuse to refuse Swinburne's proposal to come back to live at Tudor House. He could not stand the interruptions and upsets inevitable from Swinburne's increasingly irregular ways of life. He was no longer amused at the poet naked sliding down that elliptical back staircase and did not care for it when he pinched Miss Herbert's ankles from underneath the chenille table-cloth.

20

The Cheyne Walk period from 1862 to 1867 was one of achievement. Those who want to project morbid fancies into it and prefer to admire the shifts and shabbiness of earlier days resent the evidences of prosperity and success and Rossetti's enjoyment of them. But it is only sentimental to wish that the slender youth of slender means should not grow stouter.

Besides the parties held in the long upstairs room, friends were welcomed to talk and to listen to that magnetic voice as their host sprawled on a sofa in his studio, or on fine days lay on the grass under the Elizabethan mulberry tree watching the antics of his menagerie. "Lewis Carroll" called it "a memorable day" when he was introduced by Munro and invited to bring his camera to take some groups of family and friends.[89] Christina arrived "a little shy at first, and I had very little time for conversation with her, but I liked the little I saw of her". He also looked through a portfolio of sketches with a view to photographing them—"a great treat, as I had never seen such exquisite drawings before". On one occasion Ruskin let himself be photographed standing by the steps with an arm linked in his host's, while Bell Scott stood bowler-hatted beside them.

James Smetham,[90] who may have attended Rossetti's classes at the Working Man's College, hard up now and with nowhere to paint, was allowed the use of the studio every Wednesday. Frederick Shields at this time also began to come regularly to the house—a strange friend, for he was fanatically religious and puritanical. He had come up to London from the north where his father was an impoverished book-binder and he himself had tried to earn a living by colouring posters and drawing portraits in public houses at a penny a time. His first visit to Tudor House was a red letter day. Years later he wrote of the "lowliness" from which Rossetti raised him up: "his generous praise at our first interview gave me confidence . . ."

How far Rossetti retained his early influence over the older man who might be considered his *Maître*, Madox Brown, is shown by his willingness still to accept his advice. When Brown was completing his admirable portrait of James Leathart with the lead works in the background, he wrote to him:

> "Rossetti called over Thursday & saw it, he thinks it very like but proposed to cover up part of the landscape with a flower-pot on the window ledge. I have compromised by painting some rose leaves growing outside. This helps ballance (sic) the light & shade in the composition."[91]

Casual callers were never admitted and even intimates had to risk being turned unceremoniously away, for Rossetti varied his sociability with stretches of solitude when for days on end, right into the night, he would stand at his easel going without meals or snatching food as he painted. Many of the well-known oils belong to this period—too well-known in one sense, for the large luscious women with their flowery backgrounds have created the popular impression of a Rossetti type culminating in "Monna Vanna". "The women and flowers", to which Bell Scott prematurely referred, had now become the "ardent blossoms" of Swinburne's unfortunate phrase.

But before exaggerating the sensuousness of these pictures it may be noted that Rossetti did not paint the nude—there are only "The Spirit of the Rainbow" and two half-torsos. He expressly declared himself against the titillating sexuality of what he called "Ettyism". It is a sign of his vigour that he went through different phases of development. At this period he was painting beautiful women, neither ladies nor elf-girls: later there was to be a third phase, integrating the others.

The pictures of these years were often based on sketches that had been dashed off in Chatham Place, such as the "Beatrice", which was to be a memorial to Lizzie. But the properties worn by the models bear witness to the new abundance of Cheyne Walk: there are rich robes and curious pieces of furniture and many more jewels than Lizzie's strings of coral. Favourite ornaments are the pearl-shell brooch worn in the hair and the large crystal locket of "Monna Vanna", seen again in "Joli-Coeur" and "The Beloved": the robe of Lucretia Borgia is also worn by "Monna

Vanna", and a favourite piece of furniture in the background is a small brass ewer topped by a figurine. He went to enormous trouble to get the right flowers for these pictures—still Pre-Raphaelite in that conscientiousness; honeysuckles for "Venus Verticordia" were ordered from three different parts of the country but arrived "broken and faded", and after much searching he finally found what he wanted from the Crystal Palace. The roses needed came from a nursery gardener at Cheshunt "every two days at 2/6 for a couple of dozen a time". Later, he was to ask Mrs. Cowper Temple for magnolia buds and go to great trouble to keep them cool so that they did not open too soon, and when he was painting "Lilith",[92] sketches were sent to Howell and to Shields to show in which direction a branch of apple-blossom had to lean. Sometimes new properties were added to earlier pictures which he retouched and often re-named, even using different models for them: "Fazio's Mistress" had much *bric-à-brac* added to it and was re-named "Aurelia": "Lilith", which had originally Fanny for model, became "Body's Beauty" with a prettified Miss Wilding. "The Beloved", so called from *The Song of Solomon*, was afterwards re-named "The Bride", and had for model Miss Mackenzie. "Regina Cordium", for which several different models sat (including Lizzie and Mrs. Aldam Heaton), was many times copied in oil and in water-colour with variations each time.

Also from this time dates Rossetti's habit of making replicas to sell as pot-boilers. He borrowed back old pictures to copy or alter and for new ones freely asked friends to supply details he needed. Boyce had given him the sea background for "Writing on the Sand" in Chatham Place days, and was later asked to send round to Tudor House a tracing for a windmill and to find a sycamore tree that Sandys had drawn in leaf. To confuse the position further he began employing assistants. First, there was the indigent W. J. Knewstubb, whose beautiful daughter married William Rothenstein; then Fairfax Murray, an artist of some charm but of odd looks with a shock of fuzzy hair and bow legs which gave rise to much "chaff" in the circle. This question of assistants is very tricky and needs to be seen in the context of the practice of the Old Masters.[93] Of Rossetti's contemporaries Lord Leighton also employed them, and Rossetti made no secret of his search for suitable candidates. A letter from Henry Wallis (painter of "The Death of Chatterton", who eloped with Meredith's first wife) recommends a boy from Ashburton, Devon: (6th November, 1867) "He may not turn out a Giotto but he will certainly make a deucedly sharp page to yr. Worship—not hinting you in any way resemble Sir John."[94] From correspondence with a later assistant, Treffry Dunn, it appears that he was expected to be able to construct sets for backgrounds, stretch canvases, cut chalks, lay-in backgrounds, and sometimes to trace reduced figures for replicas, but Rossetti showed himself very concerned when he thought that Dunn had finished a picture for him. That these replicas and the forgeries put out by Howell's mistress, Rosa Corder, were worth making, shows the demand for Rossetti's work. Gambart, the well-known dealer, offered to represent him which, after some vituperative correspondence, he was allowed to do.

The buyers of his pictures were the north-country industrialists: Leyland of Liverpool (who owed to Rossetti the unfortunate introduction of Whistler), Rae of Birkenhead, Plint of Leeds, Craven of Manchester, Leathart of Newcastle. They were expected to pay a good advance, sometimes to lend money as well. Rossetti disarmingly tells Leathart of a debt that "nothing could rejoice me more than to liquidate it at once"—but he didn't. Often they had to buy the preliminary sketch as well. Murray Marks, the dealer, a discriminating buyer to whom Rossetti was much indebted for watching his interests in the sale-rooms, took the extras in good part when he commissioned "La Bella Mano" for a thousand guineas. He paid £400 down and then found he had bought the sketch as well:

> "April 30th 1875.
> My dear Marks,
>   I shall have finished the chalk drawing of *La Belle Mano* in a few days and should then be glad to receive its price, £120. The picture progresses well. I have now got the frame."

When Marks protested that he had never contracted for a chalk sketch, Rossetti replied that he had not charged enough for the oil. In addition, Marks found himself supplying several of the properties—the open-work table, the flower-pot for the lemon tree, the brass ewer and bowl, and innumerable bunches of out-of-season tulips, from which the painter at last selected two. Over the toilet castor Marks did demur: for it had been silver, but Rossetti gilded it over to make it easier to paint from; its restoration took some time, labour and expense, but Marks, like the rest of them, accepted the situation and gave more commissions. The heads of Mrs. Marks are some of Rossetti's most sensitive work and show that his women do not all look alike, as is sometimes suggested.

The sketches for the big pictures of water-colours from them were often sold to friends and then changed about. Boyce good-naturedly accepts an exchange:

"May 5th, 1865. . . . Rossetti sent for the study he gave me, a pencil head of Ellen Smith, said it was by inadvertence he had parted with it, as he particularly wished to dispose of it with other studies of the same picture (Bride in Song of Solomon) to the purchasers of the picture."

From an entry two weeks later, it appears that Boyce received thirteen pencil heads in exchange; two as gifts, the other eleven to be paid for. One of them was "a head of Mrs. Morris of Upton, price £10."

21

During this time at Tudor House, Rossetti was not doing much work for The Firm. He had enjoyed the experiment of designing stained glass for church windows,* but otherwise he had too much to do at his easel to devote time to arts and crafts. The Firm had expanded to include tile-making, mostly in the hands of William de Morgan; the manufacture of carpets at Kidderminster from Morris patterns; and also furniture from traditional "peasant" designs. Morris and Burne-Jones worked closely together. For tapestries and stained glass Burne-Jones would provide the willowy figures to stand in front of Morris' backgrounds of broad acanthus leaf or trailing poppy in bold and at the same time subtle colours.

These developments and some losses in Morris' private income from the tin mine necessitated greater attention to business than was possible from Upton, so that early in 1865 Morris moved to 26 Queen's Square, Bloomsbury, with his wife and their two young daughters, Jenny and May. It was gloomy after Red House, but Morris compensated what he missed in the country by priding himself on "living above the shop" like a medieval craftsman working in his own home. He could be seen in his shirt sleeves and with arms sometimes blue to the elbow from indigo, serving expensive materials to the customers who ventured into the ground floor showrooms—catering for what he pleased to call "the swinish luxury of the rich". Not an accommodating salesman: when Palgrave asked F. G. Stephens for advice on a memorial window, he added: "The lady is not *specially* artistic and hence I fear Morris & Co. (who have the reputation of taking no hints as to what employers wish for) may not answer."[95]

The hospitality of those country week-ends at Red House could now

* See Appendix G for list, p. 229.

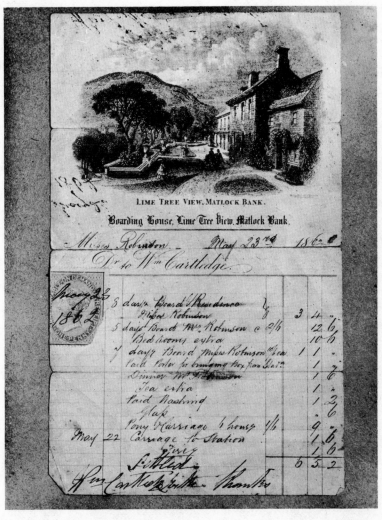

LIME TREE VIEW, MATLOCK BANK.

Boarding House, Lime Tree View, Matlock Bank.

Misses Robinson — May 23rd 1860

Dr to Wm Cartledge

			£	s	d
	8 days Board & Residence Misses Robinson		3	4	"
	5 days Board Mrs Robinson @ 2/6			12	6
	Bed Rooms extra			10	6
	7 days Board Misses Robinson & Tea	1	1	"
	Paid Porter for bringing box from Station			1	6
	Dinner Mr Robinson			1	6
	Tea extra			1	"
	Paid Washing			1	3
	Gas				6
	Pony & Carriage 6 hours 1/6			9	"
May 22	Carriage to Station			1	6
	Fire			1	6
	Settled		6	5	2

Wm Cartledge with Thanks

10. Lime Tree View, Matlock. This bill has been receipted by Mr. Cartledge who was the landlord at the time Rossetti stayed there. It shows the house as it then looked and the items charged must have been much the same.

11. Study of Jane Burden for "Guinevere"
by D. G. Rossetti

be repaid by invitations to the garden at Cheyne Walk, then covering a quarter of an acre, with tended lawns and wild patches inextricably mixed. Here Janey, "out of health" as Georgiana wrote, could recline on a *chaise-longue* and watch the little girls play hide-and-seek round the statues or venture up the trees or pet the animals of so delightful a private zoo. There would be need of caution here for the kangaroos, mother and son, might turn from fighting each other to attacking small humans, and on no account must the heavy stone be lifted off the packing-case that contained the racoon. Indoors, the parrot was to be avoided also, for it was a deceitful creature that would incline its head for a caress and then turn and nip a finger. Once on a Sunday morning after the church bells had stopped ringing, it called out, "You ought to be in church now!"

When Janey reclined in the garden, Dante Gabriel lolled beside her —that lolling which so irritated Allingham and Bell Scott—and took the opportunity to make sketches and to start on the rather perfunctory portrait of her sitting in a blue dress at a table which was seen by Henry James. He also posed her in the garden for a professional photographer he called in. "Among his finest pictures," declared Paul Nash to Gordon Bottomley. It is not easy to realise Janey's overwhelming beauty from these records of it, for without colour her gauntness is unrelieved and her statuesque quality accentuated by the strain of holding a pose for the length of time then necessary for the camera.

During this first summer of 1865 Rossetti was very busy with work already in hand. Fanny was sitting for the finish of "Blue Bower" and for "Boccacio's Fiammetta", Ellen Smith[96] for "Washing Hands", and Alexa Wilding now began to be employed regularly from July. That she had much the same build as Janey may account for Rossetti's frequent recourse to her: she could be an understudy. At this time she sat for "Monna Vanna" and "Regina Cordium", and it was from her that he made the preliminary sketches for "La Pia".

There is no reason to suppose that his models were also his mistresses; indeed, every reason against it. They were never professionals who sat "in the altogether" and expected to eke out their earnings by other services. Once the desired blonde or red-head had been found and consented to sit, he would want to draw, not to seduce her. He had his work as an artist to do and he did not need to prove his virility as a man. We know from Mrs. Gaskell's story that his approach to a woman with the right coloured hair was too direct to have any ulterior motive and there is also a record of his discovery of Alexa (or Alice) Wilding.

He had been on his way to a meeting of the Arundel Club in the

Strand:[97] "Walking quietly along amidst the hurrying folk that thronged the pavement he became aware of a young girl by his side. He turned his head to look at her and was struck with her beautiful face and golden auburn hair . . ." He followed her down a side street and explained that he wanted to paint her. She consented to come the next day to Cheyne Walk, but never turned up. "He had given up all hopes of seeing the young lady again and had even abandoned the picture when one afternoon, in company with Howell in the same part of the Strand, he again caught sight of her. He was then in a cab: telling Howell what he was going to do, he stopped the hansom in a side street, got out and darted after the girl and at last overtook her. This time he took her back in the cab with him." She was a thoroughly respectable girl: in fact, dull, although she had ambitions to be an actress.

He had enough to cope with in his relations with Fanny Cornforth. How he put up with her as he did is not easy to understand. Partly, no doubt, it was from a masculine laziness; she was useful to him and it saved looking for anyone else. Also, the seduced girl of "Found" had become the full-blown siren of "Fazio's Mistress" and he had feelings of tenderness and of duty to each image of her. His tenderness is shown in his letters to "Dear Elephant" where he rallies her when she is bad-tempered and always puts the best interpretation on what she does. When she has quite plainly stolen something from Tudor House, it is simply a trifle picked up to add to the "Elephant's Hoard".

His sense of duty came from the belief that if the Establishment of the time complacently accepted a double standard of sexual ethics, then it behoved the anti-Establishment to go to the rescue of the unfortunate and to fall over backwards in making allowances for them. Fanny represented Rossetti's duty—for he always liked his issues personified—in this respect. Even so his forbearance towards her and his generosity are extraordinary. At this time her good nature was going the way of her good looks and she was becoming more exacting in her demands for the pictures for which she sat, as well as for payments. Although she never lived in Tudor House but in rooms nearby in Royal Avenue, she was always in and out, singing at the top of her voice, and began to take offence if it was conveyed to her that she must make herself scarce. Naturally the staff objected to taking orders from her and the household degenerated into a state of squalor.

As this made entertaining difficult, Rossetti began to affect a preference for solitude. "I see no one", he wrote to Frederick Shields, who after a breakdown had retired to a remote house in the north, congratulating him "supremely on having attained at last to complete desolation as regards social propinquity . . . Nothing would suit me better, and I still hope to be an outcast from humanity one of these days."

In fact, he was a long way yet from being a recluse at Cheyne Walk. He still accepted invitations outside; to the Greeks, as he called the Ionides family and their connections; to Little Holland House where Mrs. Prinsep's "unquiet spirit" and her "outpourings" amuse him—"but she is really very nice and kind"; even to attend a fancy dress party at the Gambart's.

13 April 1866.

"My dear Madam,"
    . . . If the dress of the nineteenth century is an admissible period of costume, I shall be most happy to attend as a crysalis and so set off the more brilliant butterflies."[98]

His large dinner-parties for old friends may have been in abeyance, but there were newer friends like Whistler and Howell dropping in, and there were visits (provided due notice was given) from numerous acquaintances, from patrons, and from literary "lions" and many of whom we have little or no record. Turgenieff, for instance, called, and on one occasion Longfellow, under a misapprehension that the poet and the painter were separate people—brothers. As he left he said:

"I have been very glad to meet you, Mr. Rossetti, and should like to have met your brother too. Pray tell him how much I admire his beautiful poem, 'The Blessed Damozel'."
"I'll tell him."

In fact, Rossetti was in a state of some ambivalence between solitude and sociability. Gregarious since his student days, when he had first found himself popular, he was at the same time aware of the temptation to waste the substance of his spirit in talk: there is always Coleridge as an awful warning to all artists. He varied between withdrawal; declining, for instance, to attend Howell's wedding ("But after all, I *am* a bogie and there's no help for it") and yet welcoming anyone who might prove to be good company and keep him from dwelling on the divisions in his mind. He began to be worried about his eyesight, an occupational disease of painters whose terrors in this case were aggravated by the memory of his father's blindness, but the several ophthalmic surgeons he consulted—and, like his doctors, they were men of high distinction—declared that there was nothing organically wrong with his eyes: he needed only to rest them and to take steps to improve the general condition of his health.*

* Appendix H, p. 233.

In the autumn of 1867 he was therefore persuaded to try a country holiday and went to stay with Allingham at Lymington. He took with him "Venus Verticordia" in order to add the deep pink roses, but he was dissatisfied with those that neighbours sent in and the visit was generally disappointing. They had grown apart: Rossetti found Allingham insipid and Allingham disapproved in turn of his "need for strong savours in art, in literature and in life". "In poetry, as in other things, Rossetti turns always to what is hot in the mouth." He could not forgive him for refusing to cross over to the Island in order to visit Tennyson.

The trouble really was that at the moment Rossetti had no new interest nor, what is more important, either the leisure or the security from which to reach out towards a new interest and claim it for his own: the desideratum to make life worth the living.

Someone was wanted to set his house in order—literally—so that he would be able to turn round, rub his eyes and see in front of him the very thing he sought. His luck held when 1867 brought into his employment the young Cornishman, Henry Treffry Dunn, "come up" from Truro, like John Opie before him, to make his fortune or content to let that go if he could sit at the feet of his hero, Rossetti. It was Howell who introduced him as a pupil and in a very short time he was established as secretary and accountant and housekeeper—"Dante Gabriel's guardian angel". His excitement recalls that of Burne-Jones years before: "the fulfilment of my longed-for desire". He made the most of his opportunity to learn from Rossetti: "I began to feel how very ignorant I was upon all things save of the most ordinary kind", and with Cornish adaptability readily entered into the life of Tudor House.

There was no end to the variety of things he was expected to see about: to obtain some dragon flies and set them up in different positions as models, "also you might get me a few blue or blue-grey butterflies. These also to be set up in action, flying or resting". Or to turn to as a carpenter and erect in the garden a carved wooden staircase in Florentine style, to serve as a background for "Dante's Dream", and in the cellar lumber-room to work on the construction of a medieval-type vessel for "The Boat of Love", an unsuccessful venture which Rossetti never completed. The boat was copied from the Campo Santo frescoes. "Rossetti", wrote Dunn, "watched the building with great interest, from the laying-down of the keel line, the constructing the ribs and planking of the timbered sides and partial deck to the final little chambered poop, set high upon the stern and rudder post." Large as it was, "Rossetti had so many figures in his design comprising the boating party that it would have been impossible to have crammed them all in with ease and comfort to themselves and, moreover, it conveyed too much the unpleasant impression that the crew must inevitably swamp the craft if they all got aboard".[99] He bought books about London so as to make more interesting the walks from Chelsea into the City that Rossetti liked to take in the evenings when he could no longer paint.

There were parties again at Tudor House. Dunn has left an account of them in his *Recollections*:

> "His greatest pleasure was to gather round him those whom he liked and his little social dinners when they took place, were events to be remembered. When the party was an exceptional one—I mean as regards the number of friends invited—the table was laid in the so-called drawing room. . . . It was a beautiful room by day when the sun streamed in and lit up the curious collection of [furniture and *objets d'art*]; and at night . . . when the huge Flemish brass-wrought candelabra with its two dozen wax lights . . . was lit up and the central, old fashioned *épergne* filled with flowers, the room was filled with pleasant warmth and glow anticipatory of what company was expected."

Rossetti took great trouble with these parties and conventionally demanded "togs" when ladies were expected. An extra manservant would be employed and Howell put in charge of the "fruit and flower department". At table Howell was put next to someone quiet, and Sandys across the way so as to "cap his romances with some more racy", in order that no one was neglected. "But," wrote Dunn, "it was not really until the feast was over and adjournment to the studio came about that the night's enjoyment commenced. . . ."

22

With order restored at Tudor House, it was sometime in the spring of 1868 that Rossetti must have taken up two or three of the sketches he had made of Janey or suddenly looked at her herself with new eyes and decided that it was she who must be the model for the great new picture he had started upon, "La Pia". He was so excited that he gave a party to celebrate the event. Ford Madox Brown described the evening:

> "A great dinner was given in honour of the Topsies and we were all warned to appear in *Togs*. However, Morris at the last moment was dispatched to

Queen Square to forcibly bring back his partner, Faulkner, thirteen at table being otherwise the mishap."

But Morris had hardly gone when it was discovered that "Rossetti had miscalculated and we were thirteen without Morris". It was all "magnificent and jolly", Brown concluded, innocent of undercurrents in the story of the picture and how they would work on Rossetti's literary mind.

"It seems that in Dante's time a very beautiful lady was shut up by her husband in a castle in the Maremma and there died of poison or through the malaria . . . She said to Dante: 'He who with this ring espoused me caused my death.' "

A rather formal note to Janey in March about sittings suggests coming early, "i.e. if about one o'clock, my gratitude will commence at that hour",[100] or later, if Morris would like to come to dinner. By May she had undertaken to work some embroidery for the dresses in which she sat and for his sofa cushions. (7th May, 1868) "Between this and the dress I shall be giving you an awful lot of work." They had a common interest in small animals, for he reports: "On reading your letter I took out the little mouse to report on his condition. He is wonderfully improved & is getting quite plumped out and sleek again—only a place he had worn bare on his nose by gnawing at the trap does not fill up yet." He signs himself "Affectionately yours, D. Gabriel R."*

He also sent a pair of dormice to Jenny and May Morris at Queen's Square. In an undated note he gives directions for feeding and ends: "If you love them very much I daresay they will get much bigger and fatter and remind you of Papa and me."

Top and Janey were to stay together in Tudor House for a week or more, so that she would be at hand to sit. Morris took the opportunity to study Icelandic, in which he had become interested and to complete the first volume of *The Earthly Paradise*. He would try out new verses by reciting them in a loud voice from the back windows of the house, so that "to the neighbours he must have looked like a shock-headed sea captain shouting at nothing from the bridge".

Meanwhile in the studio that faced the garden, Janey sat regularly as a model. However solemn the subjects for which she posed, the sessions were relieved by frequent and often uproarious laughter. When Janey was sure of sympathy she could relax, for behind those amazing looks she was a very ordinary woman—that is to say, she had an unusually developed normality. She had a good brain; in fact, her reading

*See Appendix I. p. 235.

and her comments show her as what would be called "well-educated", if the facts of her schooling were not conspicuous by their absence. She also had a sense of humour (though this did not preclude self-pity and morbid attention to her state of health), and liked company: in fact, she seems to have needed amusing. She had warm feelings; was devoted to her children and competent at running her household. If we compare her, as inevitably we must, with the other women in Rossetti's life, we find that she had none of Lizzie's artistic urge and therefore none of the neuroticism that went with it, and without Fanny Cornforth's coarseness and sexual promiscuity, she yet had the same down-to-earthiness that could put a man at his ease and give him relaxation and comfort. When Rossetti began to see her *sub specie litterarum* in his usual way, she insisted on remaining a woman. She saw to it that what inspired the artist remained a comfort to the man.

With her honesty went dislike of humbug and pretension. She would have sensed that Henry James had come to look at her like a scientist examining a specimen when he called at Queen's Square:

> "Oh, *ma chère*, such a wife! . . . it's hard to say whether she's a grand synthesis of all the Pre-Raphaelite pictures ever made or they a 'keen analysis' of her—whether she's an original or a copy."

She saw through the young Bernard Shaw. There is more to his anecdote of her than he himself realised when he said that she was "the silentest woman ever I knew" and that the only time he heard her say anything was when she was presiding at one of the Sunday lunches when Morris entertained his socialist hangers-on. As a vegetarian, Shaw had refused the meat course but accepted pudding. She offered him a second helping, saying: "It will do you good; it has suet in it." Here there is speaking both the housewife proud of a good dish and the woman sceptical of a young man's food fads. Her silence said what she thought of them all.

Since her marriage, Janey had withdrawn behind that timeless face and allowed her husband's textiles, hanging in their unfashionable folds, to make a cloak of invisibility about her. It was boredom that had reduced her to silence; boredom with her beauty, boredom with her husband. Those outbursts of rage which had seemed funny at Oxford with other young men to chaff him and which his workmen at Merton Abbey later admired as harmless eccentricity cannot have been amusing in married life. She must have chosen to ignore them as well as she could. He was not the man to awaken response in her; he loved Man, not men and women. He would preach socialism but never give a penny to a beggar.

As Rossetti put it much later in a letter to Janey: "has Top perhaps thrown trade after poetry, & now executes none but wholesale orders in philanthropy,—the retail trade being beneath a true humanitarian?"[101]

Even his closest friends admitted that Morris had little sense of the value of personal relationships. Wilfrid Scawen Blunt (who certainly ought to have known) wrote of him: "One thing only, I think, he did not know, much as he had written about it—the love of women and that he never cared to discuss." And Burne-Jones repeated without disagreement the comments of Red Lion Mary on the subject.

"I shouldn't think Mr. Morris knew much about women, sir."
"Why not, May?"
"I don't know, sir, but I should think he was such a bear with them."

It is unlikely that Morris guessed the secret of those great mournful eyes "standing far apart" when he wrote of them:

> "So beautiful and kind they are
> But most times looking out afar
> Waiting for something, not for me."

What they were waiting for—had given up—was on its way to them in these days at Cheyne Walk. Here Janey was no longer the dark silent medieval woman who amazed Henry James lying on a sofa with medieval toothache in that overcast room in Bloomsbury (the Maremma of "La Pia"?) When she sat for Rossetti she became again the high-spirited girl from the Holywell stables, the romp of Red House, and he was once again the slim, dark leader of young rebels, cocking snooks at the Establishment. Together they could re-create their youth in a new image. But not altogether. Rossetti, too, had been wearing a cloak of invisibility in these latter years with threads in it of regrets and remorse, and coloured with coarseness and cynicism. It could not be shed at once; perhaps, like the shirt of Nessus, never.

All he knew from 1868 was that he wanted to draw Janey and he covered sheet after sheet with tentative sketches for big pictures. He must make up for the time lost in ever drawing anyone else. In her he had found at last the model who represented the two sides of his art— the sensuous and the mystic—but transcended them both in a new entity. Unfortunately for the peace of mind of the man and the artist, Janey was something more than the ideal model and it was not only as a painter and a poet that he wanted to immortalise her looks:

"Was I most born to paint your sovereign face
Or most to sing, or most to love it, dear?"

He was now deeply in love with Janey, set to enjoy a "regenerate rapture" at her feet. Whether it was also in her arms, there is no evidence to prove; from his poems it would appear that she must have yielded to his passion, but if she did it was only for a short period and with protests that were more and more supported by a retreat into invalidism. She liked being loved, sensuously but not sexually, and even here drew her lines. When Rossetti is looking forward to her return so that she can sit to him again, he assures her: (23rd August, 1869) "I wonder whether we shall be able to realise some sittings when you return. They shall be *such* careful, judicious, and considerate ones!"

Rossetti always took what he wanted and then generously shared it. So now, the warmer his letters to Janey, the more affectionate are his messages to Morris.

"Give my love to the dear old thing and bear in mind how much you are loved by
                              Your affectionate D. Gabriel R."

is typical. When he painted "The Portrait" he accompanied it with his most passionate sonnet, but also on the top of the frame he inscribed:

"Conjuge clara poetâ, et praeclarissima vultu,
Denique picturâ clara sit illa meâ."

The clue is to be found in a Shelleyan theory of love, summed up in the couplet from *Epipsychidion*:

"True love in this differs from gold or clay
That to divide is not to take away."

There are, indeed, other parallels between Rossetti and Shelley which serve to throw light on several dark places. Bell Scott, for instance, compared Lizzie's fate with that of Harriet[102] and Rossetti seemed "mad" even to Janey, in much the same way in which he himself wrote of Shelley after reading Hogg's biography: "S. appears to have been as mad at Keswick as everywhere else, but not madder;—that he could not compass."

But if it is possible to analyse Rossetti's emotions, what was William Morris' reaction to this devotion to his wife, whether or not it involved sexual intercourse? Did he not realise it, or realise it but not care, or did he accept it without protest because of his declared belief in principles of freedom in sexual relations, deriving from a mixture of Godwin-anarchism and sentimental communism or, even if no longer under the spell of his magnetism, did he, out of habit, accept it that Rossetti had to have his way? His biographers point to his unhappiness at this period as shown in letters to women friends and in his poems on the theme of brothers loving the same woman (the "Laxdoela Saga" as rendered in his "Lovers of Gudrun") but as biographical material poetry is very mis-leading. What could be less like Morris, for instance, than his description of himself as "the idle singer of an empty day"?

The melancholy he shows in letters to Aglaia Coronio or Georgie Burne-Jones may have been nothing to do with Janey, but due to some unsatisfactory relationship of his own elsewhere. Melancholy, in any case, must be seen in context, for Rossetti and Jane were melancholy too and reproach each other for it, indulgently. Melancholy was still accepted in the 1870's as something glamorous—an attitude surviving from the Wertherism admired by the Romantics. As few people would admit to happiness then as will admit to having time now, when to be busy is all. It was considered sensitive, not silly, to pine or repine; delicacy in health as in manners was admired. It is important to bear this in mind in reading correspondence between Rossetti and Janey, where medical prescriptions jostle protestations of devotion on the page.

Whatever "regenerate rapture" some "long inconceivable change" in Janey's attitude had brought out in 1869, Rossetti was then a man of forty-one. He had lived a full life and was no longer a boy without other cares to stand in the way of a fresh enthusiasm. He was not single-minded and the first effects of the excitement were disquieting. In trying to slough off the protective coverings—the thick skins—that had grown on them in the past ten years, both Rossetti and Janey met difficulties that reacted upon them in illness.

The insomnia from which Rossetti suffered worsened and the con-dition of his eyes worried him again. He began to wear strong spectacles, sometimes two pairs at a time on top of each other across his bridge of Michelangelo, and kept them on even when he was not at work. He considered going to Coblenz to consult a specialist there, but was per-suaded by his London advisers to try instead spells of rest in country air, so, in the autumn, accompanied by Howell, he went to stay with the Leylands at Speke Hall. "A glorious old house, full of interest in every way," he wrote to Bell Scott. "I was seedy, however, while there and did not feel well enough to go to Liverpool." Later he set off on a walking tour in Warwickshire with Treffry Dunn, going over again the route he had taken with Bell Scott in 1853, but he soon became bored: "moping and wearying for home".

These tours were too short and too comfortless to be of any benefit and he was at last persuaded by Bell Scott to come up to Penkill Castle, Ayrshire, for a month or so. He had wanted to go earlier but could not make up his mind to face the journey. "I *do hate* railways."

23

Alice Boyd had already provided hospitable holidays at Penkill for Christina and Mrs. Rossetti, and now welcomed Rossetti in September, 1868. He stayed until November and was to pay another visit the next autumn.

The house was on the site of an old castle and had been done-over in Victorian-Baronial by Spencer Boyd, Alice's late brother. The turret stone staircase does not make for warmth (Girvan, although on the west coast, seems to be avoided by the gulf stream), but no doubt at this time unlimited servants provided unlimited fires in the medievalised fire-places, and hostess and guests alike were kept warm by their raptures over Bell Scott's murals up the stairs, based on *The King's Quair*. He had decided to repeat here his triumph in the entrance hall of Wallington, but time and weather has dealt less kindly with these. Rossetti shared the excitement over the furnishings and decoration, for he contributed several enormous blue pots to it in perfect condition and some pieces of tapestry,[103] and was inspired to write his own "King's Tragedy" by Scott's murals.

While staying there, he would appear at a late breakfast, then set out on a ten or twelve-mile walk, complaining, rather unexpectedly, that Bell Scott was "not over-fond of locomotion", and in the evenings after dinner would lie sprawled on a sofa or on a rug with one knee raised, his arms behind his head, and recite or read aloud to the party. He read "a vast amount of Christina", he reported to their mother, glad that most of them knew many of her poems already.

Miss Boyd was in raptures and so was an elderly relative staying there, Miss Losh. Not displeased at having a chance to go one better than her cousin Alice, she adopted Rossetti, attending him at those late breakfasts which irritated Bell Scott as much as they had Meredith: "her daily delight was to see him smashing his eggs on the plate, to the loss of half of them, and making innumerable impressions of his tea-cup on the damask table-cloth", and supporting her devotion with offers of money. If a thousand pounds would keep him from using his eyes, he should have it. He could write poems instead of painting pictures, for Bell Scott always insisted that his real genius was for poetry. He continued to put this with a rather different emphasis in a letter to Stephens:

> "The truth is, as you know, our friend never taught himself to draw—and he fell into the habit of simply reproducing his model, peculiar upper lip, spatulous fingers or anything else. To me it is clear he will live by his poems, not his pictures."[104]

The encouragement helped Rossetti, set as it was at the same time in a soothing atmosphere of comfort and intellectual cultivation.

Under the influence of a new inspiration he had felt the urge to write poems again, or a new period of creative activity had arisen which focused on the inspiration that coincided with it. Either way, he doubted his power to respond to the new stimulus. Was he not too old for poetry? Sunk under

> "The visible burden of the sun grown cold
> And the moon's labouring gaze?"

At Penkill he could recollect his new emotions in tranquillity, treasure his new secret and at the same time in "The Stream's Secret" reveal it. His love for running water is fulfilled in the flowing metre, exactly apt to the thought, and in return the stream reflects back a picture of the human emotion he is trying to express.

> "What thing unto mine ear
>   Would'st thou convey—what secret thing,
> O wondering water ever whispering?
>   Surely thy speech shall be of her.
> Thou water, O thou whispering wanderer,
>   What message does thou bring?"

Water as it flows has seen so much. The course of love is borne along with it: sometimes smooth, sometimes rough; sometimes dark, sometimes bright with promise of happiness in sunshine and a promise of union in the final river.

"But there Love's self
  And with Life's weary wings far-flown,
  And with Death's eyes that make the water moan,
    Gathers the water in his hand:
  And they that drink know nought of sky or land
    But only love alone."

Much as he enjoyed Penkill—the comforts of the household, the walks over the glens or his burrowings in Bennan's Cave, which he described to Kate Howell as "a refuge from everything almost including oneself—the supreme bogey"[105], where he could be alone to write—he wanted to get back to Cheyne Walk.

He returned there on the 3rd November, 1868. His eyesight was not up to it, but he must resume painting. He could not keep off sketching Janey. He wanted her for "Pandora", opening her casket and letting free:

"Powers of the impassioned hours prohibited."

He wanted her also for other pictures, but the tension told again on both of them. While he was painting "Sibylla Palmifera" he had to call in Alexa Wilding as understudy. Writing to Smetham he said that the picture was "held up because poor Mrs. Morris has been very ill and unable to sit which threw me out a good deal in my work, besides being a much greater concern to me on her own account".[106]

During the summer Rossetti also worked on other important paintings: notably the "Dante's Dream", which turned out so large that it could only be hung on the staircase in the house of William Graham, M.P., who had commissioned it, and had to be exchanged for something else. He also proved how good a likeness he could get when he tried in a pencil sketch he did of Dr. Gordon Hake, the poet-doctor, whose work he had admired long ago and who now sent in a card and instantly made friends: "Rare indeed after 40", as Rossetti wrote to Scott, at the same time describing Hake as "a tall thin man of sixty with nothing in the least old about him but his white hair".[107] The friendship thus formed was to be of considerable benefit later.

And Rossetti's long-standing enthusiasm for Browning had been renewed with the appearance of "The Ring and the Book". He wrote in acknowledgement: (13th March)

"I feel as if we were in communication now even before I put pen to paper: for is not your completed thought now filling me?—in how many ways,

at what strange junctures, to recur to me for ever. Such function I have
long acknowledged as yours: but now most strongly by this confirmed and
controlling impression of your greatness when judgement should be mature
in me . . . For this great work of yours now let me thank you as for a fullness which I have lived to see: and believe me ever

Yours in greatest love

D. G. Rossetti."

But, overstrained, he was thinking of retiring to Penkill again while
Janey was abroad. She was so far from well that in July she was ordered
a cure in Germany and set off for Ems with Morris, who grumbled at the
time taken from The Firm, but brought along some verse-making to
occupy himself. Rossetti's letters[108] to her are particularly warm in affection and solicitude and there is no attempt in them to hide his feelings from
Morris. He must have been meant to see the cartoon which accompanied
the letter dated July 21st, showing Morris reading aloud from *The
Earthly Paradise* quite unconcerned—and unappreciative—as she lies
in her bath, looking very like the lady of "La Pia", drinking spa waters
from a series of glasses standing on the floor which keep pace with the
volumes of the poem on a shelf above. The letter ends: "I suppose
Bessie and Lucy (Madox Brown) are enjoying themselves vastly. Love
to them, as well as to dear Top and to your dear self——" A week
later he writes: (30th July, 1869) ". . . All that concerns you is the all-
absorbing question with me, as dear Top will not mind my telling you
at this anxious time. The more he loves you, the more he knows that
you are too lovely and noble not to be loved: and, dear Janey, there are
too few things that seem worth expecting as life goes on, for one friend
to deny another the poor expression of what is most in his heart . . .
Absence from your sight is what I have long been used to, and no absence
can ever make me so far from you again as your presence did for years.
For this long inconceivable change, you know now what my thanks must
be . . ." Presumably her health worsened for on the 10th August he
asks Morris for news and Morris replies on her behalf. By the 14th she
was well enough to write herself and Rossetti answers that "I shall bless
the name of Ems which does not take up much room in one's thanks-
giving" and goes on to tell her of Marie Spartali's sittings: "I find her
head about the most difficult I ever drew." He adds, "I have received
from America the water-colour by poor Lizzie, for which I am to give
Norton a drawing of you. It looks very fine though certainly quite
quaint enough."

In August, 1869, he returned to Penkill. "I have fled hither," he
wrote to Aglaia Coronio, "for the purpose of shooting nothing—not

even the moon—but have merely myself been shot here as rubbish quite used up."[109] He ordered sets of his poems to be set up in print as "trial books", and worked hard at revision of them. Constant letters to William Michael ask for advice, and to his mother he sends messages consulting Maria about Italian versions. He refused to be bound by any strict pre-Raphaelite accuracy: "Nazareth remains by the sea," he insisted in answer to William's geographical objections. "You know, an old painter would have made no bones if he wanted it for his background." On the other hand, for "Cassandra" he was anxious to make sure whether Hector was killed with a sword or with a spear—even if he were wrong in putting Cassandra on the walls of Troy at all.[110]

Rossetti was not overbearing and not vain, but when he wanted something he had to have it. He simply helped himself to one of Bell Scott's titles, "The Stream's Secret", for his own poem: "grabbolized it", said Scott. He might have said with Swinburne, who had to discard the title "Songs of Day and Night" when W. M. Rossetti objected it was a crib from Allingham: "Damn the minor poets, what right have they to call their titles (or their souls) their own if *we* condescend to find any use for them."

Irritated by the walks on which Rossetti dragged him out, and jealous of his personal success with the ladies and of his renewed creativeness, Bell Scott took his revenge in his autobiographical notes, published after Rossetti's death. He recounts an unfavourable sequel to Miss Losh's loan and he paints a general picture of Rossetti as a neurasthenic equally addicted to hallucinations and to whisky-drinking; to which, incidentally, he had introduced him as the only elixir to keep out the Lowlands cold. When they went to see the Devil's Punch-bowl, near Lady's Glen, Rossetti was standing near the slippery edge and suddenly drew back, ". . . put his hand in mine, an action which showed he was losing self-command and that fear was mastering him". (Did Bell Scott disapprove of suicide or of his drawing back from lack of courage?) When on one of their walks they found a wounded chaffinch, Bell Scott says Rossetti insisted it was the soul of the dead Lizzie.

In these occult references, Bell Scott exaggerates Rossetti's credulities. He might dabble in spiritualism as one of the fashions of the time, but Allingham's complaint that he went little further than having "a curiosity" about it is much more plausible. And the story that after Rossetti's departure from Penkill the party in the dining-room heard a voice in the room above them reciting poetry is hardly attributable to any super-stitiousness of Rossetti's and indeed was found to have an ordinary explanation. It did not occur to Bell Scott that somebody with a sense of humour and easily bored might have been making fun of him. A hard-headed northerner, he had no conception of the hardness he was up against in a latin: like Celts they have granite under the soft green-grey lichen.

24

Bell Scott deserves credit for the visits to Penkill that were his suggestion and for the sacrifice of the time he meant to devote to his own book on Dürer, as well as for the encouragement he gave to the writing of the poems. The complacency of the household there provided just the screen that Rossetti needed behind which he could play with fire. None of them guessed his impatience for letters from Ems nor the sort of letters that he was writing there in return.[111]

He made no secret to his friends about his anxiety over Janey's health. To Kate Howell he wrote: "My news of Janey Morris continues pretty good, but I fear the days of miracles are past."[112] And to Howell, on the news from Ems: "If this were but well, nothing could be very ill."

There was frequent correspondence with Howell asking him to find things: a particular sketch of Janey "must be found and locked away"— probably the one in which she is lying in an armchair having fallen asleep over a book which has a title clearly pencilled in, "The Defence of Guinevere".

They were also corresponding over a certain project in connection with publishing the poems, which family tradition at Penkill has it that Alice Boyd and Bell Scott were first responsible for suggesting. They realised that their encouragement of his poetry-writing was useless unless he could somehow recall the "lost" poems, as he always referred to them. They feared for his reason if he were any longer frustrated in this, for they used to overhear him in his room nearly demented as he tried to recall aloud certain lines from "Jenny". He had written to Bell Scott years before: "Some day of wild energy, I will copy 'Jenny' for you, if I can make it up from memory, but have no complete copy." It was the Penkill household, therefore, that first suggested opening Lizzie's grave to reclaim the book buried there. Howell was willing to take the responsibility for putting the operation through, if Rossetti could be persuaded to believe that Lizzie would have been the last person to mind. Would she not have deplored the gesture and rejoiced that it could be redeemed?

In order to effect the disinterment, a permit had to be obtained from the Home Office, and without consulting Mrs. Rossetti. As the Home Secretary was Bruce, now Lord Aberdare (who had been on the Llandaff Committee), Rossetti was able to use his influence with him to waive formalities.

The scene in Highgate Cemetery on the night of the 10th October, 1869,[113] ought to have been painted by some Pre-Raphaelite out for a "subject", but, like Shelley's funeral pyre at Via Reggio, it had perhaps too strong a literary flavour to inspire a good painting. By the light of torches and a fire built at the graveside, three friends watched as the workmen drove in their spades: Howell; the solicitor, Henry Virtue Tebbs; and a Dr. Williams, who took back the book to disinfect. Howell, thoroughly at home in so romantically macabre a scene, was the one to look first into the coffin and it was he who lifted the book out and reported afterwards that Lizzie's hair was still miraculously fresh and golden.

> "Even so much life hath the poor tress of hair
> Which, stored apart, is all love hath to show
> For heart-beats and for fire-heats long ago:
> Even so much life endures unknown, even where
> 'Mid change the changeless night environeth
> Lies all that golden hair undimmed in death."
>
> (Life in Love)

Rossetti wrote to tell the news to William Michael.[114] The devoted brother, who had regretted the gesture by which the book had ever been lost, but had not liked to over-rule Madox Brown who approved it, accepted the news of its rescue with matter-of-fact approval. Swinburne, with more warmth, heartily endorsed what had been done and, as one who had loved Lizzie, insisted that she would have been in favour of it too:

"I cannot tell you how rejoiced I am at the news you send me . . . I have thought often and bitterly of the loss sustained. I can say to you now, what, of course, I could never hint before, how often my thoughts have run in the line of yours as to what her own hope and desire in the matter would have been, who loved art so notably and well."

What is surprising is not Rossetti's lack of sentimentality over the affair, nor his apprehension as to what friends would think about it, but his obsessive need for the book. Considering how good his own memory was and how many other people had received copies of the poems (including Swinburne, who never forgot a line) there can have been very little that could not have been reconstructed. But Rossetti had to have the book back for other reasons: to prove that he had grown away from his own emotional gesture and because deep down he held some superstitious hope that the grave might give up its secret—what had been the motive behind Lizzie's suicide? If the book were intact, perhaps it would show that she had kept it as a pledge of love, had forgiven everything, and yielded it up to him to build a new future upon. What she thought still mattered; the golden thread of her hair had not loosened its stranglehold upon him.

The book restored to him, Rossetti pressed on still harder with revising and re-copying. But in Cheyne Walk he had to paint as well: there was so much to be done to make up for time lost.

> "And let us sup with summer: 'ere the gleam
> Of autumn set the year's pent sorrow free,
> And the woods wail like echoes from the sea."

There is a note of deep melancholy and frustration in a letter to Janey at the end of January: "The sight of you going down the dark steps for the cab all alone has plagued me ever since—you looked so lonely. . . . Now everything will be dark for me till I can see you again—— How nice it would be if I could feel sure I had painted you once for all so as to let the world know what you were but every new thing I do from you is a disappointment and it is only at some odd moment when I cannot set about it that I see by a flash the way it ought to be done." She must have been withdrawing herself on the plea of illness for he protests that he is fully aware of her suffering and only asks to be allowed to alleviate it. (18th February, 1870) "Dearest kindest Janey, . . . But I hope you believe that it is never absent from my thoughts for a moment & that I never cease to long to be near you & doing whatever might be to distract and amuse you. To be with you and wait on you and read to you is absolutely the only happiness I can find or conceive in this world, dearest Janey; and when this cannot be, I can hardly now exert myself to move hand or foot for anything. If ever I do wish still to do any work it is that I may not sink into utter unworthiness of you & deserve nothing but your contempt. I shall come up on Saturday evening and see how you are. But if I *should* be prevented then (or rather, to speak plainly, if I could resolve that it would be much pleasanter to come when no visitors were at your house) I will then come on Monday."

Sometimes the old humour breaks through:

4th February 1870

"Funny sweet Janey

A bloke is coming here tomorrow with a frame, so I think I had better take the opportunity of sending you that chalk drawing as said Bloke can hang it up. If he should happen not to come tomorrow, then I suppose it will be on Monday & I will send it then.

Dear Janey, I suppose this has come into my head because I feel so badly the want of speaking to you. No one else seems alive at all to me now, and places that are empty of you are empty of all life. And it is so seldom that the dead hours breathe a little and yield your dear voice to me again. I seem to hear it while I work, and to see your eyes speaking as clearly as your voice: and so I would write to you for ever if it were not too bad to keep reminding you of my troubles who have so many of your own . . . Thus perhaps at this moment you are suffering so much as to shut out the possibility of pleasure if life had it ready for you in every shape. I always reproach myself with the comfort I feel despite all in the thought of you, when that thought never fails to present me also with the recollection of your pain and suffering. But more than all for me, dear Janey, is the fact that you exist, that I can yet look forward to seeing you and speaking to you again, and know for certain that at that moment I shall forget all my own troubles nor even be able to remember yours. You are the noblest and dearest thing that the world has had to show me: and if no loss than the loss of you could have brought me so much bitterness, I would still rather have had this to endure than have missed the fullness of wonder and worship which nothing else could have made known to me.

When I began this I meant to be cheerful and just see what vague and dismal follies I have been inflicting on you.

Your most affectionate

Gabriel."

Such intensity of emotion could not fail to tell on his constitution. Again friends and medical advisers said he must get away from London. Remembrance of Ayrshire reconciled the Cockney to the idea of the country and he set about looking for some retreat. While he was searching, or friends were doing so for him, an offer came from Barbara Leigh-Smith, now Madame Bodichon, to lend him her house at Scalands, built since he had stayed with Lizzie at the farm on the estate.

It shows Rossetti's lack of sentimental superstition—or remorse—that he could bear the memories the place would evoke. He was driving a horse and cart over the bones of his dead, but at the same time keeping what was most precious of them, for it was exactly at this time—the spring of 1870—when his "lost" poems were about to be published and his painting had been re-vitalised under the influence of Jane Morris as a model, that he set out to collect all of Lizzie's drawings that he could find. He appealed to Madame Bodichon:

"11th January, 1870.

I have been for some time past very anxious to get back all such sketches by my late wife—however slight—as were not in my own hands: as I admire her work even more now if possible than I did years ago. I have got most of those which Ruskin had, but find that he has lost or rather, I believe, given away several. Did you happen to be the recipient in any instance? There was particularly a little pen and ink design (of a woman kneeling by a fireplace with a boy in the background) which I am very sorry to find is lost as it was done to illustrate a poem of my own. . . . I would gladly give you something of my own in exchange, if agreeable to you."[115]

Rossetti was sorry to hear that at Scalands there would also be staying William James Stillman, an American journalist, whom he knew already in London, as he would have preferred to be on his own. But in the event he found him the best of accommodating companions—"surely his name must indicate the hereditary character of race"—he "walks with me, talks with me and avoids me with the truest tact in the world".

Stillman was more than "the entirely unobtrusive man", the grieving widower of this time, who was afterwards to marry the beautiful Marie Spartali. He had taken an active part in Crete during the island's struggle for independence from the Turks and continued to carry on propaganda for it. In Rossetti's story Stillman could be cast for the villain of the piece, for it was he who introduced him to the use of chloral, the latest wonder-drug from America. But

> "in tragic life, Got wot,
> No villain need be."

Stillman took it himself for insomnia, and, of course, is not to be blamed for the excessive doses in which Rossetti later indulged, nor the whisky with which he washed it down. At this time the drug gave him relief and the country air and the general quiet very soon restored his health. "The leisure and pleasure of work in the country," he wrote, "is something new for me—no interruptions, no invitations, no anything which is the bane of studious enjoyment."

Rossetti could write approvingly of Stillman's tact in leaving him "quite to himself", but in reality this was always the last thing he wanted and soon he was taking him off for long walks and keeping him up late at night talking. "In this Sussex desert one tells all his secrets," Stillman quotes him as saying. On his side he was willing enough to be a good listener for, with his eyes open, he had fallen under the Rossetti spell. "He dominated all who had the least sympathy with him or his genius," he wrote later in a very perceptive, though not entirely uncritical, chapter of his *Autobiography*. Rossetti used him as a model too: "I think when I finish Stillman, I shall give him a nimbus and call him his Redeemer by which title he may be made to pay."

At the same time he worked at "Dante's Dream"; earned fifty guineas from the head of Sophy Burgess, the gamekeeper's daughter; made last-minute revisions to the poems after detailed consultations in correspondence with Swinburne, and wrote numerous letters to friends in influential positions to alert them about the appearance of the poems and to enlist their help in publicity. He was in some doubt what publisher to employ. F. S. Ellis was a friend who offered generous terms and already published Swinburne and Morris. With some nostalgia for Brotherhood days, Rossetti liked the idea of his sponsoring a family group and persuaded Christina to transfer to him from Macmillan. He then wrote in rueful humour to Swinburne that Morris with his tremendous energy swamped them all "as he is so fearfully prolific that one would feel like the mouse looking up at the mountain with a clear conviction that everyone thought it had given one birth in some way or other".

He was extremely indignant with anyone who did not appreciate Morris's poetry, rounding on "staunch Mac"—Alexander Macmillan—for never noticing it in his *Magazine*: (30th December, 1870) "Why in the world has Morris been left in the lurch till now? I don't know who your present editor is, but I may assure him that it is of no use sulking over good work."

As his health improved at Scalands he wanted more people about him and began sending invitations to friends, for, Stillman wrote, "Rossetti was one of the men most dependent on companionship I have ever known." As they were supposed to be sharing expenses on a 50-50 basis he decided he could not stay on, for such hospitality was beyond his means. Without rancour he accepted it that Rossetti must have what he wanted: "He was generous to the same degree of extravagance that he was indifferent to the claims of others: he made no more account of giving you a treasured curio than he did of taking it."

As Stillman had seen, Rossetti, even if it tired him, needed the stimulus of other people in order to work. The Madox Browns were invited, and so were Top and Janey. They went on expeditions together, "church crawling", and collecting wild flowers which Rossetti sent to his mother.

When Morris returned to London Janey stayed on—"in another house, lent by Barbara's brother", wrote Rossetti, registering the fact, to Scott.

Scalands was proving "of some decided benefit to her" and "she walks about like anybody else", he reported to Madame Bodichon. She was needed as the model for "Dante's Dream" and, perhaps, for the new poems of those weeks too: "Youth's Spring", "The Love Letter", "The Monochord".

Scalands provided a spring idyll that Rossetti greeted with a new gaiety in "Fin de Maggio":

> "O May sits crowned with Hawthorn-flowers
>   And is Love's month they say
> And love's the fruit that is ripened best
>   By ladies' eyes in May."

25

The year 1870 was to be yet another *Annus Mirabilis* for Rossetti: an autumnal one with colours more muted than the others and a chill wind from winter ahead blowing ominously through, but a renaissance all the same. Even if his letters to Janey in the early months are melancholy, his very yearning for her meant that his emotions were alive: he was not in that worst state of despondency when they are dead. His pictures and his poems were on top of the world again. In painting even a critical friend like Bell Scott had to admit in a letter to Holman Hunt (28th January, 1871) "Gabriel has made a great success and has lately been painting in such a way everyone even among his own circle have been surprised."[116]

When the *Poems* appeared from Ellis in April, they received extremely good notices in a wide range of journals, engineered, to quote Scott again, by the author himself "working the miracle". He certainly did make the most of friends who were in strategic positions. So did others. Coventry Patmore wrote to "Stephie": "Pop that into the Athenaeum"; and a sense of public relations is hardly one at which the present generation should cavil. The volume sold out its first thousand within a fortnight and by the end of the year six further editions had appeared, bringing in over £800 to their author, together with an undertaking from Ellis to publish a revised edition of *Early Italian Poets*.[117]

Among the numerous reviews by friends there was Swinburne's ecstatic contribution in the May issue of "The Fortnightly", which seems to have been written concurrently with his comments on the poems in letters as Rossetti had been sending them to him. In fact, Rossetti had to implore him not to praise them in print "beyond my deserts", to which Swinburne replied "I shall not—to speak Topsaically—say a bloody word which is not a blasted fact."

Rossetti was aware of the repercussions there might be and had written to Bell Scott (4th May, 1870) from Scalands: "Swinburne's wonderful paean which is a darling bit of friendly enthusiasm but simply appals me (to speak truth) for the probable result of reaction from its excessive & supernatural laudation." William Morris praised the poems in "The Academy", though he had been reluctant to write a notice at all. "I have done my review", he wrote to Aglaia Coronio, "just this moment—ugh." But whether this was distaste for the poems or because he did not want to spare time from his multifarious activities is not clear.

Colvin was full of compliments in "The Pall Mall Gazette"; Joseph Knight (Editor of "Notes and Queries" and afterwards an early biographer) in "The Globe"; Skelton in "Frasers"; Dr. Gordon Hake in "The New Monthly"; Marston in "The Athenaeum", though a very hostile review of W. M. Rossetti's "Shelley" had appeared in the January issue, written by Robert Buchanan, for which "The Athenaeum" was called "Arse-inaeum" in correspondence with Swinburne.

One of the few unfavourable notices appeared in "Blackwoods" and another in the New York "Nation", written, it was suspected, by "poetaster Lowell" and it was disappointing that the edition hardly sold at all in the United States. Emerson declared that Rossetti's poetry "does not come home to us, it is exotic; but we like Christina's religious pieces".

Friends and admirers sent their congratulations—"flooded" him "with letters". Among these was Meredith's unstinted praise:

"I have not had such a delight for years. We never meet now and my regret is that I cannot talk to you of the pleasure and pride I feel in your volume.

You are our Master, of all of us. Some of the Sonnets and lines throughout the poems, hang about me like bells . . . [Swinburne] threw flowers on you in the Fortnightly; not one was undeserved. After first finishing the book, my voice would have been as unrestrained, less eloquent.

I am ever, my dear Gabriel,
Your loving
George Meredith."

Robert Browning wrote after some delay, stiffly but with appreciation, particularly expressing his gratitude to the younger man for the sympathy he had given "when I got few enough gifts of the kind". He said frankly that he did not care for personifications: "Love as a youth encircling you gives me a turn," but added "those are nothings one is driven to, lest there seem abdication of the critical faculty; the main is masterly and conclusive, with whomsoever shall need it, of your right to all the honours in poetry as in painting, double-lived in regions new". How far Rossetti was from arrogance at this time of recognition is shown by a letter he wrote to Purnell: "Many thanks for the Newspaper cutting, which is but too friendly and flattering. As for what is said of Swinburne and Morris, I know that the volume & *élan* of their genius would always leave me far behind; and if I, as a rather older man, had any influence on them in early years, I feel in my turn that their work has duly reacted upon what I have done since."

The demand for fresh editions was brought to an end by a trade recession due to the death of Dickens (there had been nothing comparable since the death of Byron) and the outbreak of the Franco-Prussian War. Rossetti was less cosmic-conscious or, shall we say, more honest than others at the time—or since—who pretend to sympathies wider than they can support. He challenged Shields to declare whether his horror at "this truly atrocious and insufferable war" was due "simply to what all most feel or to more direct influence of a baleful kind in your immediate prospects". The Italian refused to be anything but utterly insular: it was no use expecting him to show himself *engagé*, but the attitude of the Brotherhood to the war, like their judgments of French painting, was unfortunate, as a letter from Hunt in Paris to Stephens may illustrate.

"It is amusing to hear the Prussians speak of the defeat of the French as the work of the hand of God . . . as zealous Protestants they answer on being asked for which particular sin they were punished that it was for supporting the Pope. Getting the pox, writing filthy sentimental novels, not putting Nap. in quod, keeping lorettos and drinking absinthe are nothing in comparison to the iniquity of supporting the scarlet lady. . . ."[118]

Success is a great healer and Rossetti's health, and with it his eyesight, improved from the summer of 1870. At the same time the attitude grew on him of "not giving a damn". At the Tuesday night whist parties at the Bell Scotts'—now settled at Belle Vue, opposite Battersea Bridge—he sometimes swore to an extent that shocked George Boyce, though when this happened with the Rector of Chelsea present he apologised handsomely afterwards.

His "take it or leave it" attitude to patrons and to visitors increased. Not even to please his brother and Madox Brown would he find time for the Miss Mathilde Blind they both admired. An aggressive literary lady with a strong guttural accent, she was Karl Blind's adopted daughter and had a passion for Shelley that had warmed William Michael to her. He tried to enlist Mrs. Rossetti's help:

> "Have you ever spoken to Gabriel about her work, or about his seeing her? You have I believe much influence with him and I think it looks strange his never seeing or speaking of her . . . and such a poetess as she is ought to be on good terms with him."

When Rossetti did not sufficiently admire a sonnet of hers in an anthology that Madox Brown brought to show him, Brown smashed a peacock screen as he strode out of Tudor House in a huff. Contrite and affectionate letters between them made up the quarrel. Rossetti would gladly sacrifice even a precious screen to escape an hour in a blue-stocking's company, especially one who seems to have been a re-incarnation of Shelley's own Miss Hitchener, "the brown demon".

But he had always a concern for women classed as "unfortunate". One day Luke Ionides took the Westminster magistrate, Thomas Arnold, to his studio. He was delighted with his visit and on leaving asked if there was anything he could do to show how much he had enjoyed himself. "Yes, you can," answered Rossetti. "When some very pretty girl is brought up before you, deal leniently with her." To which Arnold very properly replied that he hoped he would always do that, pretty or no.

On another occasion at one of his own dinner parties the high-pitched voice of a well-known artist was heard saying: "I had rather any day meet a lioness bereft of her whelps than a woman who has lost her virtue." Then the soft voice of Rossetti answered. "Nonsense, man, nonsense! I've met many and all very nice indeed."

Luke Ionides also tells of walking once at night with Rossetti and seeing him empty the coins from his pockets into the lap of a woman lying huddled in a corner.

Under the stimulus of his success and of his new interest Rossetti worked even harder, compulsively, as if his brush kept some evil spirit, some "bogey", at bay. He was very remorseful that in his pre-occupation he forgot his mother's birthday and wrote to "The Antique" that evening:

> "It makes me very unhappy to think that extreme worry with my work for a week or two past has put this intention [of visiting her] to flight, and

even found me oblivious of the anniversary when I saw your dear face to-day . . ."

and again,

> "I am so tired by dusk that if I do not wait an hour or so to rest before going out, I am obliged to take a cab and sacrifice my walk—without which I am done for."

When he did consent to go out to visit old friends, to attend the Burne-Joneses' parties at The Grange or the receptions which the Madox Browns now held regularly in Fitzroy Square, he did not bother with anybody except Mrs. Morris. They would sit together quite unself-consciously "wrapped in the motionless silence of a world where souls have no need of words". Edmund Gosse, as a young man, described Janey "in her ripest beauty" sitting on the painting throne at the Browns in a long unfashionable gown of ivory velvet while Rossetti "squatted on a stool at her feet", and a relation of William de Morgan's saw Rossetti at another party at Mrs. Virtue Tebbs' feeding Mrs. Morris with strawberries. "He was carefully scraping off the cream, which was bad for her, and then solemnly presenting her with the strawberries in a spoon."

Rossetti was evidently feeling the middle-aged need that comes upon even the most popular party-goers to share them with someone familiar. He wanted to enjoy the secondary and sometimes sweeter pleasure that comes from talking it all over afterwards at home in bedroom slippers over a nightcap. But that was not for him; instead, his evil spirit, his "bogey", gained upon him. The companionship he had found was not always at hand, and the need for it, and the impossibility of obtaining it, told upon his health.

Dr. Hake, over-rated as he might be by Rossetti as a poet, was to prove himself an invaluable friend when he was called in as medical adviser. He now suggested country air and prepared some rooms at Roehampton. Rossetti lingered over committing himself and suggested they would do instead for Christina, who had been seriously ill. He then toyed with the idea of going to Penkill again, to Scalands, or to Lymington, for some of the old feeling towards Allingham had been revived by a London visit in the summer. To the Cowper Temples, who invited him to Broadlands, he made the excuse of work: "I fancy my easel and I will have to be each other's cronies all this winter under pain of getting nothing done. I must be a very bad manager, for other people seem to work and enjoy themselves too, which is more than I find myself able to contrive."[119] He had got into that state when he could not make up his mind to move, like a man too hungry to eat, too tired to sleep.

PART FOUR

KELMSCOTT AND THE END
1871–1882

And then a curious respite—the interval at Kelmscott in the late summer and autumn of 1871 which, like one of its own healing walks along the young Thames in the sunshine between storms, brought relief from the tensions of the years before.

How it came about is curious the whole way through. William Morris wanted somewhere in the country for his family to live away from Bloomsbury. He saw an advertisement in a newspaper for Kelmscott Manor House near Lechlade and went down to see it. He fell in love with it—"a heaven on earth: an old Elizabethan house like Water Eaton and such a garden!" The place seemed meant for him.

At the end of the week he took Janey to look at it—and Rossetti went too. Curious, for Morris must have been doubtful whether so incorrigible a Cockney as Rossetti could ever really settle down in such "an abode of ancient peace" and even more doubtful whether he wanted him there at all. However it was, they decided on a joint tenancy, sharing the £60 a year rent. Rossetti was to move in at once, while Philip Webb started on additions to the studio at Tudor House.

In July, therefore, he went down there a week after Morris set off for the first of his visits to Iceland. His loyal biographer, Professor Mackail, son-in-law to Burne-Jones, remarks that the importance of this trip is "not wholly intelligible" and it does not become more so from Morris' comment to Aglaia Coronio on "what horrors it saved me from". If the "horrors" were connected with Janey, the letters he writes to her are unrevealing. "Dearest Janey", he opens with conventional connubial affection, and hopes she is happy, for fear of her boredom weighs heavily on him and of her "chaff"—he begs her not to laugh at Aglaia for buttering him up. Before he sails he writes: "I am very happy to think of you all happy there,—Live well and happy." Is this obtuseness or complacency? Was he a *mari complaisant*, not caring, or accepting some ultimatum from the other two by which they insisted on a *ménage à trois* under the same roof?

Anyway, oblivious of him, Rossetti papered and painted, imported furniture from Cheyne Walk and made arrangements for a gig, as housekeeping was difficult so far from the town of Faringdon. He corresponded with Penkill about buying one of their Ayrshire cows and he imported dogs which Morris, who hated animals about the place, hoped the children "would not take to". There were three in the end and the games they played with one of them, a black and tan terrier given by Dr. Hake and called "Dizzy", occur frequently in Rossetti's letters.

He found Janey a good walker—"licks you hollow", he wrote to Bell Scott—but, then, hadn't she something of the gypsy in her? He read aloud Plutarch's *Lives* and Shakespeare, wondering why Shakespeare had not written on Pompey; declaimed Browning's *Balaustion's Adventure*, but found it heavy-going and called it "Exhaustion's Adventure". He enjoyed playing with the children, who were "the most darling little self-amusing machines", and found the younger, May, particularly intelligent and beautiful. In later life she remembered him with warm affection and put on record a protest against his detractors.[120]

He brought a replica of the "Beata Beatrix" to finish and rigged up the big tapestry room as a studio, but it proved to be uncomfortably draughty even in summer. The tapestry got on his nerves—too medieval and art-and-crafty. Too Topsy-ish? "The subject is the history of Samson which is carried through with that uncompromising uncomfortableness peculiar to this class of art manufacture." He asked Howell to send material to put over it and screens as well.

When Morris wrote from Iceland that he had been greeted as a "Skald", Rossetti seized upon the ungainly Nordic word with glee. This must supersede the name of Topsy in future: "Skald" for Morris and "The Bard" reserved for Swinburne. He told Bell Scott that he hoped for some amusing stories from Morris on his return—in rather half-hearted expectation, for he thought Topsy's Nordic enthusiasm a bore. He was himself "an inveterate Southerner", as he wrote to Madame Bodichon: "In answer to your enquiry, I was just going to say I was sorry I did not know (and perceive no reflection that I hope I never may) what is to be got in Norway or further north—always besides the rheumatism and habits of swearing which I feel confident must be acquired there. You see I am an inveterate Southerner though, I fear, no particular patriot." This sympathy for North or South also divides the respective admirers of Rossetti and Morris.

"Who can take an interest in a man who has a dragon for a brother?" asked Rossetti in reference to Morris' poem, "Sigurd the Volsung".

"It's better than having a brother who is a bloody fool," exploded Morris.

His failure to appreciate William Michael is not to his credit, for William's respectability was not dullness. He had warm sympathies and a wide learning which made him good company in any congenial circle. This, as well as his broad-mindedness, comes out in his correspondence with Swinburne, which continued long after other friends had given him up as impossible.

Rossetti took a new interest in nature: the noise made by the starlings, for instance, he reports exactly in "Sunset Wings":

> "And clouds of starlings, 'ere they rest with day
>   Sink clamorous like mill waters, at wild play
>   By turns in every copse."

He wrote to Purnell when sending it to "The Spectator":

"I believe I had made up my mind not to print any more in periodicals, as it deflowers one's offspring when collected: but I don't say no this time . . . The habit of the starlings referred to in them quite amounts to a local phenomenon . . . It was new to Morris also—great rural observer—& might perhaps seem strange to some readers but is very exactly described. The noise is, as I have said, just like the wheel of a watermill or (more prosaically) like a factory in full spin . . . Let me see a proof without fail, as I am morbid about commas & semi-colons. Tell the printer to stick to my punctuation exactly."[121]

His painter's eye also took in details of the river-country round— "the drained flood-lands flaunt their marigolds"—and used them as backgrounds; for there is always a figure, or two figures of lovers, that the eye is to focus upon. The sonnet on "Spring" ends:

> "Chill are the gusts to which the pastures cower,
>   And chill the current where the young reeds stand
>   As green and close as the young wheat on land:
> Yet here the cuckoo and the cuckoo-flower
> Plight to the heart Spring's perfect imminent hour
>   Whose breath shall soothe you like your dear one's hand."

Even so, people always meant more to him than places and he would not have cared for Kelmscott or stayed there so long if he had not had a woman he admired for company. Whether their companionship extended to consummation of the sexual act would not be so all-important for him as it seems to a post-Freudian generation. His warmest letters before Scalands show that he was willing simply to be allowed to adore her and, it must be remembered, to paint her. She was of vital importance to him as a model: again difficult for a generation to understand where artists have largely dispensed with models. He may have been content to worship:

> "There kneels he now, and all—anhungered of
> Thine eyes grey—lit in shadowing hair above,
> Seals with thy mouth his immortality."

When in later years Rossetti regretted that she had refused to believe in his love for her, he may have meant that she refused to believe it would last and had therefore declined to set up house with him permanently. He wrote (1st July, 1878) of his "deep regard". "Would that circumstances had given me the power to prove this: for proved it *wd.* have been. And *now* you dont believe it." In none of his letters to her or hers to him is there any reference to happiness enjoyed together at Kelmscott which there surely would have been if they had been lovers.

That she kept the letters at all, however, shows that they must have represented memories precious to her. She was clearly not indifferent to the worship he proffered her. What woman would not prefer Rossetti's passionate lines:

> "Her arms lie open, throbbing with their throng
> Of confluent pulses, bare and fair and strong:
> And her deep-freighted lips expect me now
> Amid the clustering hair that shrines her brow
> Five kisses broad, her neck ten kisses long,"

to Morris's formal listing of her features, addressed to her in some odd moment taken from designing a tapestry or wall-paper?

> "My lady seems of ivory
> Forehead, straight nose, and cheeks that be
> Hallow'd a little mournfully
> *Beata mea, Domina.*
>
> Not greatly long my lady's hair
> Nor set with yellow colour fair,
> But thick and crispéd wonderfully.
> *Beata mea, Domina.*"

In trying to arrive at a conclusion, not about what actually happened but, more important, about the feelings and reactions of each of them it must be borne in mind how mixed-up they all were with illusions of romantic medieval love: Morris from a picture in his mind of medieval socialism and Rossetti of a *Paradiso* with a Shelleyan gloss—each as ill-founded as the other. The Guinevere story seemed to fit.[122] Morris-Arthur was more concerned with the Round Table of his fellow-workers in The Firm, Janey liked posing as Guinevere and Rossetti believed the Grael well-lost for love—it was, anyway, a loving-cup in which body and soul could be pledged as different aspects of the same principle of beauty. They none of them saw any reason to change the situation at Kelmscott-Camelot: Janey because, like any other woman, she enjoyed its complication, Rossetti because it suited him well enough, and Morris because he was not really interested. The final comment must be Rossetti's own when he wrote to Dr. Hake on the relations of Byron with his half-sister, Augusta Leigh. "Lastly, if Byron f . . . . d his sister, he f . . . . d her and there's an end,—an absolute end, in my opinion, as far as the vital interest of his poetry goes, which is all we have to do with."[123]

At Kelmscott Rossetti found a new serenity. What might seem to be a rumbling of boredom in his references to its quiet, "the doziest dump of grey old bee-hives", is characteristic of his mocking what he most cared for: favourite pictures were always "daubs": "The Blessed Damozel" became "The Blasted Damdozel", and "The Annunciation" the "blessed white eyesore". His affection for it must not be minimised, nor the idea accepted that "in some way he desecrated the sacred air of Morris' refuge". He wrote his appreciation to his many correspondents; to Bell Scott: "the house and garden—make up a delicious picture to the eye and mind"; to Shields: "a perfect paradise, and the place peaceful even to excess", and to Mrs. Cowper Temple: "This is a most lovely old place—a desert in solitude and an Eden in beauty—just my idea of a change from hateful London."[124] To his mother he wrote, "this house and its surroundings are the loveliest 'haunt of ancient peace' that can well be imagined". He encouraged the children to collect wild flowers for her, and told her of his visits to the old churches around: Kelmscott itself, which he intended to get into a picture some day, and Lechlade, in whose churchyard Shelley had written his "Summer Evening" verses:

"The winds are still, or the dry church-tower grass
Knows not their gentle motions as they pass."

Rossetti invited his friends and his family to come to Kelmscott to share his enjoyment of it. Was this to put them off the scent, to show that he could get away with anything or simply that he took what he wanted and was always generous in sharing? His very conventional mother and sisters do not seem to have found it odd that he was living in the depths of the country alone with the wife of his once close friend.

However it may have been, Rossetti at Kelmscott enjoyed a spell of life happier than he had ever known. He was able at once to work and to relax. He had no "sense of guilt", for he sent the poems he was writing to friends, even to Morris, for objective criticism, and to Bell Scott half-grumbles that he does not get as much work done as he would if he were on his own: "My walks are seldom taken alone."

> "Deep in the sun-searched growths the dragon-fly
> Hangs like a blue thread loosened from the sky:
>   So this winged hour is dropt to us from above.
> Oh, clasp we to our hearts, for deathless dower,
> This close companioned inarticulate hour
>   When two-fold silence was the song of love."
>
>   (Silent Noon.)

27

Then into this Eden there intruded the serpent, rearing himself with the poisonous hiss of an article in the "Contemporary Review" of October, 1871, called "The Fleshly School of Poetry". It was signed by Thomas Maitland, a *nom de plume* for Robert Buchanan, a neurotic and second-rate literary figure who enjoyed a certain reputation for his long narrative nature poems and was fairly regularly employed as a reviewer. He had old scores to pay off against the Rossetti coterie, as he regarded it, for in 1856 William Michael had adversely reviewed his *Idylls and Legends of Inverburne* and later called him a "poor but pretentious poetaster" while defending Swinburne against his attack on *Poems and Ballads*.

Buchanan's skit on Swinburne in *The Session of the Poets* was not unapt and in other circumstances might have amused Rossetti and his friends:

> "Up jumped with his neck stretching out like a gander
> Master Swinburne and squalled, glaring out through his hair:
>   'All virtue is bosh: Hallelluja for Landor.
>   I disbelieve wholly in everything—There.'"

The failure of his own volume, *The Book of Orm*, published a few weeks before Rossetti's much-praised poems, brought out again all his old resentments (the unkindest cut was an unfavourable comparison with *Atalanta*). Paranoically, he imagined the coterie had conspired together to have him ignored and belittled.

When the article first appeared it did not worry Rossetti unduly. "I have been surprised (and pleasantly)," he wrote to Shields, "to find such things producing a much more transient and momentary impression of unpleasantness than I should have expected—indeed, I might almost say, none at all." He mobilised friends to reply and to find out who "Maitland" was, and, more annoyed at the anonymity than at what had been said, himself wrote a counter-attack, "The Stealthy School of Criticism" for "The Athenaeum" of 16th December. This had to be toned down, but if violent, it was not unbalanced.

Buchanan replied in "St. Paul's Magazine" in March, 1872, saying of Rossetti: "Here is Euphues come again with a vengeance, in the shape of an amatory foreigner, ill-acquainted with English and seemingly modelling his style on the Conversations of Dr. Samuel Johnson." He next issued a longer version of his article in pamphlet form in May, 1872, under the title "The Fleshly School of Poetry and other Phenomena of the Day". It was this which produced in Rossetti a reaction comparable to Keats' deathblow from the "Blackwood" review of *Endymion*.

> "Strange that the soul, that most fiery particle,
> Should let itself be snuffed out by an article."

What was it that Buchanan said? Of "Nuptial Sleep"* he wrote: "Here is a full-grown man [therefore worse, he implied, than Swinburne who had been little more than a boy in 1866] presumably intelligent and cultivated, putting on record for other full-grown men to read, the most secret mysteries of sexual connection and with so sickening a desire to reproduce the sensual mood, so careful a choice of epithet to convey mere animal sensations that we merely shudder at the shameless nakedness."

He went on to bring in Simeon Solomon: "Nasty as it is, we are very mistaken if many readers do not think it nice. English Society of one kind purchases *The Day's Doings*: English Society of another kind goes into ecstacy over Mr. Solomon's pictures—pretty pieces of morality, such as 'Love dying by the breath of Lust'."

He introduced a reference to himself in order, no doubt, the better to preserve his disguise: " 'Jenny' is in some respects the finest poem in the book . . . It is a production which bears signs of having been suggested by Mr. Buchanan's quasi-lyrical poems, which it copies in style of title . . . but certainly Mr. Rossetti cannot be accused, as the Scottish

* See Appendix J III, p. 240.

writer has been accused, of maudlin sentiment and affected tenderness . . . there is not a drop of piteousness in Mr. Rossetti." Curious that this should be the same criticism as Ruskin had made years ago on a poem which is surely essentially a study in tender and unselfish pity! He ended: "In petticoats or pantaloons . . . he is just Mr. Rossetti, a fleshly person."

What had been shrugged off in October, 1871 (or years ago during *The Imbroglio*), was no matter for indifference a year later, which, it must be remembered, was two years after the publication at a time when. the paeans of praise had died down and would have been forgotten.

The accusation of sensuality and phallic exhibitionism touched the puritan in Rossetti. Bohemian as he might be in many ways, he also wanted to be respected by the respectable. He once wrote to Edmund Bates: "I don't know what copy of my poems you have lent to the Rev^d. Gentleman, but apprehend there may be things here and there in the book which might rather ruffle the nap of 'the cloth', though not a line that is vile, by God!"[125] He never published "The French Liberation."*

At this time there was something more—much more—to make him sensitive on the point. The intensity of his resentment and its reaction on his mental balance was due to the situation at Kelmscott. He wanted to keep it unbesmirched. The very fact that he had known fairly wide sexual experience made him the more anxious to keep this relationship with Janey different: to keep her on her throne and ensure that everyone respected her there. His success up to this point in making his family and his friends accept what was undoubtedly an equivocal situation must be maintained. The English-governess side of himself needed re-assurance. There was nowhere any sense of guilt towards Morris as a conventionally wronged husband—that simply did not apply—but there was frustration: the perfect companionship of Kelmscott had to be interrupted and this meant the aggravation of the loneliness at Tudor House.

> "Oh, dearest! While we lived and died
> A living death in every day,
> Some hours we still were side by side,
> When where I was you too might stay
> And rest and need not go away."
>
> (Spheral Change)

With regret for the years that had been lost, unhappy memories crowded in. And just when he was most depressed over the pamphlet, Rossetti received from Browning a copy of his *Fifine at the Fair* with a personal inscription. The inscription read:[126]

* See Appendix J, p. 241.

"To Dante Gabriel Rossetti from his old admirer and affectionate friend.
June 4, 1872. R.B."

This time Rossetti wrote off to acknowledge the volume before he
looked into it.

"June 5th, 1872. My Dear Browning. Thanks once more for a new book
bearing your name loved as of old. And even before I read it, let me say,
Thanks.

"Thanks for your warm expression of regard at this moment,
Affectionately yours,
D. G. Rossetti."

But when he began to read it he was shocked at what he could only
regard as a personal attack. If, leafing through, he started at the back
with the Epilogue, it is no wonder. What Browning wrote of the "losel"
in the main body of the poem could apply to any philanderer, but the
ghost-haunted widower of the Epilogue must have come right home to
Rossetti. It put better than he himself could, the loneliness and despair
he sometimes felt:

> "Savage I was sitting in my house, late alone
> Dreary, weary with the long day's work:
> Head of me, heart of me, stupid as a stone
> Tongue-tied now, now blaspheming like a Turk."

It was his once-adored Browning who was turning Buchanan's knife
in the wound. There is even an echo of "The Blessed Damozel":

> "All the fancies . . . Who were they had leave, dared try
> Darker arts that almost struck despair in me?
>
> 'If you knew but how I dwelt down here!' quoth I:
> 'And was I so much better off up there?' quoth she."

And after the brutal *clichés*, the diapason of her triumphant faith must
have struck with a bitterness not to be forgotten:

> " '*Affliction sore long time he bore,*' or what is it to be?
> '*Till God did please to grant him ease.* Do end!' quoth I:
> 'I end with—Love is all and Death is nought,' quoth she."

The house on which he had lavished so much care, the river he loved
to watch from the windows of that upstairs drawing-room, even the
friends who had laughed with him there, did not comfort him. The things

on which he had fed his heart had turned sour: memories haunted him in
bitterness.

> "Who, sleepless, hath not anguished to appease
> Tragical shadow's realm of sound and sight
> Conjectured in the lamentable night? . . .
> Lo, the soul's sphere of infinite images!"

28

Buchanan's pamphlet and Browning's poem—these triggered off the
breakdown, but what was the dynamite at the base? Not a sense of guilt
over his relations with Jane nor remorse over Lizzie—he refers to her
without embarrassment in letters—but the disappointment and disillusion to which any artist is prone in middle-age. Echoing the diffidence he had expressed to Holman Hunt as a very young man, he now
explained to William Michael his reluctance to exhibit publicly on account
of the "lifelong dissatisfaction which I have experienced from the disparity
of aim and attainment in which I have all my life produced as best I could".

He showed his fear of meeting "Lost Days" in the sonnet of that name:

> "Each one a murdered self, with low, last breath
> 'I am thyself—what hast thou done to me?
> And I—and I—thyself!' (lo! each one saith,)
> 'And thou thyself to all eternity'."

Rossetti had a conscience but in Art or in Love a sense of guilt was
something which he never suffered from. He took the things he wanted.
It never occurred to him to doubt that when he wanted a thing he must
have it, and no question of rights or wrongs came in. Stillman saw this
at Scalands:

> "He was the spoiled child of his genius and of the large world of his ad-
> mirers: there was no vanity about him and no exaggeration of his own abil-
> ities, but other people, even artists whom he appreciated, were of merely
> relative importance to him . . . his was a sublime and child-like egotism which
> simply ignored obligations until, by chance, they were made legal, at which,
> when it happened, he protested like a spoiled child. And he had been so
> spoiled by all his friends and exercised such a fascination on all around him,
> that no one rebelled at being treated in his princely way, for it was only
> with his friends that he used it."

Besides his personal domination, Rossetti had enjoyed success with his poems and with his pictures, but he knew they were not as good as he wanted them to be. And this is a disease for which there is no cure. As the Wordsworth he never liked put it:

"We poets in our youth begin in gladness
But thereof in the end comes despondency and madness."

Every artist must have his ups and downs: his creative periodicity; a term of fallow succeeding activity. As he aged, Rossetti, like anyone else, found the melancholic periods prolonging themselves and recovery from the trough to the crest of the wave more difficult. There is no call to search for a clue to each "down" period and far too much can be made of sexual relations. With Rossetti the position was worsened by complications that went deep into the foundations of his character. In work and in life he had to pay the price for his triple personality as poet, painter, person. Too often he let the person win against the artist when in his heart he knew what he had written once to James Smetham to be the truth: "You comfort yourself with other things, whereas Art must be its own comforter or else comfortless." It was his *credo*. At times he betrayed it by weakness of will, and retribution was demanded by avenging Furies under various forms. It was his fault that Lizzie had died, for he might have saved her; if he had not left her alone and if he had poured out the correct dose himself she would not have been tempted to take too much. It was his fault that Janey was ill and unhappy, for he should have been clearer-sighted and bolder. He should have realised where his true love lay and taken action: not yielded to illusions in willow-wood. "Guilt" and "Remorse" were accessories after the fact of his regret—regret that his character was too weak to support the weight of his personality. Or, as Watts-Dunton perceptively put it: "He was the slave of his own imagination—an imagination of a power and dominance such as I have never seen equalled. . . . Imagination is a good servant but a bad master."

With such tensions, no wonder his health gave way. The actual breakdown came on 2nd June, 1872. Even Dr. Marshall could do nothing with him. William Michael was summoned to Cheyne Walk and with the help of Dr. Hake took his brother to Roehampton. In the cab he had the hallucination that a bell was ringing and wanted to get out to disperse an encampment of gypsies whom he accused of organising a demonstration against him.

On the Saturday night he took what was intended to be an overdose of laudanum when he went to bed. Hake did not visit his room until the afternoon, as he hoped that a natural sleep would be the best possible cure, but when at length he went in to see him, he realised what had happened and sent for another doctor. Personally he thought there was no hope. William Michael went to fetch Mrs. Rossetti and Maria (Christina was bed-ridden with Graves' Disease), who were taken completely by surprise as they had not been told of the collapse at Cheyne Walk. On the way Madox Brown was informed. He undertook to fetch Marshall at once and then to come on himself.

Dr. Hake had applied ammonia to the sick man's nostrils and now Dr. Marshall ordered strong coffee. This treatment was successful, but as the patient's strength increased so his delusions returned. It was impossible to leave him unattended and a private asylum was for a moment thought of. But, as so often before, it was Madox Brown who came to the rescue, offering the shelter of Fitzroy Square. A letter to Shields makes nothing of his own generous friendship but states the position as it appeared to those close to Rossetti at the time:

"You must know that Gabriel for the last two years has been, without our noticing it, subject to fits of eccentricity, partaking of the nature of delusions. He had also been sleeping worse and worse and taking doses of Chloral every night. This state (about the time of the Buchanan pamphlet) owing to the irritation consequent on that libel, reached a state of development, accompanied by a kind of fit . . . that rendered it unsafe to leave him alone . . ."

Brown and William Michael took charge, making arrangements for a place to go out of London and for someone to be in attendance. Letters of enquiry had to be answered: one written in an un-characteristic scrawl that betrays its emotion came from Jane Morris:

"Dear Mr. Brown. Have you any fresh news? I had a letter from Mr. Scott last Saturday [crossed out] Friday, but have heard nothing since although I have written to him twice. I had such dreadful dreams last night. I can't rest today without trying all means to get news. I am to come back to town on Friday."[127]

From Brown's, Rossetti went to Scotland on 20th June to houses put at his disposal by William Graham, M.P.: first Urrard House, then Stobhall. He could not bear to be alone and when Dr. Hake had to return he sent in his place his son, George, rusticated for a term from Oxford. Nolly Brown came up, though Rossetti considered him too young and tried to persuade Stillman to pay a visit instead. Bell Scott stayed and took the opportunity to do a water-colour of the house, which he wanted Rossetti to get Graham to buy—ready to make use of a friend whom he considered "finished".

Regular letters [128] from the Hakes, father and son, to W. M. Rossetti and to Madox Brown recount the course of the illness and the almost miraculous recovery. At first he slept badly and when sitting up suffered severely from the hydrocele swelling, a condition considered by Dr. Hake to be "a useful reality among his fancies". There was an idea of Marshall coming up to operate but in the end it was done successfully by a local surgeon. He expected to be entertained by someone reading aloud and telling him amusing anecdotes late into the evening. Gradually he began to sleep better, even without whisky, although he would not admit it. (30th June) "Last evening," wrote Dr. Hake, "because Scott and I congratulated him on getting a ten-minute nap, he broke out into a Philippic against us, saying it was too bad that he should be persecuted as he is about to sleep. That he cannot lie down, but he is told he is sleeping. He can't shriek and howl always etc. He was very sorry afterwards that he had given way."

The whisky was cut down to three wine-glasses a day and later dropped entirely for claret. When he was able to take walks, his condition improved considerably, but despite the improvement there was still cause for anxiety in case some annoyance should trigger off one of his paranoic delusions. And yet he was at the same time writing business-like letters to William about securing Fanny's furniture to her in the house at 36 Royal Avenue so that creditors would not be able to claim it.

George Hake wrote to William Michael on 11th July on the difficulties of considering a holiday abroad, or a sea voyage, or even a move to another place:

> "You have no idea how he invests with undue importance the most trivial circumstance. If we start a rabbit (you know how they lie in the grass) or if a passing countryman civilly bids us a 'good night' or even a watch dog barking as we pass—all are studied insults. What then would it be if he was travelling?"

Rossetti summed up his condition best for himself when they went to watch some seine fishing on the coast. "It is an allegory of my state. My persecutors are gradually narrowing the net round me until at last it will be drawn tight."

Meanwhile at Tudor House Dunn had to hold the fort, constantly referring difficulties to Madox Brown and William Michael and sending them detailed accounts of expenditure. Was Alexa Wilding to be paid off? Millais was one of those after her as a model. She was receiving a retaining fee of thirty shillings a week. How should he get rid of the rats and mice in the studio ceiling? "Emma (the maid) hardly knows what to do. Poison leaves them about. Men with ferrets are mostly thieves and dishonest characters and the cat seems too proud."[129] Money had to be found for big bills which on no account must Rossetti be bothered with. To this end his blue pots had to be sold.

29

When the time came at the end of July that they had to leave Stobhall because Graham needed it[130] George Hake and Rossetti stayed for two days at the George Hotel in Perth while the elder Hake went off to look for lodgings. Rossetti behaved normally and no untoward incidents occurred. Rooms were found at Trowan in a farmhouse kept by a Mrs. Stewart, who charged £10 a month. Her plain fare had to be supplemented by wine and by "sardines and anchovies" which Rossetti insisted upon. Graham frequently sent presents of game.

Hake considered Trowan to be "the second place in the world in point of solitude—the desert of Sahara being the first", but so much did Rossetti's condition improve there that it was thought he should be encouraged to paint again and Dunn was accordingly sent for. George Hake did not know how to stretch a canvas and "no one could cut his chalks like Dunn", but he was alarmed when he thought that Dunn was finishing some chalk drawings that had been commissioned—it would never do to send them out as his own. Dunn was told to circulate the news in Chelsea that Rossetti was almost fully recovered so that gossip about insanity should be quashed. It was not only the man-servant who had talked unwisely, but friends who should have known better. "Sandys & Swinburne going over the whole matter at one of the tables in Solferino's Restaurant,"[131] reported Dunn.

When he arrived he found Trowan a dismal place, "one of those miserably squalid towns that one fortunately hears of oftener than meets", and attendance on Rossetti rather a strain. He wrote to Madox Brown on 13th July: "I am up by night and never was very capable of keeping up a conversation . . ." and refers to Rossetti's obsession with persecution at Tudor House and his plans to have part of a wall pulled down "and discovering the whole paraphernalia of machinery which has been erected for his special annoyance". He also deplored the scheme to return to Kelmscott in order to start work on "Desdemona". "Of course both you, I and all else will think this move to Kelmscott the worst that could be made, but I don't see what can be done to prevent it. . . ." A visit to Penkill was proposed instead but Rossetti would not consider it.

They all seem to have been anxious that the relationship—whatever it was—with Janey should not be resumed. When Rossetti sent her a letter on August 11th or 12th, Dr. Hake took it upon himself to write to her as well.[132] In the copy which he made, he says that this is the first time that Rossetti has "resumed correspondence with his nearest friends. I feel naturally very anxious concerning it and what answer you may feel it necessary to make, especially as this morning on waking he referred to his old delusion for the first time after a long silence on the subject and a great apparent improvement in many respects. As a medical man and viewing you and Mr. Morris as among Rossetti's dearest friends, an anxiety arises in my mind to learn whether his letter exhibits any sign of delusion . . . May I further take the liberty of asking you to be very guarded in your reply to him, telling him only amusing and cheering facts, not noticing in the slightest degree his delusion if he has manifested any to you . . ."

Jane replied to William Michael from Kelmscott on August 15th.

"Dear Mr. Rossetti. I am writing to you at Dr. Hake's request to tell you what I think of Gabriel's letter—it showed no sign whatever of his late distressing illness, no one could have told he had been ill. I am quite hopeful about him now. I believe he will get perfectly well, if only he can be kept in Scotland away from his work a sufficiently long time. I must tell you too that his letter was not of a gloomy nature. I have had many from his hand of a far more depressing kind. With my kindest and most affectionate remembrances to your sister. . . ."[133]

Rossetti was tougher-minded than they knew. By the end of August he had set himself to work at a copy of "Beatrice" for Graham and completed it within four days; then asked for sketches of Janey left at Tudor House to be looked out so that he could finish them at Kelmscott. He was determined to get there. He wrote to William, "Wherever I can be at peace, there I shall assuredly work: but all, I now find by experience, depends primarily on my not being deprived of the prospect of the society of the one necessary person."

On 23rd September he and George left Scotland for London. William Michael met them and took them to Euston Square to visit Mrs. Rossetti and Christina, then on to Paddington for Faringdon. They had been

careful not to alert Fanny: ". . . as well not to mention it", wrote Dunn,
or she "would be excited by the news and perhaps be rushing to one or
other of the stations".

Arrived at Kelmscott, Rossetti was mindful of the debts of gratitude
he owed his brother: "The pleasant peaceful hours at Euston Square
yesterday were the first happy ones I have passed for months: and here
is all happiness again, and I feel completely myself.

"I know well how much you must have suffered on my account:
indeed, perhaps your suffering may have been more acute than my own
dull, nerveless state during the past months. Your love, dear William,
is not less returned by me than it is sweet to me, and that is saying all."

30

"Here is all happiness again." He wanted to recapture the idyll of the
summer before—and he did, for close on two years, 1872–1874. He
responded quickly to Kelmscott's healing power and was soon at work
painting. He even considered holding an exhibition in the following
spring and consulted Howell about it: "a collection of some dozen or so
of my latest & best things".[134] He did not want to go into it with Gambart. "One leading question is, what *good* gallery could one get? All
however is quite a question in my mind as to advisability."

He started on a new "Proserpine", writing to Boyce enthusiastically:
"I am hard at work on a picture of Proserpine, which I have begun and
re-begun, time after time, being resolved to make it the best I could do.
I think I have struck out into clear waters at last & am getting on swim-
mingly with it."[135]

The picture is his truest vision of Janey. It catches her brooding
for something lost—her youth or the love that should have gladdened
it—or, perhaps, Rossetti's projection of his own sense of this.

> "Afar those skies from this Tartarean grey
> That chills me: and afar, how far away
> The nights that shall be from the days that were,
> Woe's me for thee, unhappy Proserpine."

He took a lot of trouble with the symbolism: the gleam of light on the
wall from the upper world; the incense-burner beside her as the attribute
of a goddess, and, linking painting and poem, "the ivy branch in the

background (a decorative appendage to the sonnet inscribed on the label) may be taken as a symbol of clinging memory", he wrote to Shields.

Friends and models came down to Kelmscott to sit for him: Marie Stillman, who was to remain a life-long friend of Janey's, and Alexa Wilding. Rossetti wrote to his mother when inviting her and his sisters: (24th May, 1873) "About the model, it wd. be Miss Wilding, who is a really good-natured creature—fit company for anyone & quite ladylike, only not gifted or amusing. Thus she might bore you at meals & so on (for one cannot put her in a cupboard) . . . but she is the most retiring of creatures and would not be much in the way, at least not more than was unavoidable." Mrs. Rossetti tactfully replied: "The presence of good-natured Miss Wilding would be agreeable to us instead of the contrary."[136]

May Morris, then about ten years old, is said to have disliked Alexa intensely, as so often happens when the daughter of the house has to put up with the presence of someone in that limbo between heaven and hell, the front and the back, but she sat for the couple of angel heads behind Alexa in "La Ghirlandata". "The greenest picture in the world, I believe," Rossetti declared enthusiastically to Bell Scott, "the principal figure being draped in green & completely surrounded with glowing green foliage—I believe it is my very best picture—no inch of it worse than another."[137]

Besides painting, Rossetti considered making a translation of Michael Angelo's sonnets and, for relaxation, produced a lot of nonsense verse at this time. Janey enjoyed it, for Proserpine had a sense of humour. One limerick[138] that has not often been quoted before runs:

> "There was a young fir-tree of Bosnia
> Which daily got ros'nier and ros'nier:
> It at last caught on fire
> And flamed higher and higher—
> And the angels said: 'My, but that was near.' "

He was having trouble with Valpy, one of his buyers, and with Howell's partner, Parsons, and tried to conduct correspondence with them in the third person. This breaks down on the 2nd November and he finishes: "And now let me add that if we are to be Dear Sirs (or even Sirs merely) we must be civil ones for the future. I can answer no letters which contain such phrases as 'You must' and 'I cannot allow'."[139]

His continuing interest in people around is shown by letters to Howell in which he refuses to allow any complaints to be made to the Post Office about delays in delivery as "the postmaster is a good carpenter", and, "he has been ill and had a daughter marry". For Christmas, 1873, he gave Janey a copy of Burton's *Anatomy of Melancholy* and in the top right-hand corner of the fly-leaf drew an exquisite little picture of her slightly larger than the size of a postage stamp.

At intervals he went up to Cheyne Walk: "looking extraordinarily well", reported Boyce, remarking also on the new whiskers and the beard he had allowed to grow "which has greatly changed his aspect". He even presided at a dinner-party again, memorable to the visiting Joaquin Miller, author of *Songs of the Sierras*, who wrote of "the shining and enduring glory of it. . . . I am a better, larger man because of it".

Howell's dealing was going well and Dunn was attending loyally to his multifarious duties. He had to pay the bills or, more often, put off the creditors; superintend the builders; find and send things down to Kelmscott from furniture to lost note-books and props for pictures—a theatrical jewel, "big, showy of the diamond kind" is wanted for "The Beloved". At the same time he had to try to keep on terms with Fanny, who was jealous of Rossetti's confidence in him, and sore because Dear Elephant had been courteously but very firmly dissuaded from visiting Kelmscott.

A new friendship was formed when Theodore Watts, introduced by Dr. Hake, was called in as legal adviser over a forged cheque. When he added "Dunton" to his name, Whistler telegraphed: "Theodore, What's Dunton?" A solicitor by profession, he was also a man of letters and wrote an unexpectedly good novel, *Aylwin*, in which several of his friends appear—Rossetti was D'Arcy and Howell was de Castro—but his real success was in his literary friendships. He took Swinburne into his house, No. 2, The Pines, a semi-detached villa on the way up Putney Hill, and kept him out of trouble there for the last twenty years of his life, rationing his intake of liquor and banning the even more toxic influence of de Sade. He and his wife, Clara, who was fifty years his junior, later performed the same service for Treffry Dunn.

That he exacted some payment for his services in possessiveness was inevitable. Visitors to The Pines complained of it and one of Rossetti's younger acquaintances, Samuel Haydon, was to write to Bell Scott that when he had offered to accompany Rossetti to some sea-side resort: "Mr. Watts seems so dreadfully suspicious that every one wants to withdraw him from his (in some respects, I fear, bad) influence that I repented I had offered."[140] His influence over men of such superior genius as Rossetti and Swinburne is at first sight puzzling, for he seems a fuzzy little man given to prosiness and procrastination, but there was more to him than that. A friend is worth having who could write as he did when

Rossetti was in a mood of deep depression: "As you are, even when 'out of sorts', far more interesting than is any other man when *in sorts*, I shall, of course, be delighted to accept your invitation for Sunday." His account of Rossetti in his article in "The Nineteenth Century", March, 1883, shows an exceptional sympathy, insight and tact throughout that makes it regrettable he never expanded it into the full-length biography that he was expected to write.

His account of his first visit to Kelmscott provides an amusing glimpse of William Morris as he appeared at this date. "Mouse", the Icelandic pony, had been sent to Lechlade Station to meet him.

" 'You must mind your p.s and q.s,' Rossetti warned his guest, 'he is a wonderfully stand-off chap, and generally manages to take against people.'

" 'What is he like?'

" 'You know the portraits of Francis I? Well, take that portrait as the basis . . . soften down the nose a bit, and give him the rose-bloom colour of an English farmer, and there you have him.' And then I saw coming towards us on a rough pony, so diminutive that he well deserved the name of Mouse, the figure of a man in a wideawake. When Rossetti introduced me, the manager (of The Firm) greeted him with a 'H'm, I thought you were alone'. This did not seem promising." Nor, indeed, was the rest of the encounter, in spite of Watts-Dunton joining a fishing expedition and devoting himself to talk exclusively concerned with fish and baits.

From time to time Janey went away from Kelmscott and took the two girls with her, either to stay with Morris in London or to accompany him on holidays abroad. She saw to it that appearances were kept up so that no breath of scandal should harm the good name of her family— translating the code of Courtly love into terms of Victorian respectability.

While she was away, Rossetti consoled himself by filling the house with visitors: Watts-Dunton, whose advice he now sought in place of Swinburne's on every word in his poems, and on other matters: (he asks, for instance, whether Morris' manservant can get off jury service); his mother and sisters; William Michael and his wife; the Hueffers, the Madox Browns, and the devoted Hakes. They would be packed off unceremoniously when Janey notified her return. Howell, who seems to have put off his visit from week to week in June was told on 16th July that as "Janey and the kids" were to return on the Friday he must postpone it yet again. "Just at present, however, you will judge that I shall be glad to be alone with the newcomers." He accepted this and wrote: "It must be uncomfortable enough for her (Mrs. Morris) to know that her husband and his friends can and would cripple her pleasure." These "friends" must have been the Nordic enthusiasts, for Morris had not yet entered upon his socialistic phase with hangers-on who all too clearly bored his wife. In this year, 1873, which Rossetti spent entirely at Kelmscott, Morris showed himself very restive over the situation in letters to Aglaia Coronio. He is kept from his "harbour of refuge" and has to stay in Queen's Square, where Bessie (Jane's sister) gets on his nerves, and he has not seen much of Georgie, "not from any coldness of hers, or violence of mine, but from so many untoward nothings". There is a mysterious reference to Kelmscott: "I feel that his [Rossetti's] presence there as a kind of slur on it: this is very unreasonable though when one thinks why one took the place, and how this year it has really answered that purpose."

In April, 1874, Morris wrote to Rossetti to relinquish his share of the tenancy "since you have fairly taken to living at Kelmscott, which I suppose neither of us thought the other would do when we first began the joint possession of the house". He then pleads poverty and concludes "Yrs. affectly". But is the letter less than honest? He knew Rossetti even with his large income could not afford to keep on the place and its staff alone, and his own poverty did not prevent him from staying on there when he acquired F. S. Ellis as co-tenant in place of Rossetti.

That Rossetti did consider taking over the lease on his own seems to be borne out by his request for a loan of £200 from Bell Scott, at this time a request (which like the suicide threat) upset Scott all the more when it was cancelled![141] Nothing was to be finally settled before the autumn quarter and, in July, 1874, Jane went with Morris and the girls to visit Belgium. George Hake came down to keep Rossetti company. Conditions did not appear to him on the surface to be much different from other occasions on which he had stayed, although Rossetti was slightly more fidgety again, which was not surprising when separation from Kelmscott, and therefore Janey, was imminent.

One afternoon when they went out together for a walk beside the river—and a stream was usually a sedative to Rossetti—they came upon a party of anglers peacefully fishing. Suddenly Rossetti insisted that one of them had given him an insulting look and rushed up to them shouting in fury. Hake had to drag him away and get him back home as quickly as he could.

It was the end of the idyll: Rossetti gave up his share of the house and never saw Kelmscott again. What he had written when he left Penkill, "Farewell to the Glen", took on a much deeper meaning now:

12. Jane Morris at Tudor House, Chelsea. One of a series of photographs for which Rossetti posed her in the garden in 1865.

13. Jane Morris asleep over a copy of *The Defence of Guinevere* by *D. G. Rossetti*

14. MR. AND MRS. MORRIS AT EMS
by D. G. Rossetti

The letter quoted on page 126 mentions the volumes of *The Earthly Paradise* keeping pace with the glasses of mineral water.

15. "TO JANEY, CHRISTMAS, 1873"

This drawing appears in the right hand top corner of the fly leaf to Burton's *Anatomy of Melancholy* given by Rossetti to Mrs. Morris.

"And yet, farewell! For better shalt thou fare
  When children bathe sweet faces in thy flow
And happy lovers blend sweet shadows there
  In hours to come, than when an hour ago
Thine echoes had but one man's sighs to bear
  And thy trees whispered what he feared to know."

31

The Tudor House, to which Rossetti finally returned from Kelmscott, had begun to show a wear and tear in common with its tenant. Outside it was discoloured and overgrown with creepers as if in sympathy with the encroaching grey in Rossetti's hair and the beard which he had allowed to grow untrimmed. Inside, the hangings of the room provided a dark background for his fits of depression: the Fifine widower entered upon his Epilogue.

But that is to be too literary about the situation as it really was. In the summer of 1874 it was still not too late to rub up the brasses, tidy the junk that littered the floors, and clean the curtains and tapestries. He set about putting the place in order. He did not intend to shut himself up completely and still welcomed friends who were faithful and buyers who were serious. "I do not tout among strangers," he wrote to Howell, "to see if they will buy, and should not be at all pleased to learn that he [Grant] had kindly called in to see the pictures but thought on the whole he preferred something else."[142] Brother-artists would be admitted, if he knew when to expect them. Someone as modest as William Linnell wrote to a friend (11th August, 1874), who offered to make an appointment, expressing his great pleasure at it but adding, "would it not be making too much fuss about our coming to inform him of it beforehand? If we take our chance of finding him at home, we might make another opportunity if unsuccessful first time. As you think best, however. . . ."[143] He engaged a new couple for staff: "both", he wrote to his mother on 26th September, "seem to be very respectable, though the cook is rather obese and Hogarthian".

Whether or not he realised the break with Kelmscott was final he could at least know that it did not mean a break with Janey. In their relationship they had arrived at an understanding which was to endure for the rest of their lives. It was not the fresh vital joy of their youth which they had allowed to escape them nor the troubled "regenerate rapture" of middle-age, but a settled understanding, so that from henceforward their letters to each other take a lot of background for granted and dwell on trivialities important to each other as only long-standing lovers can, or two people who have, to their regret, shared an unconsummated love-affair. Ironically, their relationship can be summed up in Morris' words, implicit in much of *The Earthly Paradise*, but set out clearly at the end of his life in a letter to Faulkner. After stating that a married couple should be *free*, he continues: "But I should hope that in most cases friendship would go along with desire, and would outlive it and the couple would still remain together, but always as free people."

Some change in Morris's attitude from the end of 1874 can be seen in letters to Aglaia. They become at once less complaining and more reserved—he does not need tea and sympathy from her any more, although letters of later date to Georgie Burne-Jones still complain of depression. If he had won in expelling Rossetti from Kelmscott and from too frequent association with Janey, it was a woeful victory, for Janey, parted from her lover, became even more aloof from her husband. It was with Rossetti, not with her husband, that she retained the friendship of which Morris wrote in *News from Nowhere*: "We know the unhappiness that comes of men and women confusing the relations between natural passion and sentiment, and the friendship which, when things go well, softens the awakening from passing illusions. . . ." On his side, he never saw Rossetti again and into Rossetti's old teasing of Topsy there entered a note of bitterness, distressing to their friends: "If you gird at Top," Burne-Jones complained, "I grow impatient and feel cross—if it's before strangers, I feel explosive and miserable." But perhaps Ned, with troubles of his own, was ultra-sensitive or now got on Rossetti's nerves, for he wrote of him to Janey after a visit: "His style in conversation is getting beyond the pussy-cat and attaining the dicky-bird." Rossetti's references to Morris in letters to Janey although teasing about his new political interests are not ill-natured.

Rid of Rossetti from Kelmscott, Morris set about securing other freedoms. In August he proposed dissolving the partnerships in The Firm and becoming its "sole Lord and Master".[144] As he had been for some years its mainstay, doing most of the work and seldom leaving the premises (although there was first Warrington Taylor, then Wardle as manager) this did not seem unreasonable, but the proposed share-out of the assets was more open to question. Madox Brown protested vigorously that the original partners were being unfairly treated. Rossetti, although sympathising with his old friend, refrained from the controversy which Burne-Jones feared when he wrote: "I must say I feel ashamed of the remarks of a philosophic world at the spectacle of a set of friends breaking down in this humiliating way—if it goes to law and new anxieties begin for us in that vague region I must say it will be damnable." Watts-Dunton, called in to advise, told Rossetti that "a single meeting between you and him [Brown] and Morris would, I think, put all things right. But it is not easy to see what you, doing alone, would avail". He also says that the manager, Wardle, had made it clear to him that he was not to consider himself as acting for the Firm ("which I knew all along") as the Solicitors instructed were Messrs. White & Co. of Budge Row. But Madox Brown's protest proved effective and Rossetti accepted his share and devoted it to a "member of the Morris family". This meant that it was invested for the benefit of Janey with Watts-Dunton as trustee. He wrote to him (25th March, 1875)

"I find the investment [word deleted] plan would be much preferred; but it seems to be much doubted by the divinity concerned whether so large an income as £50 could be obtained from the sum securely. Do you think this is certainly attainable? When you have kindly drawn up the draft you spoke of, I fancy it would be better not to *send* it here, lest it should fall into other hands than my own: but rather to *bring* it some time when you are able to come and dine."[145]

Again in April:

"I think the sum had better lie at your bankers till we talk it over. The Divine One and her offspring are likely to be staying here from tomorrow (Friday) till Monday evening. . . ."[145]

From this it is clear that, when Janey came to Tudor House, she often brought May and Jenny with her. There was nothing furtive about their relationship. Aglaia Coronio was aware how often she sat and lent embroideries for the backgrounds. She herself came with her brother, Constantine Ionides, to see pictures, and their help was enlisted on behalf of Smetham. Marie Stillman also sat and Alexa Wilding, for he was completing several large pictures—"The Blessed Damozel", "La Bella Mano", "The Sea-Spell", "Mnemosyne", and starting on "Venus Astarte" from Janey. There is no sign of "running down".

He got in a small Italian boy as a model and wrote about him to amuse Mrs. Rossetti: "he highly appreciates *Torrone*, but on my giving him *Panetone*—that queer loaf—he said in a startled tone: 'Quanto coasta questo?' I replied: 'Non credo molto', and he rejoined 'Crederei quasi niente?' Such was his verdict on that comestible."

Little is known about Rossetti's male models, but as a good host he seems to have taken pains to entertain them. Sir Johnston Forbes-Robertson as a boy sat for Eros in the second "Dante's Dream" and remembered that to get the correct pose he had to lean over a cushion on a couch. "At the first sitting I remember he said, 'I am sorry, my dear Johnston, there is no beautiful creature for you to kiss.' I can feel my youthful blushes now," and he goes on to say how pleased Rossetti was when a butcher-boy model for the man in "Found" said he understood the whole incident. "That tells me the picture is right."

Inevitably some old friends had dropped away. There had long ago been a re-grouping of the Pre-Raphaelite Brothers and in the 1870s the close friendship with Swinburne was broken. He took his dismissal with dignity, writing to William Michael: "Many thanks for your note. I shall of course take every precaution against a meeting. It is of course a grief to me to be debarred from showing the same attention and affection as friends who can hardly love him better—as indeed I think no man can love his friends more than I love Gabriel . . ." Later he burst out with some of his extravagant abuse that was as hyperbolic as his praise even while Watts-Dunton was trying to keep the door open by exchange of news and asking for presentation copies of books.

Other friends had by now formed ties which prevented them from dropping in upon each other as young men do and Rossetti would not accept compromise. "Life is a coin", he wrote in a note-book, "which we once shared together, but which has now quite passed from my pocket to yours—doubtless rightly enough. Only I desire no half-farthing of its small change." Even William Michael could not always be on hand when required for he was now married and, again inevitably, had moved away from his old home, for Lucy as a wife had not been able to continue to share a house with Mrs. Rossetti and Christina.

Rossetti did not make it easier to keep up with acquaintances by his refusal to go to their houses. In this he was not abnormal; many gregarious people in middle-age begin to shun society from a revulsion against its wastage of time and a realisation that social gatherings do not suffice to keep loneliness at bay; the candle-light becomes powerless to dispel the encroaching gloom. Well aware that popularity would slip if he did not exert himself to retain it, Rossetti preferred to revert to the withdrawal of his schooldays, but in isolation the man of middle age became a prey to paranoid obsessions he could not always overcome.

At this time, if he shed some of the old circle, there were still others to join it—William Sharp (later a novelist as Fiona McLeod) and Joseph Knight, both to be early biographers; and the young blind poet Philip

Bourke Marston, son of Dr. Marston; and Comyns Carr, who, introduced by Hake, testified to the magnetism of the host "coiled up on the sofa in his studio after dinner". "[I] can hear the deep tones of his rich voice as he ranged widely over the fields of literature and art, always trenchant, always earnest, yet now and again slipping with sudden wit and humour into a lighter vein." He insisted that a picture should be a painted poem; overpraising artists (particularly his friends) if they acted on this and undervaluing others. Of Millais he declared: "I don't believe since painting began there has ever been a man more greatly endowed with the mere painter's power", and of Burne-Jones: "he has oceans of imagination and in this respect there has been nobody like him since Botticelli", but of Albert Moore he said: "often pretty enough, but sublimated café-painting and nothing more".

There was no break with the first and best of friends, Madox Brown. Poor Bruno was to suffer a tragic loss in November, 1874, in the death of his son, his high hope, Oliver. Rossetti had always appreciated the boy in spite of some tiresomeness he had experienced from him at Kelmscott, and it was of his sympathy that the broken-hearted father said: "It is always Gabriel who speaks the right word."

This thoughtfulness shows in the letters that he found time to write to Canon Dixon of the "Oxford and Cambridge Magazine" days, in acknowledgment of two volumes of his verse (26th May, 1874). "Is it a compliment or the contrary to tell a man whom one has known for 18 years that one had no idea till now of his possessing first-rate powers? ..." He then goes on for some pages to pick out individual poems and comment on them, ending: "Many thanks (though tardy ones) my dear Dixon, for so much good work. Surely there must be more in store by this time and no one will be better pleased to read it in due season than myself."

No wonder Dixon replied: "I never received and assuredly never expected to have received such a letter ... Your approbation makes up for everything."

It was a misleading picture which Bell Scott, now wearing a grey wig attached to his skull cap, gave when he said that from the spring of 1874 Rossetti "has lived within the house, never even going into the street, never seeing any one". It was simply not true. The new admirers coming to call might well be represented by Philip Marston, when he exclaimed in a letter to Oliver Madox Brown: "What a supreme man is Rossetti! Why is he not some great exiled king that we might give him our lives to try to restore him to his kingdom!" And there was still to come Hall Caine to give his time and attention to this service.

So much for Rossetti, sunk in a drugged lethargy or finished as an artist. His health, physical and mental, was impaired, but the spirit still survived it and shone out through a gloom that would have enveloped anyone of less vitality.

32

A regular pattern of living established itself in the three or four years following 1874, periods at Tudor House alternating with visits to the country. There had been an idea that his mother and Christina should keep house for him in Cheyne Walk, but it had fallen through. At the time Rossetti wrote frankly about it to Watts-Dunton: "This would be in many ways a great gain. I have some misgivings as to whether my habits as regards exercise, etc., might not scare them and there is the question of Fanny who, although she may not always be there, is at times almost necessary to me."[146] If Janey had proved as much a *Dame Lointaine* as Lizzie, no wonder he still needed Fanny. But in general he was interested in women more as symbols of beauty from an erotic than a sexual angle. He had his lusts of the flesh and indulged them, but they were subordinate to other interests. He was no "womaniser". The levity of a Don Juan would have shocked him, and he was no collector like Casanova. He needed three kinds of loving: family as well as what Victorians called "sacred and profane", and at times it seemed that he succeeded in securing them all and integrating them in his life and in his art. He was happiest when he could domesticate Guinevere, but circumstances would not always permit.

He left London for Aldwick Lodge, Bognor, in October, 1875, and stayed there till June, 1876. The place was chosen largely for Janey's benefit as she needed sea-bathing and this would persuade her to come. In November she sat for the finishing touches to "Astarte Syriaca" and for once there is a sharpness in a letter from Rossetti to his mother when he asks for more books for them to read together, Horace Walpole's *Correspondence*, among others. He was not pleased with the selection she had previously sent to Janey. November 28: "The books you sent Mrs. Morris are in perfect safety at her house but with the exception of *Louis XIV* (and of this she already knew by other books) the selection was not a lucky one for her, as she takes no interest whatever in the Royal Family & *Vicar of Wakefield* & Macaulay's *Lays* had long been known to her. The D'Arblay book was new to her & a great boon & she has since read *Evelina* (of which in these glutted days a new railway edition has nevertheless just appeared) with great pleasure. In fact I think the amusement she derives from it is very beneficial in giving her strength for the sittings."[147] He also read Burns through and, loyal to his old passion for Keats, wrote to Bell Scott: "What a grand saying is this of Keats in one of the letters in the Haydon book: 'I value more the privilege of seeing great things in loneliness than the fame of a prophet.' "

Janey remained at Aldwick Lodge until December when she left in order to spend Christmas with her daughters. Rossetti wrote them a humorous letter on 22nd December referring to some family jokes from Kelmscott days: "A mind (of no common order) has conceived, for your benefit, the idea of isolating from a well-known series of the British Drama, all Fiends, Spectres, Vampires, and other persons of any interest."

After more in the same strain he signs himself "The Third Grave-Digger".

"P.S. Ha! field, I know thee now."[148]

For Christmas he invited his mother and Christina, angry that Maria was not allowed to leave her Sisterhood for a night under a brother's roof. Alexa Wilding was to be there and Dr. Hake with George, besides his two other sons, Edmund and Henry. They found the house "packed for the festive week" as the Polidori Aunts had come and also Watts-Dunton. But, Dr. Hake wrote "the holiday was made cheerful, less perhaps by the host himself than by his guests". Filling the house did not fill his mind or vision.

Janey was needed for that and off and on she came to stay again. May came with her while Jenny remained with her father. "I won't press you to come back," he wrote, but hoped she would return home for Easter, which she did.

While at Aldwick Lodge, Rossetti heard that the neighbouring house, Aldwick Place, belonging to a "Baron" Alfred Grant, was for sale.[149] To Howell he wrote jocosely that he might kill two birds with one stone: "Didn't you once tell me you had some idea he wanted pictures of mine? Suppose he were to give me the place for a daub or two—he gave £5,000 for it." But later he was very indignant when Howell proposed certain terms: "If he [Grant] wishes for pictures of mine, you know my plan, and I shall not certainly be harried or worried by him more than another. My view is, that he, or anyone, is favoured in getting a work of mine, *because* I never hurry it, but even take back and recommence it if I am dissatisfied, and give my best in the end & *am sure to give it in good time*, which means the time to make it good."

Rossetti's patience with Howell had worn thin and about now he finally broke with him. He had ignored Burne-Jones' agonised appeals to do so years before when he said that he could not bear Rossetti continuing to countenance him "after the injuries he has done me and the miseries your disastrous introduction of him has brought about."[150] Howell must have done something worse than lie or cheat over a business deal: perhaps Ned's anguish was connected with the incident when Howell introduced to Georgie a Greek lady with whom Ned was secretly in love. When Ned came in and saw her he fell against the mantelpiece from shock, giving his forehead a permanent scar. She is referred to as "Madame Z" in correspondence: her name was Marie Zambaco. Ned proposed a suicide pact with her. They went so far as to walk into the Serpentine together, but he turned back, afraid of catching a chill.

Rossetti had not so much developed a new moral disapproval of Howell's nefarious dealings as become sick of their repercussions. He could not bother any more with the clamour of dealers and patrons who had been promised the same picture several times over or been fobbed off with duplicates and "copies". Indeed, he took the trouble to write a letter to "The Times" repudiating water-colours signed with his name, which had been appearing for sale in a certain print-shop. It was all too tiresome and he felt strongly now what he had written to Howell, half in jest, in 1874: "As regards our friendly relations, I have only to say that I consider you, after nine or ten years intercourse, a very good-hearted fellow and a d . . . d bad man of business."

Rossetti stayed on at Bognor with George Hake, who was straining at the bit, in hopes that Janey might be able to return, also because he wanted to keep out of the way during the libel action which Buchanan brought against "The Examiner". He was afraid he might be involved and that under questioning some reference to the disinterment of his poems would come out.[151] Worry over this did not improve his health or his spirits and he had increasing recourse to chloral and to whisky. When, by July, it was clear that Janey could not return, he himself went back to Cheyne Walk for a spell.

His old arbitrariness had increased with the years and he insisted all the more on appointments to visit him being made in advance. On the first occasion when Bell Scott arranged an interview for his protégé, Edmund Gosse,[152] Rossetti received them and read aloud "(I had heard it twice before) his unprinted poem of Rose Mary. This might be simply to get over the time, because he never spoke of Gosse's poems." But next time, when Gosse took his fiancée, Nellie Epps, with him, presumably without an appointment, "they were kept waiting in the parlour

and there received a message that Mr. Rossetti could not see them."
It was surely unreasonable of Bell Scott to expect Rossetti—or anyone
else—to be interrupted at his work by almost total strangers. When he
was painting or when he was showing pictures to possible buyers he
had to insist on privacy: once he much regretted it that while he was
selling "La Donna della Finestra" to Ellis, Dunn had turned away the
Cowper Temples who had also come to buy it, but this could not be
helped. When he did consent to receive visitors, he was completely
gracious to them and put them at ease. In this he was very different
from Morris, as Bell Scott found when he put Gosse together with him
at a dinner-party, explaining that Gosse was interested in Scandinavian
things and had been to Norway. "After various long silences Gosse
tried his best to get up conversation but it was of no avail. He brought
up the subject of Northern literature. Morris was eating a date at the
moment but he managed to ejaculate: 'Well, yes, I don't know much
about it myself. I try my hand at it too! Will you take a date?'"

Morris as a dinner guest did not impress Cambridge when he dined
in Hall. Lady Jebb described him as a "rough, self-centred, passionate,
odd, almost wild man". "Mr. Magnússon tells me that he and Morris
agree in thinking that the supreme joy is to get away from all the restraints
of conventional life to Iceland, or to Central Africa. I can never quite
believe in a man who *tells* you what a charming child of nature he is,
what agony it is to him to have to dress like other people, to use knife
and fork, and to wind up his watch."

33

In July Rossetti left London again. This time he accepted an invitation
from the Cowper Temples to stay at Broadlands while Janey was at Deal
with May and Jenny. The amenities of Broadlands have been described
by a guest of a very different sort—F. W. H. Myers—who had been
asked there three years earlier when his hosts were interested in physical
research: "What hours of spiritual nurture", he wrote, "have I lived
through in the long drawing-room from which beyond estrade and
portico the broad lawns sloped in sunlight to Test's crystal flow! . . .
Changeless without, the immemorial forest trees and deep-shadowed
isles of lawn, through which if some fair girl-guest chanced to wander,
her beauty took something of sabbatical from the stately day."[153]

Rossetti was quite as appreciative, though his letters are never flowery period pieces. He had been allowed to bring George Hake with him and to keep to a separate wing when the house filled up with fifty or so other guests in August for a clerical conference. But he was not the hermit that he intended to be: he was delighted to find a sister of Alexander Munro's installed there as a governess and the old charm that had won Miss Losh still worked. He also made a conquest of a Mrs. Georgina Summer, "of the noblest antique type" who sat for "Domizia Scaligera", and he made a crayon sketch of Mrs. Cowper Temple that he intended to present to her but which her husband insisted on paying for.

He was able to work on a version of "The Blessed Damozel", for in one of several letters to Dunn which deal with money matters (cheques to pay the rent gone astray, alterations to the studio to make more room for hanging cupboards and stoothing for silence), he wrote:

"They set about finding my babies for the baby head in the 'Damozel'. First came a workhouse baby—I spent a day in drawing it but it wouldn't do. Then they found me a truly noble little fellow, son of a parson near here. Of him I at once made a successful drawing (which I have promised to the delighted parents), and yesterday painted his head right off into the picture at one sitting very successfully. It is as good as anything there . . ."

The visit improved his physical condition and in some sense boosted his morale, but his insomnia, if anything, worsened. "I endure nights of utter unrest", he wrote to his mother. When he began to feel pains in his limbs, he decided he must return home. Hake concurred with this, writing to William Michael about "the lassitude and despondency due to chloral and so fatal to work".

In London, Marshall insisted on his undergoing a two-night penance of abstention from chloral. Mesmerism was tried instead to induce sleep, but was unsuccessful. Presumably, after this, Marshall allowed small doses of the drug again, but never did it occur to him that the chloral might not be the source of the trouble. For one thing it was—and is—a harmless drug (the spirits he washed it down with were more dangerous), and for another it must be remembered Rossetti never took drugs as an indulgence: they were a necessity, for if he could not sleep he could not work; if he could not work he could not live. In a letter to Shields from Herne Bay on 21st October, 1877, he put the position clearly enough for himself: "as to the eternal drug, if I suffer at times from morbidity, it is also possible for others to take a morbid view of the question". He protests that his work has not deteriorated during the previous five years, in fact that "La Bella Mano", "Sea-Spell", and the "Roman Widow" are "amongst the brightest I ever produced". Rumours of his being dependent on any drug must be denied: "if an opinion was to get abroad that my works were subject to a derogatory influence which reduced their beauty and value it would be most injurious to me and would in reality be founded on a foregone conclusion as to the necessary results of such a medicine, and not on anything really provable from the work itself."

His psychological tensions were aggravated at this time by news of the tragedy that had afflicted the Morrises. It was during this summer of 1876 that Jenny became epileptic—a condition that was hereditary in Morris' family.[154] He must have been aware of this, and, as he was undoubtedly devoted to his daughters, turned for comfort to Janey. His poem "Near but Far Away" may refer to this time:

> "She wavered, stopped and turned, methought her eyes,
> The deep grey windows of her heart were wet,
> Methought they softened with a new regret,
> To note in mine unspoken miseries."

Pity was not enough to kindle passion:

> "But truth fell on me
> And kiss and word I knew, and left alone,
> Face to Face seemed . . . to a wall of stone,
> While at my back there beat a boundless sea."

Overwhelmed with grief herself, Janey would withdraw away from husband and from lover. Rossetti tells Watts-Dunton that not hearing from her is "making me quite ill and unable to work".

But from the next year (1877) a regular correspondence between them every week was resumed, perhaps because Rossetti appealed to her when he knew he had to undergo an operation for hydrocele made dangerous by his having delayed attention to it. Marshall was sent for to operate immediately and insisted on a spell of convalescence away from London. He went, therefore, to Herne Bay in August with Madox Brown for travelling companion. Here again his mother and Christina came to stay, but Maria had died the previous November (1876), serene in her Sisterhood. Shields was a visitor, and William Michael and Lucy would have been welcome but there was no accommodation for their baby and its nurse.

Janey managed to come for a short time and sat to him for what was to be his last water-colour—"Bruna Brunelleschi".[155] Again he borrowed books from his mother to read with her. Fanny Burney's *Diaries* she enjoyed: "More delighted than I think I ever knew her to be with any book", and they re-read Horace Walpole's *Correspondence*, and later Haydon's *Correspondence and Table Talk*.

She then took the two girls to Italy in November for the winter of 1877–78. She was in bad health again, so much so that Rossetti said of her handwriting: "It reminds me of poor Lizzie in days gone by." Instead of cures she had been recommended to try warmer climates. It is curious that she had to apply to Rossetti for the money to pay for these expeditions, even if it were to be drawn from the investment made by Watts-Dunn from The Firm's money. At one point Rossetti seriously considered renting a house to share with her in Italy, asking Fairfax Murray, who was in Genoa, to look out for something.[156] "How I wish," he wrote to Janey on 2nd December, 1877, "that I could look with you on all you are seeing", but he seems to have had an obsessive need to not-visit Italy. Only in verse did he wish to accompany her to the land of his ancestors. In 1869 he had written:

> "If in my life be breath of Italy
>   Would God that I might yield it all to you!
>   So, when such grafted warmth had burgeoned through
> The languor of your Maytime's hawthorn tree,
>   My spirit at rest should walk unseen and see
>   The garland of your beauty bloom anew."

While away Janey had evidently asked him to look at "The Retreat" on Hammersmith Mall, which Morris was anxious to take. Rossetti reported that it was not to be recommended as it was liable to flooding from the river. (19th April, 1878) "It is good news indeed that the iron medicine has done you so much good. I thought it must, but view the taking it on lumps of sugar as a very nasty way. I hope now you will really be fit to enjoy Venice, and that the damps of that sojourn may prepare you somewhat for the Hammersmith house, which I really do not think a wise choice, if *you* are a person to be at all considered in the matter."

The Italian visit did little good either to Morris or to Janey. Morris described to Aglaia and to Georgie Burne-Jones his own attack of gout and Janey's collapse in Venice on 2nd May, 1878. This he put down to the weather, "very dull and close, which may have something to do with it". He was not sorry to return: he felt a hostility to southern

Europe and longed "rather for the heap of grey stones with a grey roof that we call a house north-away". There was a lot of work waiting for him too; he was in the middle of his dyeing period and active in Anti-Scrape with rumblings ahead of his socialist activities. "He will be the Odger of the future, my dear Janey", teased Rossetti; Odger being a Trade Union agitator.

34

Not only was there anxiety over Janey to aggravate Rossetti's over-wrought mental state but there was chronic irritation provided by the distrust that Fanny aroused in his friends and the suspicions of her dishonesty to which he would not admit.

From Herne Bay he wrote to Dunn to collect together his letters lying about Tudor House and put them "in the iron safe outside the studio", as several had mysteriously disappeared—not so mysteriously in a household free to Howell and to Fanny and of which he had himself lost the front door key. But he would not blame Fanny. In letters to Watts-Dunton he nearly always put in an enquiry after her and uses Elephant terms. "Could you look in to-morrow? If Elephant here, she wd. go soon & we could talk."[157] It was Watts-Dunton whom he asked to go and investigate what was happening at 96 Jermyn Street after receiving a letter from Fanny in which she conveyed that she had moved there with her lodger, John Schott, and that it was an hotel. "I keep three servants and an accountant and Mr. Schott still interests himself for me . . . I took this step thinking I should never be with you again and thought it a certainty."

She was leaving what she felt was a sinking ship, equipped with pictures that she insisted were hers. In view of the attitude of Rossetti's brother and other friends towards her, perhaps she was justified in feeling she must make some provision for a doubtful future. William Michael wrote to his wife after a visit to Tudor House: (17th August, 1877) "F. turned up yesterday, much to the derangement of all rational projects for G's welfare. She was in a very obstructive mood yesterday, but I hear better today."

She was bad for him when she was there and she neglected him when he needed her, but he retained his affection for her and forgave her desertion. When he had to think of returning to Tudor House he wrote to Watts-Dunton:

"The situation is in every way a perplexing one ... Utter solitude if I return to such in London may be well-nigh fatal: and F.'s society mitigates it only in a slight degree, even if still to be reckoned on. Besides if it should chance that she has really embarked on something of an advantageous kind, it wd. be a serious responsibility for me to break it up, considering the uncertainty of my own prospects of permanently assisting her."[158]

With all the disturbances there must have been in these frequent moves, let alone his ill-health, it is remarkable that Rossetti found the time he did for his family and for old friends. He offered financial help to the Maenza family with whom he had stayed long ago in Boulogne, and he took as much trouble ordering a sealskin coat for his mother as if he were arranging the costume of a model. He canvassed friends to buy Smetham's pictures as he had gone out of his mind and his family had no support. Telling Janey of this, she must have offered to help, for he writes to her (10th February) "I will not hear of your being mulcted for poor Smetham's sake." He drafted carefully a four-page letter to his sister-in-law, Lucy, warning William against publishing his revolutionary verses: "several of William's truest friends, no less than myself, were greatly alarmed at the tone taken in some of his sonnets respecting 'tyrannicide'."

He kept up with Miss Munro[159] after the meeting at Broadlands and invited her two schoolboy nephews (the sons of Alexander) to Tudor House, though afterwards he apologised to her that "they must have found me dull and spiritless, for I was not very well on the day they called, which, however, you must not suppose to be always the case with me by any means".

Of Henry Munro's chemical experiments he wrote: "Chemistry is a branch, as indeed I told him, which might at present be made of great advantage to art, as Holman Hunt's researches into the manufacture of colour proves but too clearly."

He found time to advise Schott's son, Cecil, on drawing.*

"I think your last drawing of your mamma is much the best you have done. However it is a little larger than life, which you should avoid. The whole face, from top of forehead to point of chin, ought not to be more than $5\frac{1}{2}$ inches ... you ought to try some 3 quarter faces, as you can do profiles easily now and you should attempt something more difficult."[160]

He also fixed him up as art assistant to Shields. Schott himself became yet another factotum at Tudor House employed on various errands,

* See Appendix K, p. 242.

including house-hunting for Miss Herbert. Rossetti described him as, "really one of the best men I ever knew—most moderate and orderly in every habit of life". That he married Fanny shows she must have kept some of her former attractiveness; although Vernon Lee called her a "Vealey Woman".

In these years Rossetti's pictures were fetching such substantial prices[161] that it is inexplicable why he should always have been hard-up and in debt to Brown and William Michael for "petty cash", even if he had had no bank account until Dunn took over and people helped themselves liberally to the money thrust in the bureau drawer. He tried to disentangle the situation. On looking through his cheque-butts: "I found certainly an overwhelming sum of expenditure which is neither rent, living servants, nor work expenses but salaries of various kinds and gifts pure and simple," he confided to Scott, whose opinion in private was that Fanny robbed him "regularly and mercilessly". On Rossetti's finances, Scotus was to say the pharisaical last word when he wrote to James Leathart: "Of course I would not like to be like our friend D.G.R. making more than twice my income and as deep in debt as ever—but short of that I envy men who have no fears about spending, who are not always looking into the dark."[162]

With it all Rossetti continued to write and to paint. He put so much into each effort that it was no wonder he suffered from exhaustion; on finishing "The King's Tragedy", for instance, he admitted that "it was as though my life ebbed out with it".[163] He has been accused of sloth and of procrastination but the marvel is how much he managed to get through in pictures, poems and private life. Another attempt to produce a finished "Found" was made this year. Already commissioned by MacCracken and Leathart it was now promised to William Graham for eight hundred guineas. Shields was mobilised to lend a *papier-maché* lay figure "if this can stand up and fix its arm & hand in a position, if it be more convenient to you to spare this than the stuffed one . . ." and Mrs. Shields is asked if she can "pick up a promising bonnet shape on the way".[164] Dunn was to look for second-hand clothes: "the woman should wear something with a pinkish tinge, I suppose, to balance the sky —also a mantle of some sort—pretty showy but seedyish". This version was also to remain unfinished but other important pictures worked upon and completed within the following year were "The Day Dream", a new "Salutation of Beatrice", "La Pia", and a replica of "Dante's Dream" with predellas.

His pictures were constantly in request for Exhibitions but he seldom consented to show them. He had made an exception in Manchester in 1878 in aid of the new Art School to be opened there, but he refused

Miss Heaton in Leeds, and also Sir Noel Paton, the King's Limner, in Scotland although "always a generous friend to my work".

His refusal to take part in another project in 1877 led to consequences disastrous to the reputation of the whole Pre-Raphaelite movement. He was urgently invited to show at the first Exhibition to be held at the Grosvenor Galleries. He declined to do so—and so did Madox Brown— with the consequence that the recognised leadership went to Burne-Jones. It was, therefore, his anaemic ladies drooping in unco-ordinated compositions that from now on set the standard of what was—and is— popularly supposed to be Pre-Raphaelitism. It was the Grosvenor Gallery that was greenery-yallery.

What was intended to establish Pre-Raphaelitism marked the complete break with its original ideals: there was neither a robust romantic medievalism in it nor a contemporary story-with-a-moral and small trace of the technique that Madox Brown had brought from the Nazarenes. There is similar irony in the fact that by now Morris' *folk-lorique* productions were accepted but could only be bought by those rich enough to be able to furnish their houses from his fashionable shop in Oxford Street.

35

The correspondence between Rossetti and Janey from 1878 over to 1881[165] is that of old friends, affectionate and understanding in triviality. There must have been many more letters than have survived, for when she asks him again for an address that he had given her, she says: "To wade through a drawerful of your letters would be the work of a day for me." Her general tone is lulling, as if to cool off any warmth in his.

"It always rejoices me to see your loved writing. I know that your living, loving hand has rested again on lines addressed to me," he writes in September, 1878, and, again (1st October), "My dear Janey, I must write another line merely for the sake of some communication with you, for there is naught of news . . ." He is always at pains to send her "news", particularly amusing gossip about friends they have in common, "as I know you love a laugh". This often concerns the Stillmans or the vagaries of Fairfax Murray's wife in dealing with their babies. They also discuss people in the news—Janey confesses to a passion for looking at the other side of newspaper cuttings for odd stories—and, once, referring to *Erewhon*, he says Samuel Butler was a "great friend" of

16. JANE MORRIS
AS "PROSERPINE"
by D. G. Rossetti

I never reared a young Wombat
  To glad me with his pin-hole eye,
But when he moot was sweet & fat
And tail-less, he was sure to die!

17. Rossetti mourning his wombat (self-portrait).

Nolly Brown's. "What I chiefly remember of him is that he had eye-brows which were exactly like two leeches stuck on his face." He tells her about a housemaid at Cheyne Walk who is going home to spend "her Papa's birthday *en famille*. I asked her what her Papa was & she told me—a gummer of postage-stamps! Ye Heavens! Could it not be done in the cradle? & the man has 10 kids & presumably has kept them in this profession! So England seems to care for its own sometimes, whatever Top may say". Apologetically he reports progress on work he has in hand. He is pathetically anxious not to be a bother to her (27th July, 1879) . . . "I have always divided between the unwillingness to press you & the knowledge that if I do not hear, I shall get sorely troubled about you." On her side she gives news of her own health and is as solicitous for his; also worries if she does not hear; makes excuses for not calling and once apologises for not giving notice beforehand that she intended to come.

"I am really vexed that I came in yesterday. I shall never do such a thing again, but I did so want to see for myself how you were and I have no means of finding out unless I come—for my part, I should be only too glad to see a truly friendly face when I am too unwell to go out. I only wished to cheer you, if possible: pray forgive me if I made any other impression on your mind . . ."

and she encloses photographs "of my big babies who were so little and comic not long since". One letter in which she refers to Christina's poems, saying "They seem very funny as far as I can understand them: I still find difficulties with poetry, as you can imagine", has been sometimes quoted as instance of Janey not caring for poetry; in fact it is Christina's Italian translation of *Sing Song* to which she is referring. At the time she was trying to learn the language.

In November, 1879, Morris had decided to take "The Retreat", and changed the name to "Kelmscott House" as he considered "Retreat" sounded like a private insane asylum. It had been occupied by George Macdonald for the past twelve years. The stables that inspired Diamond's home in *At the Back of the North Wind* were converted into a theatre where the eleven Macdonald children acted plays against a backcloth designed by Edward Hughes, a nephew of Arthur. Macdonald's study "with a touch of my art," wrote Morris, "could be one of the prettiest in London" and he fitted up a tapestry-loom in his bedroom for his private use. In Rossetti's earlier report he had said that Macdonald's room was "made fearful to the eye with a blood-red flock paper and a ceiling of blue with gold stars". Knowing much more about ordinary people than the socialistic Morris he had also reported that the kitchen was too inconvenient for any good domestic to tolerate. But Morris was not to be put off.

Rossetti handed over to Janey most of his own furniture left at Kelmscott: "all will come in in the new big house", he wrote.

From further up the road by the river it was not difficult for Janey to send notes. Her first letter complains of the work to be done: "I am doing nothing myself except feeling tired and lying awake at night." (It is clear, by-the-way, from Morris's letters planning the house that they did not share a bedroom.) Later, she wrote: "I am grieved indeed to hear of your bad nights—mine are improving. I expect I was overtired and anxious to get things straight, and moreover I have got used to the noise of the river-steamers, which seemed at first to go on all night." When it was not illness it was the weather that prevented her going down to Tudor House: they both make an unconscionable fuss about it. On 4th April, he writes: "Dearest Janey, Long absences and many disappointments have inured me to missing the sight of you, and to-day at least it was best I should miss it as the weather is not fit for your being out to any distance." Again, on 2nd June: "My dear Janey, you would be a joyful sight to me, were I not so sorry a one for you. But I hope we may meet yet this summer—as yet weather still looks uncertain. I have felt a good deal out of sorts lately & my work has not much prospered. A little later there may be rather more to show. I am afraid, my dear Janey, you have found me an afflictive phenomenon & I feel I truly am so." He then goes on to give news of Graham and of the predellas he is working on for his "Dante's Dream".

The next day he writes to apologise for his lack of cheerfulness. "My dearest Janey, I fear I wrote last night in a stupid, disconsolate way calculated to make you uncomfortable. But I think it will be best to defer meeting for a little, particularly as this is the blessed Whit Week [when the river road was crowded] and most because of the daily drenches."

What was the matter with Janey is not known and there is no mention of any doctors she consulted: she was of strong physical build and, it would seem, of a placid disposition, yet she was sent to drink Spa waters, she had a "collapse" in Italy, she was often confined to a sofa at home, sometimes with what sounds like asthma. In February she had written to Rossetti welcoming the return of spring: "or more correctly the disappearance of the horrible darkness of winter. I can breathe without gasping and you can paint without bad language". She mourns the death of her cat: "My dear old pussy, Jack, succumbed to the cold a few days ago. We buried him in the garden. Alas, poor Pussy! We never shall look upon his like again . . ." In the letter following she says that she had begun to chirp too soon about weather "but you know what a babyishly hopeful creature I always am". Rossetti sent her prescriptions and medicines: (17th June)—"You dont tell me whether you tried the bottle I sent. I suppose you sniffed and scorned it." But in July he was in a "down" mood and writes: (13th July) "My dearest Janey, My mind has been dwelling ever since we met on your gentle kindliness & my dullard state. As I told you, I have become so subject to depression that this has been my main reason for not laying hold of any appointment lately till next week." He adds that he does not even visit his mother for fear of depressing her. No one knows better than the social success what it is like to be a wet blanket. On 15th July, he again apologises for melancholy: "As I have not got a line from you, I will not believe that you are worse in health, but only that you did not know what to say to my Jeremiads. Pardon, I'll never do it again. But I had been thinking troublesomely & did not duly reflect that it is one thing unbosoming onself in words and another putting it in ridiculous black & white. I write now chiefly to tell you that I had had in these bad days what must be called the rare luck to sell the picture of you, 'La Donna della Finestra'. Ellis has bought it."

In reply, after congratulating him, she goes on, "as to sitting again I should be too happy to feel myself of use again to any human being, but it is scarcely likely that my back will improve with age. I will not despair yet and you may be quite sure if at all possible I shall let you know".

When she travels up to Naworth Castle[166] with her daughters for a visit she at once reports to him her safe arrival, and, later, that she has decided to stay on longer. She consults him about a possible cure at Ramsgate: "I hear that there are sea-weed baths at Ramsgate for people of a delicate constitution. One is made into a kind of pie with the sea-weed, when it is supposed that one absorbs vast quantities of ozone by this means. Do you happen to know of this? . . . [For a journey to Italy] could any of that money be got at for the purpose, supposing I could not raise any? Enough of my health."

He answers her on 2nd August:

"My dearest Janey,
   It was a very serious relief to me to get a letter from you this afternoon. I opened it with the greatest anxiety to see whether you had been able to write yourself, & was much cheered when I read that you had 'roared with laughing'. Since getting the lecture back with Lucy's address & no card from you, I had been feeling very anxious indeed. In your letter, you treat

my poor admirer (the lecturer I mean, not yourself—we are but two perhaps, he & I) with silent scorn. I grow more & more into the weakness of being thankful to anyone who will give me a little praise. Alackaday! it is much better, no doubt, to view all admirers merely as Slaves of the Ring, which is the current fashion. The above passage you will consider cynical, so don't allude to it.

I suppose ·Top never gave one farthing to Keats's sister, but then he writes long epistles on every public event. Now there I'm at it again—as Shields says to himself (as he confessed to me on my chaffing his peculiarities) when he feels the hyena laugh surging up within his guts. The name of Shields reminds me of an incredible narrative which is nevertheless true. . . . This rambling has filled a few sheets but I fear is not worth your reading. I must ask Murray to show me his baby's photo. I daresay he thought it wd. gnaw at the aching core of my babylessness, & would not therefore produce it. . . ."

During this summer Morris was much at Kelmscott, where the weather was propitious for his fishing and he could spend days "bugging and blaspheming in a punt". (Both Rossetti and Morris accused each other of swearing unduly.) The girls joined him there, while Janey went to visit Cormell Price and his sister. Later she wrote to Rossetti from Kelmscott House to rally him on taking offence:

"I cannot weigh the exact meaning of every word before writing, nor can any human being foresee what construction you will put on the most ordinary phrasing. Surely you know as everyone else does what a violent influenza cold does for one's appearance. You have sometimes refused to be seen under such circumstances and you must pardon a woman if she has the same dislike of being seen with a red nose and the rest. . . . Now pray do not worry about trifles. I am looking [sic] to seeing you soon and shall not forgive you if you upset yourself all for nothing at all."

Surely here is speaking the tomboy imprisoned in the cast of Guinevere. Kindly at the same time as sensible: the games-mistress not above feminine foibles, sorry for herself when no longer able to romp but still generous with her sympathy to others.

Janey's limitations did not trouble Rossetti. He wanted the beautiful form to paint and the feminine commonsense for company. In considering their relationship, it must not be forgotten how well they got on together as companions. They shared a sense of humour and an interest in the trivialities which are so important a part of daily life. They enjoyed gossip about friends or about people living at close quarters to them—the maids or the Kelmscott villagers. Both of them were dependent on companionship, however much they might protest a love of solitude. Stillman observed this about Rossetti, and in letters to Janey on the choice of Kelmscott House, Hammersmith, Morris is at pains to assure her that it will not prove too far out for visitors.

At a deeper level, Janey could respond to Rossetti's manic-depression: she could romp and she could roar with laughter, but her melancholy also matched his, even if she rallies him on it, and hers is—to us— inexplicable. When comparing herself with Marie Stillman she wrote: "So much has happiness done for the one, and misery for the other." It is difficult to see what that misery was: life with Morris may have been exasperating and perhaps frustrating but not tragic.

In intellectual interests she could also keep pace with Rossetti. They had read unexpected books together at Kelmscott and Bognor and Herne Bay. Once they find each has been reading Coleridge independently. Rossetti had written: " 'The Three Graves' is one of the finest poems in the world—possessing absolute invention and exquisite pathos: of course, it begins in the middle and never finishes." To which she replied: "The remarks you make on it would apply to most of his things, his incompleteness must annoy you, I think, but there are marvellous verses scattered through his works." Rossetti also sent her Cottle's *Coleridge* with the comment that Buchanan's attacks were largely plagiarised from two sources: "a most spiteful but most amusing letter of Lamb's to Coleridge (towards end of Vol. I) & the other Southey's attack on Byron which occurs in the Appendix".

Janey showed appreciation of his pictures with girlish enthusiasm, telling him how she had insisted on unpacking for herself the box in which he had sent her some drawings and decided to hang them over her bed "so that I may always have the pleasure of feeling them near me in bed and seeing them when dressing and undressing. . . . Thank you so much for thinking me still worthy of making so lovely a present to, it is a great pleasure and more in this life."

In the spring of 1880,[167] Rossetti was adding verses to "Sister Helen" and writing poems again. Janey asks to see the Beryl Songs for "Rose Mary" and assures him "You must feel sure how welcome your work always is to me and there is little pleasure left one in this world." She took a lot of interest in the choice of flowers in her hand for "The Day Dream", whether they were to be snowdrops or jonquils: (21st February) he writes: "—one word to say—so many thanks for the lovely snow- drops. I should like of all things to paint those of your sending, but am obliged to-day to go on with the hair which is in a state that will not wait". He puts them in a cool place and then looks up in Gerard's *Herbal* to find out how the leaves should be drawn. Later he writes to Shields about what he calls the "Sycamore picture" and then comes back to Janey to consult with her whether snowdrops or primroses would go with a "fairly advanced spring sycamore".

No letters from Janey have been found between March and December but she must have written and also visited Tudor House to sit, for he wrote to her regularly, apologising for "dullness", begging for sittings, thanking her for her interest. (14th April) "P.S. Don't look up anyone else on the same day, I dont like to be 'come on' to." Sometimes there is a joke: "Davies is an honest fellow & was smit all of a heap when he first saw you in a gallery lately."[168] These culminate in the letter of 27th November: "I felt deeply the regard so deeply expressed in yr last letter. I may claim to deserve it on the ground only of an equal regard—would I could say of any worthy result! The deep-seated basis of feeling as expressed in that sonnet, is as fresh and unchanged in me towards you as ever, though all else is withered & gone. This you wd. never believe, but if life & fate had willed to link us together, you wd. have found true what you cannot think to be truth when—alas—untried!"

In December Janey writes that she is planning to go to Italy with the Howards—an occasion which caused Morris to declare that she must pay her own way as he "can't be owing money to Earl-Kin"—and leaving the girls to house-keep for their father. Janey and the Howard family crossed the Channel in January, 1881, and on hearing of their safe arrival, Rossetti wrote (25th January, 1881) to "rejoice" at it.

"Whether you possess a progeny any longer, I am not aware, as Stephens told me on Saturday that Jenny & May had taken Holly to instruct him in the art of skating. . . .

"I write merely because I like to think your eye will rest on the writing. I can only hope that when I hear from you again and again write, I may have something to say.

"Of what jumble respecting the localities of my native land my envelope may be guilty, I do not venture to surmise."

From Bordighera Janey asked for the addresses of the Stillmans and of Fairfax Murray in Florence as they were going on there, although for the time being she was looking after the Howard children on her own while their parents returned to England to fight in the General Election campaign.

36

There had always been someone to come to Rossetti's rescue and there still was. In 1881 it was to be a young man undecided between the careers of architecture and writing who afterwards became a figure of some note, best-seller and publicist—Thomas Henry Hall Caine. He had sent Rossetti a copy of a lecture on his poems which he had given in Liverpool, and after many letters had passed between them, in which Rossetti shows himself a sympathetic and stimulating critic, the young man was invited to call at Tudor House—a Royal Command.

He found the place shabby, but inside he recognised a king as other subjects had done before him. "Holding forth both hands and crying 'Hulloa' [Rossetti] gave that cheery hearty greeting which I came to recognise as his alone perhaps, in warmth and unfailing geniality, among all the men in our circle. It was Italian in its spontaneity and yet it was English in its manly reserve: and I remember with much tenderness of feeling that never to the last . . . did it fail him when meeting with those friends to whom to the last he was really attached."

In July, 1881, he took up residence at Tudor House. Rossetti had consulted Janey about it: (21st July) "Your cheerful view of my taking a house-mate cheers me also. Caine is a particularly good fellow." Later he wrote again to her: (19th August) "I find him good company & he never talks politics." Treffry Dunn, whom he supplanted, had been rather harshly treated. When he could not secure arrears of salary due to him he had gone back to Cornwall to work on the new cathedral at Truro and to draw portraits. At first Rossetti wished him well and then unreasonably accused him of desertion. Fanny had made mischief and worked on Rossetti not finding him amusing enough. He had begun to tire on the long evening walks and became sleepy sitting up into the small hours. Crossly, Rossetti wrote to Watts: "He comes to collect his goods (his d—d bads) to-morrow." But there was a reconciliation later, when Dunn undertook in January, 1882, to lay-in pictures that Rossetti owed to Valpy and he kept up with William Michael, for several years helping to settle up affairs at Tudor House.

An arrangement generously intended to provide free board and lodging to a struggling young writer with intellectual conversation in the evenings, inevitably turned into a post as agent, companion, nurse—all gladly accepted and, without, it is fair to say, any idea in mind of the uses to which he could later put the material he was collecting. At the time it seemed as if his service might continue for years, and in what he was to write later he showed both discretion and generosity. He has often been unfairly treated by other biographers.

For a young man from the provinces life at Tudor House must have presented some awkward problems to his inexperience. There was Fanny Cornforth, for instance, who seemed to have the run of the place and yet caused an upset whenever she appeared. Was he to try to conciliate her—unlike Dunn, who had not been able to conceal his dislike and had suffered for it? Or was he to discourage his host from seeing too much of her, by taking him out for walks and keeping him talking late in the evenings? And was it his responsibility to turn her away if there were other visitors expected? He must have marvelled at the way Rossetti kept the strands apart that went to make up his tangled life, for he knew that there was another lady who took precedence of everything—the famous Mrs. Morris. He never saw her, for when she was expected he would be sent a courteous note asking him to dine in his room.

To Hall Caine must go the credit for selling to Liverpool the bigger "Dante's Dream" and getting Rossetti to finally finish the ballads, "The White Ship" and "The King's Tragedy". All the spring and summer of 1881 he encouraged Rossetti in negotiations with Ellis to publish a new volume of *Ballads and Sonnets* and to re-issue the *Poems* of 1870. Both sold well and received good reviews, but did little to cheer their author. Old friends had not been forgotten in sending out presentation copies. Shields had his and Aglaia Coronio also, and Watts-Dunton put in a claim for Swinburne, as if he refused to allow the door to be slammed on their friendship of years before.[169]

"Sonnets with me mean insomnia," he had once written to Christina, and it seemed that now he had put them—and the emotions they enshrined—into print he had little interest in them. Memories he found bitter rather than sweet and he disliked having to use tact in making certain changes in the text. Of importance biographically in the poems is the deliberate mystification employed (abetted by William Michael) in dating them and changing certain words. In the titles "Love" is played down: "Love's Pageant" became "Beauty's Pageant", for instance, and "The Love-lamp" became "The Lamp's Shrine". More significantly dark hair is changed to fair to disguise the references to Janey Morris. A line in "Venus Victrix", for instance,

"O'er poet's page deep-shadowed in thy hair?"

has an alteration to "gold-shadowed".

Even so, Janey was worried lest she should be recognised, for Rossetti wrote to her:

"Unless you think me quite without feeling, you must know what I felt on reading the first of all your letters that had any bitterness for me. You will let me answer your question. I apprehend nothing whatever from criticism and Watts who knows the press all along considered it out of the question. The poems attacked now have taken their place in the language, and the Revue which attacked them had quite lately an article in emphatic praise of the Sonnets which were far more open to criticism and special application than those now added. However though I can be certain of my own mood, it is intolerable to have any uncertainty as to yours, or to think you incensed against me. Every new piece that is not quite colourless will be withdrawn and the book postponed. . . ."[170]

He told Ellis to hold up the printing, undertaking to pay for any alterations made in the type set up.

On Janey's return from abroad in May, 1881, she paid frequent visits again to Tudor House. Her letters become short notes, undated and without opening or end.

"Wednesday, I will come about 12 o'clock then, but I can't, won't wait beyond 1 for my dinner. I can eat anything at that hour, no dainties mind. I can stay all the evening till 9 about. I shall have to call at Ned's on my way back to take up Jenny where she will stay the day."

Others are like it: there must be no extra preparations, she can eat anything now, she will leave at a certain time. There are no letters from Rossetti for the period except in July when Janey had evidently been ill again, as he writes (15th July) "Watts relieved my mind last night after seeing you. I had fancied you might be quite prostrate when I did not hear from you. Watts was enraptured with the enormous democratic obesity of Top. O for that final Cabinet Ministry which is to succeed the *Cabinet d'aisance* of his early years!" He then goes on to offer to lend her Hogg's *Life of Shelley*: "You must *roar*, in spite of the heat and the devil himself." But in August he gives vent to his disappointment that he had not heard from or seen her. If she was well enough to have gone to watch the second voyage of the Ark (from Kelmscott, Chiswick, to Kelmscott, Lechlade) she could surely have sat—or reclined—for the hands in his picture? But he remembers in time that he is only a suppliant and ends: "I have not the least claim on your consideration, but if you withdrew it, it is the only one of many withdrawals which will go to my heart. The rest passed by unheeded. If you read this letter, do not answer harshly, for I cannot bear it." As a P.S. is written: "Of course it did not fail to occur to me whether you would again grasp the isolated interval in town here, but I did not venture to think it in the least likely, particularly as Caine is now with me."

Rossetti's health was worsening. He claimed to have discharged an enormous quantity of blood during bouts of coughing, and although this was regarded as hypochondria even by William Michael, the fact that he could fancy it was evidence of his neurotic condition. The "mere fantasy" to which he was prone was part of the disease. Christina's sympathy was the most perceptive: "It is trying to have to do with him at times," she wrote to William Michael, "but what must it be TO BE himself?" His doctors once again ordered a holiday from London and Hall Caine arranged a visit in September, 1881, to the Vale of St. John, Keswick, which he knew well. But it was not a success. "Kelmscott," he wrote to Janey on 23rd September, "is absolutely populous as compared with this district, and excitements are not many," and concludes by saying that he never could "write a landscape letter".

He was beyond trying to get comfort from a Wordsworthian communion with nature, although he insisted on climbing Golden Howe— perhaps as a gesture of defiance to that poet's memory. When Caine was anxious, he reassured him: "Don't be afraid, I always go up on my feet and come down on a broader basis." The walks became shorter and shorter, and, unfortunately, the "nurse" who accompanied them, for so was Fanny euphemistically called, revealed to Rossetti that Hall Caine had been giving him plain water at night instead of chloral. This had disastrous effects and the situation was made still worse by Fanny suddenly taking herself off back home. He wrote in very weak spidery handwriting to Janey on the 4th October to thank her for some books she had sent him: "I still continue in a state of much bodily weakness & exhaustion, though I take walks daily and have even climbed a mountain here when first I arrived 1200 ft. high—— A dozen copies of my book have been sent me. Do you like me to send one & to what address? Or two, for yourself & Top?"[171]

It was useless to prolong the visit and Caine, overwrought himself by the worry and responsibility, was glad to pack up easels and canvases and have other "traps" stowed into a special saloon which was sent round to the wayside platform so that they would not have to sit about on draughty platforms before getting into the Scotch express at Penrith.

On the journey Rossetti sat up all night, dressed in his coat and hat and gloves as if he were to get out at the next station, while Caine did his best to keep up talk that would distract him. But when it flagged, Rossetti began to speak himself and revealed more of the story of his life than he had ever told to anyone before.[172] Caine does not tell it all in his reminiscences, but says that it concerned Lizzie's death and the note he found beside her—"a message that left such a scar on his heart as would never be healed".

There was remorse for any suffering he had caused her, and for his action in retrieving the book of poems he had buried in her coffin. But when the whole story was told there was more to it than that. Caine concludes:

". . . if I had now to reconstruct his life afresh from the impressions of that night, I think it would be a far more human, more touching, more affectionate, more unselfish, more intelligible figure that would emerge than the one hitherto known to the world. It would be the figure of a man who, after engaging himself to one woman in all honour and good faith, had fallen in love with another, and then gone on to marry the first out of a mistaken sense of loyalty and a fear of giving pain, instead of stopping, as he must have done, if his will had been stronger and his heart sterner, at the door of the church itself."

When they reached Tudor House, Rossetti exclaimed: "Thank God! Home at last and never shall I leave it again."

37

The return to Tudor House did not bring restoration to health. And from this time there is no more mention of Jane Morris. No letters from either side are extant, nor is there any record of her whereabouts in Morris's correspondence quoted by his biographers. Somewhere she must have been lying on a sofa, sick whenever she tried to get up, but whether it was at home or in some English seaside resort or on the Continent there is nothing to tell. Nor whether she had ever loved Rossetti or only been in love with being loved.

Rossetti can have had little wish to hold on to life and yet some spring in him endeavoured to go on with things; to work, to take an interest in the outside world and be patient with old friends and grateful to them and to his family for their loyalty to him. Often irritability overcame him and he would snap the heads off people if they bored him or turn them away if they called at the wrong moment. He had never been easy: he had always had his ups and downs or, for those who believe that things are explained by calling them names, he was a hypomaniac in whom there was "hidden a small depressive component", and he was also one of those "cycloid melancholics in whom there is a vein of humour". So much for his jokes.

He was not an angel. But he had a heart as well as brains and when he upset those who were kind enough to be fond of him he was sorry. In 1872 he had written to Dr. Hake in apology: "I have been in trouble ever since to think of the sulks you found me in the other day, but I knew I had your forgiveness. I had just scratched out a hand in a picture for the 3rd time!" In these last years as he endured worsening health he needed all the more to know he had "forgiveness" from friends—and so he should from a biographer.

> "... vain, snarled up, and sneazy
> No one is really interesting until
> To love them has become no longer easy."
> (*A Note for Biographers*, Vernon Scannell)

During November a professional nurse had to be called in to supervise regular meals for him and early bed times. He asked to see a priest in order to make a confession and receive absolution.

"A new idea," wrote Bell Scott, the candid friend, "which caused us painful agitation. I mention this hallucination as I have related previous ones . . . We thought his mind wandering or that he was dreaming. But on its earnest repetition with his eyes open I, for one, put him in mind of not being a papist and of his extreme agnosticism. . . ."

William Michael, a lifelong rationalist, deals with this more sympathetically: "My brother was unquestionably sceptical as to many alleged facts and he disregarded formulated dogmas and the practices founded upon them. . . . On the other hand, his mind was naturally prone to the marvellous and the supernatural, and he had an abiding and very deep reverence for the person of Christ." To his wife he had written in 1877 that if dogmatic or organised religion would help his brother then he considered it would be a benefit, although he (like herself and Madox Brown) could never become a believer.

Rossetti had a feeling for the necessity of some force to unify and give meaning to the diversity of the universe; besides an emotional regard for the legends and outward forms of religious observances which sometimes degenerated into superstition. Perhaps what his mother and sisters believed so devotedly might be true: whatever inspired their attendances at Christchurch, Albany Street, had given a serenity to their lives. In one of his fragments of verse he wrote:

> "Would God I knew there were a God to thank
> When thanks rise up in me!"

And on personal immortality he wrote about "Cloud Confines" to Bell Scott with Shelleyan pantheism: "I cannot suppose that any particle of life is extinguished, though its permanent individuality may be more than questionable. Absorption is not annihilation: and for the special atom of life to be re-embodied (if so it were) in a world which its own former ideality had helped to fashion for pain or pleasure. Such is the theory conjectured here."

It is not known when the professional nurse left, but she must have had a lot to contend with as Rossetti became stronger and it became more difficult to keep Fanny away from him when she called. Frederick Shields, who had been devoted in his attendance, absented himself in protest.[173] Pathetic notes from Rossetti begged him to return:

> "Nov. 15 1881. The loss of your friendly society is very serious to me. I am still very ill. Yours affec.
> Nov. 22. Wm. has told you that I shall be alone tomorrow. Let me implore you to come. I am still very ill. Your affec.
>
> D.G.R."

He wrote desperately to William Michael (with several biblical quotations) to lament her influence and to beg him to strengthen the nurse's hand by instructions that "*no one* is to interfere with, much less over-ride her instructions or circumvent her vigilance in restraining him. Privately the old housekeeper seems to be under the spell of that woman but it will be most unwise to say a word about this to G under the circumstances."

William Michael had to remind Shields of "seventy times seven" and beg him to show Gabriel his forgiveness by continuing to call.

By December he was strong enough to receive visitors—indeed they were essential to keep him from moping—and on the 11th Dr. Westland Marston and Philip were with him for the evening. Hall Caine, who was present, wrote:

> "he seemed much cheered by their bright society: but later on he gave those manifestations of uneasiness which I had learned to know too well. Removing restlessly from seat to seat, he ultimately threw himself upon the sofa in that awkward attitude which I have previously described as char-

acteristic of him in moments of nervous agitation. Presently he called out that his arm had become paralysed, and upon attempting to rise that his leg also had lost its power".

"Nonsense, Rossetti, you're only fancying it," Hall Caine protested, but when he tried to hold him up, realised that he was indeed stricken and hurriedly sent for Dr. Marshall.

One of the things Marshall insisted upon was that the chloral, which had been allowed again in small quantities, often diluted with water, must be stopped entirely, and to this end a newly-qualified young doctor, Henry Maudslay, was brought into the house to take charge and to administer morphia when necessary.

Burne-Jones was among those who called to enquire: "with his delicate and spiritual face full of affectionate solicitude". When he dined with Caine in the studio he pointed to an unfinished picture on an easel: "They say Gabriel cannot draw, but look at that hand. There isn't anybody else in the world can draw a hand like that." He had remained loyal to the man he had admired so much; although their ways had parted and he continued to the end to feel the loss of his first hero. Having in mind the favourite Macdonald phrase, "Bare is my back for the lack of a brother", he declared, "The worst of it is, I've no longer Rossetti at my back—he has left me more to do than I've strength for, the carrying on of his work all by myself." It was to be Burne-Jones who filled in the sky for the background of "Found" in the most complete version of what was almost the first and the last of Rossetti's pictures.

Bell Scott wrote of the new attack in his autobiographical notes: "[he] was carried upstairs to bed and never came down again". He also had an unnecessary passage on these last months: "The picture I have drawn had been a painful one to witness and has been only less so to indicate in narrative, even carefully omitting the most repulsive elements of the scene." Bell Scott would have deserved it if Rossetti had taken him for the original of his fragment:

> " 'Was it a friend or foe that spread these lies?'
> 'Nay, who but infants question in such wise?
> 'Twas one of my most intimate enemies.' "

He was disappointed that this year (1881) he had to put off joining the family at Christmas dinner for their annual reunion, an event by which his letters to his mother show that he set great store. When the day arrived he hated the thought of being alone and begged Hall Caine to stay with him. This he did, putting off dinner at Bell Scott's.

On 29th December, Rossetti managed to write to Miss Munro in a weak and down-sloping hand telling her that he was confined by an illness which shows no sign of abatement. "My illness is a total privation of power in the whole of the left side of the body. There is a slight improvement now in the power of stepping round the room, though but slight. The left arm unfortunately is quite paralysed and holding out no prospect of work in the future as yet. This is a melancholy letter . . ." but he offers to let her bring a friend to show round his studio even if "it is not worth it, one or two new things to see there not quite finished. But if she really wishes to come, of course, this would be possible".[174]

In early January he made the effort to go round to his mother's at Torrington Square, though he writes after one of them to apologise for being such "poor company" when he is there—a recurrent tragedy of home. When it is the only place that offers shelter it is also a shelter that is no longer home: a place grown out of; a shell of dead memories.

To fit in with a pattern that was working towards completion, a *Nunc Dimittis* thread was contributed by Sharp, who insisted on reading to him the verses that Buchanan, himself broken in mind and body, dedicated to Rossetti in his novel, *God and the Man*.

> "Pure as thy purpose, blameless as thy song,
>   Sweet as thy spirit, may this offering be:
> Forget the bitter blame that did thee wrong,
>   And take the gift from me."

Threads of the pattern come out brighter here and there. When the doctors once again insisted on his leaving Chelsea—was he, like his father, to end in exile?—an old friend came forward to put a house at his disposal. This was Thomas Seddon, who was designing a sort of garden city at Birchington-on-Sea and offered his own bungalow there as readily as he had once offered the commission for the Llandaff triptych.

Rossetti with Hall Caine and a nurse left Cheyne Walk on 4th February, 1882. The old humour that had entertained the little Morris girls was still there. Hall Caine's young sister, Lily, was accompanying them to the sea for her health, and while they waited for a porter at Victoria Station, Rossetti looked up at the notice board of the London, Chatham and Dover Railway. "Why, Lily, they knew we were coming. That stands for Lily Caine and Dante Rossetti."

No sooner had they arrived, however, than Rossetti wanted to go back. Not unnaturally, for a planned suburbia was hardly likely to be a congenial background for the Bohemian Cockney of Italian parentage. Hall Caine had to insist on staying on, if only for the sake of Lily, but he had a hard time of it trying to reconcile Rossetti to the place and having to keep him entertained on his own. "The latest complaint," he reported to Watts-Dunton, "is that I do not talk enough. He has been saying: 'It was not formerly the case that I was the only man to whom there was nothing to say.' He is remarking that I find no difficulty in talking to William and Watts and 'that damned old beast, Scott'."[175] His irritability subsided as his health worsened. He had to spend more time in bed. When Mrs. Rossetti and Christina arrived, the "Antique", now eighty, found energy to take her turn at sitting up throughout the night when needed. The local vicar became a regular visitor, which must have pleased Mrs. Rossetti (was that why he was made welcome?). Madox Brown was away in Manchester working on the Town Hall murals, but Watts-Dunton and Shields came regularly and Leyland, shirt-studs flashing, drove over from Worthing.

Once, passing through the district and not to be denied, came Howell. To him must go the credit of having been about the last person to make Rossetti laugh:

> "What are you doing now?"
> "Buying horses for the King of Spain."[176]

Rossetti's constitution, however it had been abused, was not defeated yet and his mental powers held firm. He managed to finish certain pictures, a replica of "Proserpine" and a "Joan of Arc", and undertook some sketches of his father for a statue which the citizens of Vasto, his birthplace, wished to erect. He composed the two "Sphinx" sonnets[177] to accompany a memorial to Nolly Brown, which, with "Jan Van Hunks", were to be his contributions to a joint volume with Watts-Dunton.

He enjoyed reading aloud, his voice as vibrant as ever, and he wrote letters. He entered upon a correspondence with Joseph Knight, who had published an article on his poems in "Le Libre", and with the French critic, Chesneau, who wanted information about the P.-R.B. for a forthcoming book on *La Peinture Anglaise*. He still tried "working the oracle" for those he admired. In November, 1881, he had written to Stephens: "I am quite rejoiced to find that you are going to write on Brown's new works—undoubtedly his masterpieces. *Do* be strong and enthusiastic in your best style."[178]

18. ROSSETTI AT HIS EASEL
by Frederic Shields

19. MORRIS AT HIS LOOM
by E. Burne-Jones

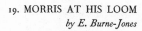

6 March
1868

10. CHEYNE WALK
CHELSEA

My dear Janey,

Next Wednesday was
the day I hoped to
see you, but I think
perhaps to secure
my finishing something
I am about before-
-hand, I had better
say Friday – i.e. 2
days later. On
Friday next then

20. A letter from Rossetti to Jane Morris.

Late in March, William Michael came down. He had to accept the doctor's report that there was little hope of recovery. "I came away from the bungalow with a firm conviction that my brother had not long to live, coupled with the feeling (I do not scruple to admit it) that, rather than so luminous intellect should be reduced to feebleness or torpor, it were far better to die."

He left on 2nd April, meaning to return on the 7th, Good Friday, but received a telegram recalling him on the Thursday. Watts-Dunton was summoned too. Shields came on the Saturday as well as the faithful doctor friend, a beloved physician indeed, John Marshall. A move back to Chelsea was tentatively suggested, but Marshall must have known it was unlikely ever to be carried out. William Michael wrote a long letter to his wife, Lucy, detailing Rossetti's symptoms. He is amazed at the recuperative power shown by the composition of the "Sphinx" sonnets—"whose secret will perhaps be very soon told to himself". On the Saturday, although Dr. Harris does not expect him to last out the day, he was able to make a new will under Watts-Dunton's direction, for William Michael had suddenly realised that the last one had left everything to Lizzie and her brothers would have been the beneficiaries. It is short and simple;* family and friends are remembered and to "my friend, Mrs. William Morris of Kelmscott House, Hammersmith" are bequeathed "three of the largest and best of the chalk drawings for the subjects of which she sat that are now hanging in my studio at Cheyne Walk, Chelsea aforesaid to be selected by her also the profile head of her in chalk now hanging over the mantelpiece in the studio".

The pattern was to stop repeating. What remained was the care of friends. On Sunday—Easter Sunday—when the times for each one to sit up with him through the night had been arranged, two sharp cries were suddenly heard from his room. When they went in they found Rossetti had collapsed in a stroke. Fittingly the last note on him comes from his brother's diary: "He died 9.31 p.m. the others—Watts, Mother, Christina and nurse in room; Caine and Shields in and out; Watts at Gabriel's right side, partly supporting him."

* See Appendix L, p. 244.

"The Past is over and fled:
　Named new, we name it the old:
　Thereof some tale hath been told,
But no word comes from the dead:
　Whether at all they be,
　Or whether as bond or free,
　Or whether they too were we,
Or by what spell they have sped.

　Still we say as we go;—
　　'Strange to think by the way,
　Whatever there is to know
　　That shall we know one day."
　　　　　　　　(Cloud Confines)

SOURCES AND REFERENCES

For the sake of brevity I am giving shortened versions of the names of the Collections from which unpublished material has been quoted in the text. Material from Mrs. Helen Rossetti Angeli appears as (Mrs. Angeli): from the adopted grand-daughter of Holman Hunt, Mrs. Elizabeth Burt, as (Mrs. Burt): from Miss Ellen Heaton, lent by the executors of K. O. Heaton as (K. O. Heaton): from Alexander Munro and Miss Munro (Mrs. J. A. R. Munro): from Mrs. Janet Camp Troxell as (Mrs. Troxell): the Library of the University of Texas, Austin, as (Texas): the Library of Duke University, Durham, N.C., as (Duke). The letters from Rossetti to Jane Morris, which were put on reserve for fifty years from her death in 1914, and became available in January, 1964, are referred to as (B.M.). Other letters in the Ashley Collection, bought from T. J. Wise, are referred to as (Ashley, B.M.).

Correspondence addressed to F. G. Stephens and bought from Mr. T. A. Iggulden by the Bodleian Library, Oxford, is referred to as (Bodleian). These papers were bequeathed by Colonel Holman Stephens to his partner, Mr. Iggulden's father.

Published correspondence is not noted but references are given to magazine and other printed sources where these have not been quoted before or are not readily available.

In several instances in these References I have taken the unusual step of explicitly disagreeing with conclusions reached by Professor Doughty in his biography of Rossetti (*A Victorian Romantic*, published by Muller in England and the Yale University Press, U.S.A., in 1949 and republished with a few alterations in 1960 by the Oxford University Press). He often proffers hostile interpretations of Rossetti's motives which can be disproved by the facts. It seems to me extraordinary for a biographer not to give his "hero" the benefit of the doubt. To show that I am not alone in this, may I remind readers of the letter which the late Sir Sydney Cockerell saw fit to send to "The Times" pointing out errors in the biography (particularly with regard to Mrs. Morris, page 372), and concluding: "Because it seemed to me that Professor Doughty failed to recognise Rossetti's stature and concerned himself so largely with his weaknesses and with the elaboration of a scandal, I insisted that no mention should be made in the preface of my having overlooked the text." It is in order to try to redress this balance that in this book—far less ambitious—I have used even trivial new material to emphasise such aspects of Rossetti's character as his generosity, his remembrance of old friends who had fallen on evil days, and the almost miraculous way in which his faculties—*pace* Professor Doughty and William Bell Scott—survived illness and depression.

CHAPTER 1

1. Letter of 13 September, 1836 (Mrs. Angeli).

CHAPTER 2

2. Bell Scott: in the *Autobiographical Notes* in two volumes, edited by W. Minto, 1902, there are not only unmarked omissions from Rossetti's letters quoted but also alterations made in them, intended presumably to improve upon the writer's punctuation, grammar or vocabulary. In Rossetti's first letter, for instance, quoted on page 243, vol. 1, in the 13th line, Scott has: "I read this and felt grateful but unsatisfied." What Rossetti had written was: "I read this and felt grateful but my desire was unsatisfied and seemed for some time to remain so." Other alterations and unmarked omissions will be noted in other letters quoted here. The originals have been seen by the author in Mrs. Troxell's Collection.

3. Deverell's father was appointed in 1842 administrative assistant to William Dyce, Director of the Somerset House School of Design, London.

4. Letters to Deverell from MS. at the Art Gallery, the Henry E. Huntington Library, San Marino, California. The MS. is entitled "Memorial Notes by Frances C. Deverell with introduction by W. M. Rossetti and Illustrations." The illustrations are sketches by Rossetti drawn on the letters, one of which, the group at Hannay's, is reproduced here. (H.M. 12895—H.M. 12982, Rossetti.)

5. Collinson to Hunt (Mrs. Burt).

6. George Palmer "pottered about" with a stick much longer than himself. He is said to have had "special charge of the Portland Vase at the time a crazy brute smashed it with a sun-dried brick from Nineveh". (Stephens to W. M. Rossetti.) From 1887 the Blake book was in the possession of W. A. White of New York, whose daughter, Mrs. Frances White Emerson, generously gave it to the British Museum in 1957.

CHAPTER 4

7. To Holman Hunt (Mrs. Burt).

8. According to Holman Hunt's *Pre-Raphaelitism* there were two separate sessions at Millais' house.

9. F. G. Stephens' quotation from *The Germ*, No. 4, under title of "Modern Giants" by Laura Savage.

10. Letters to and from Holman Hunt, *passim* (Mrs. Burt).

11. Extracts from letters to Stephens from F. G. Stephens Collection (Bodleian).

CHAPTER 5

12. This account of the evening comes from Holman Hunt's article on Rossetti in *The Musical World*, July 5th, 1890.

13. Letters to Stephens (Bodleian).
14. Letter to Holman Hunt (Mrs. Burt).
15. Tupper letters to Stephens (Bodleian).

CHAPTER 6

16. *The Illustrated London News*, May 4, 1850, p. 306.

Town Talk and Table Talk

Has any casual reader of art criticisms ever been puzzled by the occurrence of three mysterious letters as denoting a new-fashioned school or style in painting lately come into vogue? The hieroglyphics in question are "P.R.B.", and they are the initials of the words "Prae-Raffaelite Brotherhood". To this league belong the ingenious gentlemen who profess themselves practitioners of "Early Christian Art", and who, setting aside the mediaeval schools of Italy, the Raffaeles, Guidos, and Titians, and all such small-beer daubers—devote their energies to the reproduction of saints squeezed out perfectly flat—as though the poor gentlemen had been martyred by being passed under a Baker's Patent—their appearance being further improved by their limbs being stuck akimbo, so as to produce a most interesting series of angles and finely developed elbows. A glance at some of the minor exhibitions now open will prove what really clever men have been bitten by this extraordinary art-whim, of utterly banishing and disclaiming perspective and everything like rotundity of form. It has been suggested that the globe-shape of the world must be very afflicting to the ingenious gentlemen in question. Sydney Smith said that Quakers would, if they could, have clothed all creation in grey. The "P.R.B." would be bolder still, for they would beat it out flat, and make men and women like artfully-shaped and coloured pancakes. A.B.R.

17. Letter to Stephens (Bodleian).
18. It is not true that Rossetti never showed his pictures again in public. In 1857 Madox Brown was instrumental in organising a mixed Exhibition in Russell Place, Fitzroy Square, which the critics referred to as a Pre-Raphaelite Exhibition and to this Rossetti sent "Dante's Dream", "Mary Magdalene", and other pictures. He also showed in Liverpool in 1858, 1861, 1862, and 1864. This was in order to support the old Liverpool Academy, which was undermined by the rival Society of Arts and finally closed in 1862 (*The Burlington:* November, 1963). In 1859 the Hogarth Club, of which he was a founder-member, held an Exhibition to which he sent "Mary in the House of John".
19. Hunt's letters to Stephens (Bodleian).
20. Letter from Hunt to Combe (Mrs. Burt).
21. Hunt's letter to Lowes Dickinson (Bodleian).
22. Hunt's letters to Dickens (Mrs. Burt). Also see, The University of Texas *Studies in Literature and Language Quarterly*, Spring, 1964.

CHAPTER 7

23. Extract from George Boyce's Diary in *The Old Water-Colour Society's Annual Volume*, 1941.

CHAPTER 8

24. Letter to Hunt (Mrs. Burt).

25. The MS. of Brown's *Diary*, (the Pierpont Morgan Library).

26. In the first study for "The Last of England" the woman had a shawl, not a bonnet. This sketch, bought by Samuel Bancroft from Fanny Schott, is now at the Wilmington Art Centre, U.S.A.

27. W. M. Rossetti on Elizabeth Siddal's drawings: "The first design of hers, which I find mentioned was from Wordsworth's 'We are Seven' (January 1853). In 1853–4 she painted a portrait of herself. Other early designs are—pen and ink drawing of 'Pippa and the Woman of Loose Life' from Browning's drama, a water-colour of the 'Ladies' Lament' from the 'Ballad of Sir Patrick Spens', a design of 'Clerk Saunders', which afterwards she developed into a water-colour. By 1854 she had also produced designs of Rossetti's 'Sister Helen', 'The Nativity', 'The Lass of Lachroyan', and the 'Gay Goshawk'—the latter two for a Ballad book. Two water-colours, 'La Belle Dame sans merci' and the old design of 'We are Seven', were in hand at the beginning of 1856. There was also a design, pen and ink, of two lovers seated *al fresco* and singing to the music of two dark Malay-looking women while a little girl listens. As to Miss Siddal's own designs, I may mention besides those already specified: 'Jepthah's Daughter', 'The Deposition from the Cross', 'The Maries at the Sepulchre', 'The Madonna Child with an Angel', 'Macbeth taking the dagger from his Wife who meditates Suicide', 'The Lady of Shalott', 'St. Cecilia', 'The Woeful Victory'. The St. Cecilia was evidently intended to illustrate Tennyson's poem from *The Palace of Art*. It is a different composition from the same subject treated by Dante Rossetti but, like that, it certainly indicated the death of the saint; a point which does not appertain to the poem, and I have no doubt it preceded Rossetti's design and therefore this detail of invention properly belongs to Miss Siddal." An album of these put together by Fairfax Murray is now at Wightwick Manor, Wolverhampton (National Trust).

CHAPTER 9

28. Passage on *Maud* quoted from *D. G. Rossetti's Comments on Maud* by M. L. Howe in *Modern Language Notes* (John Hopkins' Press, Baltimore, May, 1934). This also contains quotations from letters to Allingham (now at Pierpont Morgan Library, New York) omitted by G. Birkbeck Hill, editor of the *Letters* in 1897.

29. Reference to Mrs. Browning in letter to Deverell (Huntington).

30. Extract from letter to Allingham (Pierpont Morgan).

31. Letters to Ellen Heaton (K. O. Heaton).
32. Letter from Madox Brown to Hunt (Mrs. Burt).
33. Ruskin's letters (K. O. Heaton).
34. On Ruskin to Bell Scott (Mrs. Troxell).
35. For reference to Mrs. Browning I am indebted to Mr. Philip Kelley.
36. In 1862 (January 7th to March 10th) Rossetti took his class on Mondays, 8–10 p.m. He would hardly have heard of it and offered his services if it had not been for Ruskin, but at the same time there is no basis for Professor Doughty's sneer: "The wisdom of pleasing Ruskin was doubtless a stronger influence than social idealism." Ruskin wrote in *Praeterita*: "Rossetti was the only one of our modern painters who taught disciples for love of them." A prospectus shows that he continued as a member of the Council after he gave up teaching. Professor Doughty says that Ruskin cancelled his lessons in painting from Rossetti because of "deep disgust" over a three-cornered transaction involving Miss Heaton. But Ruskin cancelled only one lesson because "I find my eyes today quite tired with an etching I expected to finish and haven't", and he expressly makes another appointment: "shall we say Saturday next for our lesson" and signs himself "Always affectionately yours".

Chapter 10

37. In 1871, when it was proposed to erect a public monument to Gabriele Rossetti in Florence, some Italian admirers asked for his body to be moved from Highgate Cemetery to Santa Croce. Professor Doughty comments that Rossetti was the only one who disagreed with his mother's refusal, "the rest, less partial than Gabriel to exhumations, whole-heartedly agreed with her".
38. To Hunt (Mrs. Burt).
39. This portrait is now at the Fitzwilliam, Cambridge.
40. Letter to Hunt (Mrs. Burt).

Chapter 11

41. After the Cathedral was bombed in 1940 the triptych was rescued and housed in the National Museum of Wales. It was brought back in 1958 and in a new frame is to be found in the small Memorial Chapel under the West Tower. In their 1958 restoration, the Cathedral authorities again showed themselves advanced in commissioning the *Majestas* by Epstein.
42. That Fanny assumed the name "Cornforth" is stated in a letter by her husband, John Schott, to Samuel Bancroft, Jnr. (Wilmington Arts Centre).
43. I am indebted for the following particulars of C. J. Faulkner to Mr. Peter Bayley of University College, Oxford, who found for me the University College Record of 1930–1931, edited by Sir Michael Sadler. Faulkner was elected Fellow in 1856, resigned in 1861, but returned in 1864. During the interval, besides keeping the books for the Firm, he entered the office of a

civil engineer where "he drew rivets by the thousands in plans for iron bridges". In 1880 Philip Burne-Jones came up to University College, and in 1883 it was through Faulkner that the Russell Club were permitted the use of the Hall on the occasion of Morris' lecture on "Democracy and Art", for Faulkner, known as "The Fogger", had by now become an active socialist.

Dr. E. H. Lendon (1866–70), who as an undergraduate remembered Faulkner, described him as having a "rather forlorn aspect" and mocked by the "young bloods who used to jeer at his Birmingham boots". As Bursar it was part of his duty to re-paper the men's rooms and "I remember his complaining that the young Philistines used to take off Morris's lovely paperhangings". Although a double first, he failed "Divvers" (Divinity Moderations) for including Isaiah among the Twelve Apostles. That he retained as a Fellow some Pre-Raphaelite humour is shown by entries in the College Betting-book in his name. "That the dolphin was the same animal as the porpoise", "That Miss Ellen Terry will not dine at The Master of Balliol's table on the occasion of her visit to Oxford with Mr. Henry Irving", "That no one in the Common Room at the moment will name one half of the apocryphal books of the Old Testament".

44. Professor Doughty is incorrect in stating that Morris "never produced more than one oil painting". Mrs. Troxell shows there were two; and that the picture called "Sir Tristram after his illness in the Garden of King Mark's Palace recognised by the dog he had given Iseult" existed only in Rossetti's imagination. "Tristram and Iseult" was the picture commissioned by Plint, unfinished in 1861 and whose present whereabouts are unknown: the portrait of Jane Burden as Queen Guinevere, later called "La Belle Iseult", somehow came into the possession of Oliver Madox Brown (Nolly) from whom Rossetti bought it by pictures in exchange, for which he apologises "such an exchange as would be in my power, which could merely be represented by some chalk head or other, or something of that sort" (see *Life of O. Madox Brown* by John Ingram). Mrs. Angeli rescued it from a closet and hung it in her bedroom until W. M. Rossetti gave it to the Morris Trustees who gave it to the Tate.

CHAPTER 12

45. Quotations from Val Prinsep in *Magazine of Art*, February, 1904.

46. Swinburne's introduction to Rossetti. "An Oxford friend, Mill, who knew Jones and Morris and through them Gabriel, introduced me to them, and Gabriel almost instantly asked me to sit (or stand) to him—but the intended 'fresco' never was even begun." (Ashley, B.M. 1427.) But later Swinburne wrote to Monckton Milnes (15th October, 1860): "Rossetti has just done a drawing of a female model and myself embracing, I need not say, in the most fervent and abandoned style." This was for the cover of *Early Italian Poets*, see illustration, facing p. 48.

47. The undergraduate quoted is the Rev. W. Tuckwell, *Reminiscences*. It is he who gives the story of looking for models in church.

48. On Jane's character. "I fancy that her beauty must have weighed rather heavily upon her. Her mind was not formed upon the same tragic lines as her face: she was very simple and could have enjoyed simple pleasures with simple people, but such delights were not for her. She looked like the Delphic Sybil, and had to behave as such." *Time Was*, by W. Graham Robertson.

49. St. Michael's: Oxfordshire Record Society, 1954. Visitation 1854. No return was made for St. Michael's, which was re-opened after restoration by Street in 1854. [Had Morris worked on it himself?] The Bishop noted on this occasion: "Trouble about the step on which communion Table: Metcalf afraid of being called a Puseyite. Happily arranged all at luncheon of amity at Lincoln." Diocese Book F.365B.

CHAPTER 13

50. Now an Old People's Home called The Lindens. Two wings have been altered but not so as much to change its appearance and the terraced garden is the same as in the illustration. It is now in a built-up area, but was then next to a farm with open fields all round and the famous lime tree flourishing a little way below down the steep hill.

51. Letter to Mrs. Julia Cameron (Mrs. Troxell).

52. Hunt's letters to Stephens on Annie Miller *passim* (Bodleian).

53. To Boyce (University College, London).

54. Professor Doughty comments on the marriage "as if fearing Lizzie might die in mortal sin, Gabriel hastened the arrangements for the wedding". It is most unlikely that either of them felt in this way and Rossetti's letter of 17th April certainly shows no sign of it.

CHAPTER 14

55. Writing before his marriage Burne-Jones says he is very frightened "and shouldn't be surprised if I bolt off the day before and am never heard of again" (Mrs. Angeli).

56. To Alexander Munro (Mrs. J. A. R. Munro).

57. Hunt to Stephens (Bodleian).

58. To Bell Scott (Mrs. Troxell).

CHAPTER 15

59. Rossetti's translations have never been properly appreciated. They deserve a study to themselves but, meanwhile, there may be quoted here passages on them from *The Last Romantics* by Graham Hough (1949). He says "it can be argued that his *Early Italian Poets* is his most valuable contribution to poetry. In the first place the job needed doing. Dante, his

predecessors and his contemporaries, by some accident, had never made their impact on English poetry . . . The slightest acquaintance with the pre-Dantesque poems, however, is enough to show the fantastic difficulty of rendering this often obscure and fine-spun verse, and the astonishing fidelity that Rossetti achieves".

60. Hunt to Stephens (Bodleian).

61. Woolner to Stephens (Bodleian).

CHAPTER 16

62. Rossetti also executed a portrait of her in stained glass. See Appendix G.

63. No contemporaries mention meeting James Siddal at the Rossettis although he claims to have been there. His address on 25th July, 1859, was 8 Kent Place, Southwark, given on his father's death certificate. On the 13th November, 1904, it was 63 St. George's Road, Camberwell. From other letters it is clear that W. M. Rossetti helped to support both him and his brother Henry ("Harry"), who died in 1908 in a workhouse. James was then established in lodgings with a niece in the Old Kent Road. He died 21st February, 1912 (Mrs. Angeli).

64. Account of the Sablonière from *La Vie aventureuse de Rimbaud* by J. M. Carré, 1929.

65. The note described by Mrs. Angeli in *Rossetti, His Friends and Enemies.*

66. The two missing entries from Minto's edition of the *Autobiographical Notes,* 1902, pages 64–5: "Mrs. Siddal Rossetti, little accustomed to the cares and habits of domestic life, willingly conforming. She had taken to the fastest ways and to self-taught proclivities in her assumed views of morals and religion which he [D.G.R.] only laughed at: and she had become a genius, etc." Later: "What was said or done at the Inquest I know not, but the impatient creature's wildly expressed notions had borne fruit: she had pinned a written statement on the breast of her nightshirt and put an end to her troubles, real or imaginary. Time is the great physician, etc." (Mrs. Troxell).

CHAPTER 17

67. On Rossetti's grief over his wife's death: "It is a strange fact that some individuals who have had previous attacks either of depression or mania may survive the impact of bereavement without any breakdown at all: yet they may break down spontaneously at a later date with little or no reference to the event in question." *Clinical Psychiatry* by Ian Skottowe, 1953 (page 144).

68. Letter from James Siddal (Mrs. Angeli).

69. Mrs. Witty, a grand-daughter of James Hannay, tells me that Rossetti confided to Hannay that he had poured out too strong a dose.

70. Letters from Burne-Jones (Mrs. Angeli).

71. Letters connected with The Imbroglio (Mrs. Angeli). This began with Holman Hunt telling Madox Brown that at Monckton Milnes' house Swin-

burne had declared that Rossetti thought nothing of procuring abortions daily. Faced with this by Madox Brown, Swinburne became "painfully excited". Burne-Jones, called in, also reported that Swinburne was in "a most excited and distressed state" and wanted to meet Madox Brown at Burne-Jones'. When Madox Brown confronted Hunt with the story, he denied it. Writing from the Lushingtons at Ockham Park on 12th October, he said: "Swinburne is perfectly correct in saying that he never spoke to me of Rossetti at Monckton Milnes." Brown was not satisfied and wrote (13 October) "You cannot expect me to take the whole blame of the incorrectness on myself. . . . I warned you that Swinburne's statements on matters of this nature must be received with extreme caution, owing to his habit of reckless exaggeration in order to astonish people." Hunt also said that he had heard such stories from other sources but does not name them.

72. W. M. Rossetti contributed an article on the Leathart Collection to an extra number of the Art Journal, Part 11, Jubilee Series, 1849–1899. "It was a shock to several persons, myself among them, to hear of the death in August, 1895, of Mr. James Leathart . . . my acquaintance with him had dated back to a remote year, perhaps 1855." Of Rossetti's work Leathart owned "Paolo and Francesca", "Salutatio Beatricis", "A Christmas Carol", and "Burd Alane". Of non-Pre-Raphaelites the Collection comprised pictures by Albert Moore, Bond (of Liverpool), G. T. Chapman, William Davies, Etty, Albert Goodwin, Alfred Hunt, Legros, Noel Paton, Ewbank, Shalders, David Scott.

73. Letter to Leathart (Mrs. T. H. Leathart).

74. This and other letters to Browning (Mrs. Troxell).

75. The memorial fountain has a bust of Rossetti, not a bronze medallion as stated by Professor Doughty.

76. Meredith on *Harry Richmond* (Texas). This and full texts of other Meredith letters will appear in the forthcoming edition of his letters, edited by Professor C. L. Cline, to be published by the Clarendon Press, Oxford.

CHAPTER 18

77. Letters to Madame Bodichon quoted by courtesy of Mr. Philip Leigh-Smith.

78. Letter to Red Lion Mary (Mrs. Angeli).

79. From *New Writings by Swinburne, or Miscellenea Nova et Curiosa*, edited Cecil Y. Lang.

80. Several sympathetic letters from George Eliot to Rossetti appear in her *Letters*, edited by Gordon Haight (Yale and O.U.P.) and it is known that she and Lewes cut Buchanan after the "Fleshly School" attack. In a letter (18 February, 1870 at Duke University) from Rossetti sending her the *Pandora* sonnets and several photographs of pictures, he goes to some trouble to explain his intentions in his *Hamlet*: "I fear it results in what a good many even sympathetic spectators might find puzzling and intricate.

As regards the dramatic action, I have meant to make Hamlet ramping about and talking wildly, kneeling on one of the little stalls and pulling to pieces the roses planted in a box in the angle—hardly knowing all he says and does, as he throw his arms wildly this way and that along the ledge of the carved screen. . . ."

81. Letters to Howell from Rossetti when not published in *Pre-Raphaelite Twilight*, Mrs. Rossetti Angeli, 1954, are quoted from the collection at Texas University.

82. Letter to Anderson Rose (Berg Collection, New York Public Library).

CHAPTER 19

83. Whistler extracts from three letters at Texas. See Appendix F for other references.

84. On Courbet to Bell Scott (Mrs. Troxell).

85. Letter from Inchbold (Bodleian).

86. Letter to Madame Bodichon (P. Leigh Smith). The artist was Edward Thompson Davis, 1833–1867.

87. Letters on Gurney Patmore (Bodleian).

88. Letter from Arthur Hughes (Duke).

CHAPTER 20

89. From Lewis Carroll's *Diaries*.

90. On James Smetham, the late Randolph Hughes pointed out that Professor Doughty is inaccurate in saying that he was "among the students attending Rossetti's class at the Working Men's College in 1855". It is unlikely he was at the classes as he was a student at the Royal Academy in 1843 and by 1851 had become a teacher of drawing at the Wesleyan Normal College in Westminster. Also Randolph Hughes ascertained from the Librarian of the Working Men's College that there was no record of Smetham there, either as a student or a teacher. He might, of course, have gone there unofficially to meet the lecturers, as Burne-Jones did, over a cup of tea and a bun.

91. Madox Brown's letter (Mrs. T. H. Leathart).

92. Roses for "Lilith". In an unpublished passage of his MS. Dunn records an amusing visit to Ruskin's garden at Denmark Hill, on Howell's suggestion, to collect the required white roses which he knew to be clambering over the garden wall. Ruskin was welcoming but soon "took against" Boyce, who had accompanied the others, girding at him for his picture of old Battersea Bridge, recently shown at the Old Water Colour Society, because he had introduced into it two or three black cats. "These cats seemed to act upon Ruskin pretty much as a red rag does to a bull for he chaffed poor Boyce unmercifully about them. 'Cats on a wall! Cats on a wall! Whenever I see a drawing by you there are sure to be cats on a wall.'"

Howell had meanwhile disappeared in order to have a smoke further off in the garden, but when Ruskin saw him he called out: "There you are again vitiating God's atmosphere." Some of Ruskin's architectural studies and "some very choice things" were inspected before they returned to Chelsea.

93. On the question of copying by an assistant, there is a relevant letter from Dr. Hake to W.M.R. (11 August, 1872): "Rossetti, when I mentioned about Dunn being engaged on chalk drawings, got alarmed and seemed to think that these were going to be finished by Dunn for the owners. He said that would never do to send them out as his own." (Mrs. Angeli). Cp Doughty, page 245 . . . "their [the replicas] ever increasing number as the years passed—particularly after he employed 'assistants' and contributed, it is thought, little beyond his own signature to these replicas". What is surprising is the way that patrons wanted replicas of other people's pictures.

94. Letter from Wallis (Texas).

CHAPTER 21

95. Palgrave's letter (Bodleian).

96. According to an unpublished passage in Dunn's *Recollections*, Ellen Smith was a laundry-maid in a place close by whom Rossetti accidentally met and, being struck with the suitability of her expressive face for a picture of some sort, he induced her to sit for him. She "sat for several of his sweetest pictures ('A Christmas Carol', was one) until the poor girl got her face sadly cut about and disfigured by a brute of a soldier and then, of course, she was of no more use as a model." (Mrs. Troxell).

97. Meeting with Alexa Wilding from Dunn's MS. (Mrs. Troxell).

98. Letter to Madame Gambart (Texas).

99. Dunn's MS. (Mrs. Troxell). Other particulars about Dunn from his *Recollections*, and *Life with Rossetti* by Gale Pedrick, 1964.

CHAPTER 22

100. This letter, 7th May, 1868, is the first preserved in the B.M. reserved collection. Others will be referred to as (B.M.).

101. Letter on "Top" & trade. (B.M.)

102. W. Bell Scott wrote to Holman Hunt (19 February, 1887): "D.G.R. was a very limited subject of enquiry compared with Shelley, but there has been a great deal written about him already and it is not very likely that while Shelley's behaviour to Harriet is sifted to the last syllable, D.G.R.'s history in relation to Lizzy will be allowed to remain untouched . . . My burst of ill-temper when [Lushington] was here gave me a great deal of trouble afterwards . . . Our friend read with unbounded admiration some verses addressed by Shelley to Harriet, swearing eternal devotion to her, whom a year after he leaves to drown herself. Simply the enthusiastic and

superlative style, as the speech of a lover to his mistress, took our friend
so that he thought of nothing else. I broke down and hurt the feelings
of one of the most amiable men God has made." (Mrs. Burt).

Chapter 23

103. A letter to Alice Boyd, preserved at Penkill, sent with three pieces of embroidery, reads: "I wonder if they would fit at Penkill into any of those
ingenious Chinese puzzles of arrangement which share with the reproving
eye-brow the softer palpitations of W.B.'s soul. They are, No. 1, History
of Joseph and Mrs. Potiphar (!!!). No. 2, Abraham entertaining angels to
which is added Hagar in the wilderness with an angel directing her attention
to a London pump. No. 3, Christ and the woman of Samaria." (Miss
Courtney-Boyd).
104. Bell Scott's letter (Bodleian).
105. To Kate Howell (Texas).
106. To Smetham (V. and A. Library).
107. On Gordon Hake (Mrs. Troxell).
108. Letters to Jane Morris, *passim* (B.M.).
109. To Aglaia Coronio (Mrs. Troxell).
110. I am indebted to Professor Pharr of Texas University for pointing out
that there is no authority in *The Iliad* for Cassandra appearing on the
walls of Troy.

Chapter 24

111. Letters to Morrises at Ems (B.M.).
112. To Kate Howell (Texas).
113. The date of the disinterment was probably 5th October. Mrs. Troxell
has the bill for two guineas from the Funeral Co. dated 5th October, 1869.
This might, of course, have been an estimate. D.G.R. told his brother
that it was "the 6th or 7th, I forget which", but on the evening of the 7th
he was reading the poems after dinner to W.M.R. and Madox Brown.
114. Writing to Madox Brown, D.G.R. said: "I have told Janey & Scott &
Dunn", but to Swinburne he omitted Janey's name.
115. Letters to Madame Bodichon (Mr. Leigh-Smith).

Chapter 25

116. Bell Scott's letter (Mrs. Burt).
117. This appeared in 1873 under the title *Dante and His Circle*.
118. Hunt to Stephens (Bodleian).
119. To the Cowper Temples (Pierpont Morgan Library).

CHAPTER 26

120. In her *Collected Works* of her father, May Morris wrote: "It seems to me
the duty of anyone who ever came into contact with Rossetti (even, as I
did, only in childhood) to lose no opportunity in passing, of stressing
the fineness of his character—especially in these days when he is written
of by people not altogether equipped for the task. . . . Stillman writes
especially of his generosity to his young friends, of which we have heard
before in my jottings: . . . Mr. Mackail's recent *Life of Morris* does great
injustice to Rossetti without in any way exalting his friend, for Rossetti
always urged Morris to follow his artistic tendencies . . . he was absolutely
free from personal jealousy." She goes on to quote Dr. Hake also on the
"justness" of his mind and adds: "Coming from these different sources,
what higher tribute could be paid to the largeness of mind and heart of
one who is always pictured as in the coils of dissensions and annoyances
about money."

121. To Purnell (Sotheby's Catalogue, 3rd Dec., 1952, copied by Randolph
Hughes).

122. Rossetti did not always take the Arthurian legend seriously. In a letter
to Swinburne (9th March, 1870, B. M. Ashley 4995) he gives an account of
seeing "the French Lancelot at Molini's . . ." "Lancelot, accompanied by
his friend, Galahalt [not Galahad as rendered by T. J. Wise] tells of his
deeds and is begged by Galahalt to kiss the Queen in his presence." She
demurs as her ladies are there. Rossetti finishes: "The funniest part is the
wind-up of the incident, which is, not that the Queen and Lancelot go to
bed together, but that he and Galahalt do so! What this may mean I do
not pretend to fathom, but most commend it to the correspondents of the
provincial paper from which I have to thank you for further inimitable
extracts. The provincial form of All Souls could only have been discovered by a Bulgarian Columbus." The newspaper was an imaginary
publication called "The Bogshire Banner".

123. To Hake (Ashley B.M.).

124. To Mrs. Cowper Temple (Pierpont Morgan).

CHAPTER 27

125. To Bates (Pierpont Morgan).

126. Browning's inscription and letter to Browning (Mrs. Troxell).

CHAPTER 28

127. Letter from Jane Morris (Mrs. Troxell).

128. Letters from Dr. Hake and George Hake, *passim* (Mrs. Angeli).

129. Letters from Treffry Dunn (Mrs. Angeli). Dunn wrote of Alexa (or Alice,
as he calls her) Wilding in the MS. notebook of his *Recollections*: "She

had a deep well of affection within her seemingly placid exterior. She was one of the few Maries of the Sepulchre who journeyed down to Birchington-on-Sea when she could ill afford it so that she might place a wreath on Rossetti's grave" (Mrs. Troxell).

<h2 style="text-align:center">CHAPTER 29</h2>

130. Letters from Dr. Hake to W.M.R. show that they had to leave as Graham wanted the house for a salmon-fishing party (Mrs. Angeli). Professor Doughty assumes that they left because even the beautiful scenery "could not curb Rossetti's restlessness".

131. Dunn's letters *passim* (Mrs. Angeli).

132. Dr. Hake's copy of his letter to Jane Morris (Mrs. Angeli). Rossetti's letter to her is not amongst those preserved at the B.M., showing that there were some that she destroyed. Rossetti's family evidently thought that Jane's influence was bad, for there is a story that after Rossetti's death, when Madox Brown accidentally met her, he did not cut her. He explained this to his daughter and son-in-law, saying, with one of his usual malapropisms: "It was not for me to heap coals of fire on her head."

133. Jane Morris's reply (Mrs. Angeli).

<h2 style="text-align:center">CHAPTER 30</h2>

134. Letters to Howell, *passim* (Texas).

135. To Boyce (University College, London).

136. On Miss Wilding (Mrs. Angeli).

137. To Bell Scott (Mrs. Troxell).

138. I am indebted for the limerick to Mr. Roger Lancelyn-Green.

139. To Parsons (Mrs. Angeli).

140. From S. J. B. Haydon (Mrs. Troxell). He was a sculptor, then solicitor, then print-seller. W.M.R. says he was often at D.G.R.'s studio, but he seems to have been against Watts-Dunton, as a letter from D.G.R. to Fanny says: "He shall *not* sever me from my best and truest friend" (undated) (Mrs. Troxell).

141. In his autobiographical notes, Bell Scott (vol. 11, 178–9) says "had he done this to try me? I fear this semi-insane motive was the true one". But, as Mrs. Troxell points out, the request was made at the time Morris repudiated the co-tenancy: also from Rossetti's letter in her possession, it is clear that here, as elsewhere, Bell Scott's "editing" weights the evidence. The letter of April 19, 1874, quoted on page 179, ends: "You know I am not an unreasonable debtor & you may rely on having it again very soon indeed—in a month at farthest—probably before. I have let the day run to the last postage-time before I could summon impudence enough for this request, so must end here." In the corner Scott noted that he sent the money on Monday, 20th April. The next letter from Rossetti, dated 21st

April and paraphrased by Bell Scott, runs: "My dear Scotus, Very many thanks for your prompt & kind reply. Today however some tin has come earlier than I looked for it & I am thus enabled to return your friendly enclosure, not less thankfully than if I had needed it. Your affec. D.G.R." What is there "semi-insane" here? Incidentally, the speed of the postal service in those days between Kelmscott and Penkill may be noted.

CHAPTER 31

142. To Howell (Texas).

143. Letter from W. Linnell (Texas).

144. Professor Doughty states that "partnership in The Firm was merely formal, being limited to the investment of some five pounds apiece and the making of an occasional design for a stained-glass window". He cites no authority for this and it contradicts Mackail, who says "each of the members holds one share and on the 11th of April the finance of the company began with a call of £1 a share"; and "in January, 1862, a further call of £19 a share was made on the partners". This makes £20 apiece, not £5. Whether the partners actually paid up is another matter. Much work besides designing stained glass was undertaken.

On the 24th of October, 1874, Morris wrote Rossetti the following letter: (Mrs. Angeli)

My dear Gabriel:
I enclose a copy of our last night's resolutions: I do not see how Brown can object to them. As to myself I can't doubt that you will support this peaceful way of settling matters: in fact 'tis the only way left to get out of the deadlock: so will you kindly write a word formally approving of the resolution. As to the naming of the arbitrators, my own private idea of the way of doing it is that Brown should name one and I another and that the third should be some stranger to us both; I am going to write him and tell him as much.

Marshall bore his execution with much indifference and good temper: I suspect he smelt the advent of the golden shower and was preparing to hold his hat under the spout.
I am yours ever William Morris.

Thomas Wardle afterwards married the notorious Madeline Smith, who had been acquitted on a *non proven* verdict in Scotland for the murder of her seducer. Rossetti was interested in the case and once wrote to Watts-Dunton, "when my sitter came, I rejected the first Becky Sharp which leaned too decidedly toward Madeline Smith, and have put a much better one in hand, with an upward tendency towards Lady Macbeth" (Library of Congress).

145. Letters (March & April, 1875) to Watts-Dunton (Library of Congress).

CHAPTER 32

146. To Watts-Dunton (Ashley, B.M.).

147. To Mrs. Rossetti (Mrs. Angeli).

148. To Jenny and May Morris (Ashley, B.M.).

149. To Howell, *passim* (Texas). "Baron" Grant (1830–1899) changed his name from Gottheimer and was given the title of Baron by the King of Italy as a reward for his financial services in connection with the Galleria Vittorio Emanuele at Milan. He was a company promoter and sat as M.P. for Kidderminster. As an Art collector he specialised in Landseer, paying £10,000 for "The Otter Hunt" in 1874.

150. From Burne-Jones (Mrs. Angeli). Incident quoted from *Pre-Raphaelite Twilight* by Mrs. Angeli.

151. With regard to this action George Hake wrote to Watts-Dunton (15th February, 1876) about a paragraph in *The Hornet* saying "Mr. Swinburne, Mr. Dante Rossetti, Mr. O'Shaughnessy and other poets will be subpoenad". Hake wonders or not whether to tell D.G.R.: "not daring to tell him and yet running the risk of deeply offending him by not giving him time to decamp to Italy". He wrote again on 4th May: "The chief annoyance of the trial is, thanks to you, at an end, yet he [D.G.R.] dreads things may come out in the course of it which would not only compromise him but lead to popular agitation against him. One thing, for instance—you know the circumstances which led to the *recovery* of his MS. poems? If not, my father will tell you. This weighs on his mind much and he fears it coming publicly out at the trial" (Mrs. Troxell).

152. Bell Scott on Gosse from autobiographical notes unpublished by Minto (Mrs. Troxell).

CHAPTER 33

153. On Broadlands from F. W. H. Myers, *Fragments of Inner Life*, privately printed, July, 1893. Published by the S.P.R., 1961.

154. Bernard Shaw wrote: "Morris's rages were eclampsias. His lack of physical control when crossed or annoyed was congenital and not quite sane." *The Observer*, November, 1949. "Eclampsias" normally refers to epileptic seizures in pregnant women.

155. Rossetti wrote to Janey, 27th February, 1878, about "Bruna Brunelleschi": "I did not want it to be talked about among strangers by your name, so had christened it Bruna Brunelleschi, of course bearing on the dark complexion—I did think of calling it Vittoria Colonna, who I find was *certainly* the original of those heads by M.A. [Michael Angelo], which are portraits of you: but I thought it would not do to tackle Mike" (B.M.).

156. To Fairfax Murray (Mrs. Troxell).

Chapter 34

157. To Watts-Dunton (Worcester College, Oxford).

158. To Watts-Dunton (Ashley, B.M.).

159. Letters to Miss Munro (Mrs. J. A. R. Munro).

160. To Cecil Schott (Wilmington Art Centre). Letters concerning the Schott family bought by Samuel Bancroft were bequeathed by his family to the Wilmington Art Centre, Delaware, U.S.A. Some of these were not used by Professor Paul Baum in his *Letters*, 1940. See also Appendix G.

    Fanny evidently claimed to have sat for many more pictures than she actually did. A letter from Fred Schott, another stepson, to Bancroft after visiting George Rae's Collection and seeing "Monna Vanna", "The Beloved", "Damozel of the Sangrael" and some early water-colours—for none of which was she the model—wrote: "My mother is delighted to think that you saw Mr. Rae's examples which are with a few exceptions from herself."

161. Rossetti's prices were not high by contemporary standards although there was a boom immediately following his death. He certainly lost by refusing to exhibit at the Grosvenor Gallery and was handicapped by none of his subjects being suitable for reproduction as prints. "The popular framed steel engraving, once the duty on glass had been abolished in 1845, became a distinctly English feature of life and its impact on taste something peculiar to these islands. . . ." A dealer like Gambart paid 5,000 guineas in 1860 for the copyright of Holman Hunt's "Infant Saviour in the Temple". Rossetti's highest fee was for "Dante's Dream": £1,575 from the Walker Art Gallery, Liverpool. Quoted from *The Economics of Taste*, G. Reitlinger.

162. From Bell Scott to Mr. Leathart (Mrs. Leathart).

163. To Hall Caine. Mrs. W. M. Rossetti (Lucy Madox Brown) wrote to *The Athenaeum* (25th July, 1885) that when she and her husband paid one of their last visits to D.G.R. he was walking in the garden "and as we never interrupted these walks, we awaited him in the studio. . . . On entering he greeted us with his usual cordiality, and then asked my permission to write a memorandum for a minute . . . he explained that he had just finished *The King's Tragedy* in the garden and liked to write it at once. . . . Many will feel with me the needlessness of the apology, and admire alike the perfect poetry and the perfect courtesy".

164. Letters to Shields (Duke).

Chapter 35

165. Jane's letters, *passim* (Mrs. Troxell) and Rossetti's, *passim* (B.M.).

166. Jane's hosts at Naworth were George and Rosalind Howard, later Earl and Countess of Carlisle. George Howard, a Liberal M.P., was an amateur painter as well as a patron of *avant-garde* art. In the memoirs of Sir Sidney

Colvin (see *The Colvins and their friends*, E. V. Lucas) he quotes Lady Carlisle's shyness on first meeting Morris in 1870. "He was rather shy— and so was I—I felt that he was taking an experimental plunge amongst 'barbarians' . . . He lacks sympathy and humanity, tho'—and this is a fearful lack to me—only his character is so fine and massive that one must admire—He is agreeable also—and does not snub me—This I imagine may be attributed to Georgy [Burne-Jones] having said some things in my favour . . ." Rosalind, Countess of Carlisle, became later a very formidable figure. As a temperance enthusiast legend has it that she poured all the wine from the cellars down the drain. A pastel sketch of her by Rossetti is at the Ashmolean, Oxford, presented by her daughter, Lady Mary Murray, wife of Professor Gilbert Murray.

167. In view of the space which Professor Doughty devotes to Christmas, 1879 (pages 609–10) and his conjectures that "the ties were loosened" between Rossetti and Janey on account of his "increasing age and illness" and her own recovery while with the Howards at Naworth and in Italy it is essential to quote in contradiction here from the B.M. reserved letters and from Mrs. Troxell's Collection.

At Christmas she wrote of May that she is "very tall and excessively delicate: I think will not drag through a long life. So much the better for her . . . As bright a New Year as is possible dear Gabriel I wish you with all my heart" (Mrs. Troxell). (The reference to May is very surprising to anyone who remembers her sturdiness in later life!)

On 29th December Rossetti answered: "Your letter is true and tender as always," and tells her how on Christmas Day in spite of the incredible weather, "my good mummy nevertheless turned up with one of my Aunts and spent the day very pleasantly looking at pictures & the evening in Xmas pudding etc.". He then encloses a copy of the sonnet "just made" —"Pleasure and Memory", later called "Ardour and Memory".

On this sonnet he asks her, January 30th, 1880, whether it was "conceivable that you put some inconceivable construction upon it?" as she had made no acknowledgement of it. "Of course I have no pique or vanity about so mere a trifle, but merely put the question, as I say, because of what happened (inconceivably to me) long ago. . . ." (B.M.). To this she replied (Mrs. Troxell) "I am quite grieved at my stupidity as regards the sonnet—the truth is I was ill when I received it and would not trust myself to make any remarks on what struck me most at first, its extremely woeful character. . . ." The rest of the letter refers to her reading of Coleridge as quoted in the text. This hardly indicates that she was in too good health to bother with Rossetti any more!

That he took her complaint about the "woefulness" in good part is shown in his letter of the next month (5th February, 1880) enclosing the three "Beryl" songs: "In copying them I perceived them not to be merry, so if that quality is your present favourite in poetry, I fear they will find no favor (sic)." This is not American usage: the "u" in such words is usually omitted by Rossetti and his contemporaries.

168. This is William Davies of Liverpool.

CHAPTER 36

169. From Worcester College, Oxford.

170. In the Catalogue of the Ashley Library, Volume VII (1925), T. J. Wise described this letter as "an A.L.S. of four octave pages addressed to Swinburne by Rossetti—obviously written in 1872", but Mrs. Troxell shows it is much more likely to have been written to Jane Morris in May, 1881. Mrs. Angeli agrees with her and says as it was only a draft it could well have been picked up by Watts-Dunton and mixed with Swinburne's papers. It is obvious from the contents that Wise's interpretation is an error. Rossetti and Swinburne had parted forever before June 2nd, 1872. Messages were exchanged through Watts, but there were never any circumstances under which such correspondence as is indicated here could have taken place. The *Review*, which attacked the poems, and "had quite lately an article in emphatic praise of the Sonnets", was the *Contemporary Review*, which in September, 1880, had an essay by James Ashcroft Noble on David Main's *A Treasury of English Sonnets*, in which Rossetti was called "undoubtedly the greatest of living sonneteers". This dates the letter definitely not as 1872, but as 1880–81.

171. Extract from the last letter in the series preserved at the British Museum.

172. This testimony is written off by Professor Doughty as follows: "It was during that dreary journey—if we accept Caine's unconvincing account, given many years later—that Rossetti, usually so reticent, revealed to this very new acquaintance, whose relationship to him was almost that of a menial, what he had apparently hitherto never spoken of to any of his intimate, life-long friends, the secret of his life's frustration, his passion for Janey." It is surely no uncommon occurrence to confide in a stranger what has been kept from intimates. In what way was Caine a menial?

CHAPTER 37

173. Letters to Shields (Yale).

174. To Miss Munro (Mrs. J. A. R. Munro).

175. Hake's letter (Ashley, B.M.).

176. Howell anecdote from *Pre-Raphaelite Twilight* by Mrs. Rossetti Angeli.

177. The Sphinx sonnets have not been found. Professor Doughty lists them in his Manuscript Sources, but without saying where they are.

178. To Stephens (Bodleian).

CHRONOLOGY WITH PLACES OF RESIDENCE

1828	May 12	Born at 38 Charlotte Street, London.
1835*		Family move to 50 Charlotte Street.
1837		Attends King's College School.
1842*	Summer	Attends Cary's Drawing Academy.
1843		Visits Boulogne.
1846*	July	Proceeds to R.A. Antique School.
1848	January	Meets W. Bell Scott.
	March	Becomes pupil to Ford Madox Brown.
	August	Shares a studio with Holman Hunt in Cleveland Street.
	September	Pre-Raphaelite Brotherhood formed.
1849	March	"The Girlhood of Mary Virgin" shown at the Free Exhibition.
	September	Visits Belgium and Paris with Holman Hunt.
	December	Takes studio at 72 Newman Street.
1850	January	First number of "The Germ".
		Meets Elizabeth Siddal through Deverell.
		Moves to 74 Newman Street.
	October	Visits Sevenoaks with Holman Hunt.
1851		Shares studio at 17 Red Lion Square with Deverell.
		Family now at 38 Arlington Street.
	May	Shares studio at 17 Newman Street with Madox Brown.
1852	November	Moves to 14 Chatham Place, Blackfriars Bridge.
1854		Meets Ruskin. Period of water-colours.
		Visits Hastings.
1855		Visits Paris to join Lizzie. Sees the Brownings there.
1856		Meets Fanny Cornforth. Llandaff commission. Introduction of Edward Burne-Jones by Vernon Lushington.
1857		At Oxford for the Union paintings. Then goes to Matlock to join Lizzie.
1858		Working on Llandaff triptych.
1859		Morris marries Jane Burden and goes to live at Red House, Bexley Heath. Rossetti paints "Bocca Baciata" from Fanny Cornforth.
1860		Marries Elizabeth Siddal at Hastings. Honeymoon in Paris. Foundation of the Morris Firm.

*These dates are given by W. M. Rossetti in his *Memoir*. Professor Doughty changes them but does not cite his authorities.

1861		Publication of *The Early Italian Poets*.
1862	February 10	Death of Elizabeth (Lizzie) Rossetti. Stays with family now at 166 Albany Street, then takes chambers in 59 Lincoln's Inn Fields. Spends Christmas at Newcastle upon Tyne with Bell Scott.
	October	Settles at Tudor House, 16 Cheyne Walk, Chelsea.
1863		Prosperity at Tudor House. Period of large oil paintings, mainly with Fanny Cornforth as model.
	September	Goes to Belgium with W. M. Rossetti.
1864		Success continues and much party-giving in Chelsea.
	November	Visits Paris with Fanny Cornforth.
1865		Morris and family move from Red House to Queen Square, Bloomsbury. Mrs. Morris begins to sit as model, also Alexa Wilding.
1866		Re-touching of pictures and making of replicas.
	October	Visits Winchelsea with Sandys.
1867		Arrival of Treffry Dunn as art assistant. Eye-sight troubles.
	September	Visits Allingham at Lymington.
1868	Spring	Paints "La Pia" with Mrs. Morris for model. Begins writing poetry again.
	August	Visits Speke Hall with Howell.
	September	Walking tour in Warwickshire with Dunn.
	September–November	Visits Penkill Castle, Ayrshire.
1869		At Tudor House working on "Sibylla Palmifera". Morris and Janey go for cure to Ems.
	August–September	Visits Penkill again.
	October	Recovery of the "lost" poems.
1870	April–May	Visits Scalands, Robertsbridge.
	April 25	Publication of *Poems*.
1871	July	With Morris as co-tenant takes Kelmscott Manor, near Lechlade.
	October	Attacked in article on "The Fleshly School" in *The Contemporary Review*.
1872	June	Collapse. Stays with Dr. Hake, then Madox Brown in London. Goes to Scotland to Urrard House and Stobhall (both lent by William Graham, M.P.), then to rooms at Trowan, Crieff.
	September	At Kelmscott again.
1873		Improved health at Kelmscott. Writing sonnets and painting pictures: a new "Dante's Dream", "The Blessed Damozel", "La Ghirlandata".

1874	July	Leaves Kelmscott. Returns to London.
1875	October	Holiday at Aldwick Lodge, Bognor. Mrs. Morris sits for "Venus Astarte".
1876	July	Returns to Tudor House.
	August	Visits the Cowper Temples at Broadlands.
1877	May	Illness.
	July	Convalescence at Hunter's Forestall, near Margate.
	November	Returns. Money troubles with Fanny Cornforth (now Mrs. Schott).
1878		Troubles with creditors and impatient patrons.
1879		Paints Mrs. Morris in "The Daydream".
1880		Finishes "La Pia". New young friends among callers.
1881	August	Hall Caine comes to live at Tudor House.
	September	Visits Keswick.
	October	Publication of *Poems and Ballads*.
1882	February 4	Leaves for Westcliff Bungalow, Birchington-on-Sea.
	April 9	Death.

ACKNOWLEDGEMENTS

I have many friends among descendants of the Pre-Raphaelites as well as students of the period to whom I am indebted for generous co-operation. First and foremost must come Mrs. Helen Rossetti Angeli, with whom it has been the greatest pleasure and privilege to talk of "Uncle Gabriel" and "Aunt Christina" and to take advantage of her remarkable memory of events and people with whom she was so closely connected through her father, William Michael Rossetti. I have, in addition, to thank her for allowing me to quote from material of which she holds the copyright and for making available to me the invaluable note-books concerning Rossetti and Swinburne, bequeathed to her by the late Randolph Hughes. Information provided in her own published books has also, of course, been drawn upon. I have often enjoyed the ready hospitality of Mrs. Angeli's daughter, Mrs. Imogen Dennis, and taken advantage of her talent for recognising likenesses in portraits and for digging out treasures from unlikely places.

To Mrs. Janet Camp Troxell, of New Haven, Connecticut, in addition to her magnificent generosity in allowing me to use the material in her possession, I also owe the experience of a first visit to the United States, made wholly delightful by her hospitality. Mrs. Troxell established her reputation as an expert on the period by her work in *Three Rossettis* (Harvard, 1937) and by contributions to *The Colophon*, New York. Her collection is recognised as a leading one on both sides of the Atlantic. She not only allowed me to see and to use her papers—first editions, corrected proof sheets as well as letters—during my visit, but also put at my disposal articles she had herself prepared on Mrs. William Morris's letters to Rossetti as well as on Morris's pictures and the transactions of "The Firm".

It is also a pleasure to acknowledge the help received during many pleasant meetings with Mrs. J. A. R. Munro, who gave me access to the correspondence of Alexander Munro, and with Mrs. Elizabeth Burt, who allowed me to use her Holman Hunt papers. To Miss Evelyn Courtney-Boyd I am grateful for permission to use papers at Penkill: to Mrs. T. H. Leathart for letters to James Leathart: Mrs. Dorothy Garratt for particulars of her late father, Dr. Robert Steele; Colonel Rudyard Russell for the trouble he took in tracing correspondence with Miss Heaton: Mrs. Witty for information about James Hannay and access to his diaries: Mr. Philip Leigh-Smith for copies of letters to Madame Bodichon.

For help in finding illustrations and for unfailing sustenance of the spirit in moments of crisis or discomfort on Pre-Raphaelite expeditions I must thank

Mrs. Virginia Surtees, who is engaged upon a *Catalogue Raisonné* of Rossetti's pictures.

For the use of pictures hitherto unpublished I am indebted to Mrs. Rossetti Angeli (Mrs. Morris asleep in an armchair), the Warden of All Souls (Morris at his loom), Mrs. Victor Kennett (Annie Miller), Mr. Kerriston Preston (Elizabeth Siddal), Dr. R. R. Wark, Curator of the Art Gallery, the Henry E. Huntington Library (group from letter to Deverell).

I am also grateful for information and references given me by Dr. Joseph Dunlap (the Morris Society, U.S.A.), Professor Cecil Lang (Syracuse, U.S.A.), Professor W. D. Paden (Kansas, U.S.A.), Professor Lionel Stevenson (Duke, N.C., U.S.A.), Professor George Worth (Kansas, U.S.A.), Mr. Peter Bayley, Mr. John Bryson, Miss Jane Douglass, Dr. S. C. Dyke, Mr. Malcolm Elwin, Mr. Ronald Fuller, Dr. L. W. Hanson, Mr. Philip Henderson, Mr. Wendell Stacy Johnson, Mr. Philip Kelly, Mr. Roger Lancelyn-Green, Mr. Roger Peattie, Mr. A. C. Sewter, Mr. Michael Stillman, the executors of the late Gerald Henderson for access to Violet Hunt's papers, and my daughter Anthea.

Grateful acknowledgements to the Editors are also due for permission to quote from articles of mine in "Apollo", July, 1963 and March, 1964, and "The Times Literary Supplement" of April 5th and 12th, 1957, and February 1st, 1964.

In the United States I received from Librarians and the staffs of Universities a full measure of that hospitality and generosity for which Americans are renowned and should like to express my very sincere appreciation of it. For giving up time to finding material and then making it available to me, I must particularly thank Professor C. L. Cline of the University of Texas, Austin, Texas, and Professor Lewis Patton of Duke University, Durham, N.C., as well as the staffs of the following Institutions: The Art Gallery, the Henry E. Huntington Library, San Marino, California. The Pierpont Morgan Library, New York. New York Public Library: Berg Collection and M.S. Division. Wilmington Art Centre, Wilmington, Delaware. The Library of Congress, Washington, D.C. Duke University, Durham, N.C. University of Texas, Austin, Texas. Schaffer Library, Union College, Schenectady, N.Y. Yale University Library, U.S.A.

For courteous and ready assistance I have also to thank the librarians and staff of the following Libraries, Institutions and Art Galleries in Great Britain: The Bodleian Library, Oxford. Worcester College, Oxford. The Society of Antiquaries, London. The British Museum, London. University College, London. The Library of the University of Glasgow, Scotland. The National Gallery of Scotland. The Library of the Victoria and Albert Museum, London.

APPENDICES

APPENDIX A

SOME LETTERS FROM ROSSETTI

I. Rossetti's letter to Deverell

By kind permission of the Art Gallery, Huntington Library, California, I am able to reproduce in full the letter on which Rossetti's sketch of the group at Hannay's was drawn.

V (HM 12910)
(envelope postmarked Aug. 30, 1851)
addressed to Liverpool Arms, Kingston Hill, Kingston-on-Thames.

17 Newman Str.
Saturday.

Dear Deverell,

I know it is a shame that I have not yet answered your last friendly missive —I therefore send as a propitiatory offering, the enclosed cartoon—— It will inform you (at least it ought to) that little Read is come back at last, and spouting "Inez" among us as of old. The reunion represented was held the other night at Hannay's. There were a great number of fellows present besides those represented, but the paper is such beastly stuff to draw upon, that I had not the pluck to put every one in, and I fear that some may already be un-recognizable, since it was impossible to alter anything or go over a line.

Hunt, as I suppose you will see, has been up in town. He has worked upon his picture returned from the R.A. & means, I believe, to send it to Birming-ham—Millais was likewise here the other day, both being in aspect something like the "sun-dried bricks" of Nineveh. I wonder you have not managed to meet them out there.

What do you think? Read made in Florence the acquaintance of Browning; & that stunner being in London at present, we called on him together. He had heard speak of me by Read, & remembered also perfectly our correspondence about "Pauline". He promised to call on me forthwith, which, however, he has not yet done. In person he is short but so well made that he scarcely looks so: his head is most stunning, & even handsome in the common sense of the term. I also saw Mrs. B. who, I am sorry to say between ourselves, is as un-attractive a person as can well be imagined. She looks quite worn out with illness, & speaks in the tone of an invalid. Probably, however, one might manage to forget this if one got into animated conversation with her. Their child seems healthy enough.

William is still at Newcastle with Scott. Before he went I rashly engaged
to write his things for the "Spectator", owing to which they have sent me in
various orders for Exhibitions of Sketches &c—I wrote one (on the trash at
Lichfield House) but have written to say I cannot undertake any more after
these.

I am not doing anything & probably shall cut Art as it is too much trouble.

Yours most sincerely,

D. G. Rossetti.

II. Rossetti's letter to Allingham

The question of plagiarism looms large in the relations between artists of this
period. Rossetti seems to have been particularly concerned with it over the
subject of "Found", as an omitted passage in one of his letters to Allingham
shows. Here, incidentally, it is noticeable that Millais expected to be waited
upon hand and foot and also that as early as 1854 he was being teased for his
snobbery: a letter is addressed to him at Chatsworth.

On page 47 of the published *Letters to Allingham*, after "put in a design I
have made of *Found*", read "Only certain consequences haunt me, which may be
shadowed forth in a rapid dramatic action—'Miching Mallecho—it means
mischief'," all omitted as well as following:

Scene 1 (Aug. 1854)

Robert St. Adelphi

Michael Halliday Esq.—*solus*

Hal. (writes) "I've got the Folio back at last from that lazy wretch Rossetti.
In spite of your prophecy, he really *has* put in a design. The subject is"—
(Halliday proceeds to describe subject and design at length. Then goes on)—
"I hope you'll be back, as you promise, this day week, and that I will see you
at Collins's in the evening. Meanwhile I am yours sincerely, M.H." (He folds
up letter, and addresses it, "John Everett Millais, Esq., A.R.A., Chatsworth,
Derbyshire." Scene closes.)

Scene 2 (Sept. 1854)

Hanover Terrace, Regents Park.

Charles Collins, Esq.   Michael Halliday, Esq.

John Everett Millais, Esq., A.R.A., P.R.B.

Mil. Ah, Halliday, how rum about that design of Gabriel's.

Hal. What's rum?

Mil. Why, that he should have got the same subject that I'm going to paint.
        Did I show you my sketch for it? O, didn't I?

Hal. No, that is odd.

Mil. Ah, you, Collins, it was you that saw it, just before I went into the
        country.

Col. Let's see—I don't remember—at least I'm not sure—I don't know.

Mil.   Well, if you don't know, what's the good of your talking about it? What's the good of sitting in the corner of that sofa with all your clothes on, if you've nothing to say? Stupid little fellow—you're as bad as my mother. Go and get me one of your pocket handkerchiefs and wake up. (Exit Collins.) And I say—just tell your mother to get tea.

Enter Frederick George Stephens Esq'. P.-B.R.

Steph.   (shakes hands with Millais) How are you, old fellow? Looking stunning. Where's Collins?

Mil.   O, he's gone out. I am very glad to see you, old boy. What are you doing?

Steph.   (shakes hands with Halliday) How are you, old fellow? (To Millais) Design.

Mil.   Going to paint it?

Steph.   Yes. (A pause.)

Mil.   Going to put your design in the Folio?

Steph.   Put one in.

Mil.   What is it?

Steph.   "Death & the Riotours" from Chaucer.

Mil.   O, of course, I remember your beginning that when I painted "Isabella".

Steph.   Yes. (A pause.)

Steph.   Ah! have you seen Gabriel's design in the Folio, *Stunning!*

Mil.   No, but Halliday told me. We were talking about that. Ah! it was you, Stephens, that I showed that design of mine to.

Steph.   Which? that in the Folio? Yes! *Stunning!*

Mil.   No—one I did some time ago like Gabriel's, about a woman and a market gardener—finding her in the street.

Steph.   O. No. O. Let's see, though, was it one that wasn't mounted yet?

Mil.   Yes, that was it. (Re-enter Collins with handkerchief.)

Steph.   O, yes, I remember. *Stunning.* (To Collins) How are you, old fellow?

Col.   (shakes hands with Steph.) *How* are you?

Mil.   There, Collins, Stephens remembers that design of mine. (Takes handkerchief from Col.) Ask him—— Don't you, Stephens? There, go and sit down again.—When's that tea coming?

Col.   Soon, I hope.

Hal.   Are you going to paint that design of yours then?

Mil.   Yes, I've got the canvas. My brother couldn't come tonight because he was drawing the perspective for me.

Hal.   It'll be a bore for Rossetti.

Steph.   Ah! sorry for old Gabriel.

Mil.   Lord bless you, he'd never have painted it, you know. You know him. Is he coming hear (sic) tonight, Collins? Ah! he always keeps out of my way. I'll tell you who saw my design and said it was the finest thing he ever saw in his life, Allingham. Ask him.

Steph.   He's gone to Ireland.

Mil.   Ah! When's he coming home?

Steph.   Don't know. (A pause.)

Mil.   (to Steph.) O, my dear fellow, you'll see when I paint this picture, it'll come the loveliest thing you ever saw in your life. I know of a bri(ck) wall to paint in it that's perfectly heavenly. (Goes on to describe brick wall at length.) Ah! you wait till it's finished, Stephens—you'll say it's wonderful, I know.

Steph.   Stunning, old fellow.

Servant (entering) If you please, sir, tea's ready. (Scene closes.)

Scene 3 (May 1855)
Athenaeum Office.
Hepworth Dixon, Esq.—*solus.*

Dix.   (writes) "Our readers will remember that there was one picture in the Royal Academy last year, in reviewing which, while we stated our strong objections without reserve, we did full justice at the same time to the striking originality of the artistic conception. We allude to Mr. Holman Hunt's work entitled *The Awakened Conscience*. Yesterday, at the private view of this year's exhibition, there was no picture which attracted more notice than one to which the same objections present themselves, but to which also it would be impossible to deny the merit of perfect originality in the artist. We speak of Mr. Millais' *Found*. Our readers know that we are not defenders of the School, but it must be universally acknowledged that no living painters except Mr. Hunt and Mr. Millais could have conceived the subjects of these two powerful works." &etc. &etc.

(*Dix. finishes article, and rings bell. Enter Servant.*)

Dix.   Is the boy waiting for copy?

Serv.   Yes, sir.

Dix.   Give him this. (Scene closes.)

THE END.

III. Extract from Rossetti's letter to Holman Hunt on "Found"

Jan. 30th, 1855. . . . I can tell you on my own side, of only one picture fairly begun—indeed I may say, all things considered, rather advanced: but it is only a small one. The subject had been sometime designed before you left England, and will be thought by anyone who sees it when (and if) finished, to follow in the wake of your "Awakened Conscience", but not by yourself, as you know I have long had in view subjects taking the same direction as my present one. The picture represents a London street at dawn, with the lamps still lighted along a bridge which forms the distant background. A drover has left his cart standing in the middle of the road (in which i.e. cart stands baa-ing a calf, tied on its way to market) and has run a little way after a girl who has passed him wandering in the streets. He has just come up with her and she, recognising him, has sunk under her shame upon her knees, against the wall of a raised churchyard in the foreground, while he stands holding her hands as he seized them, half in bewilderment and half guarding her from doing herself a hurt. These are the chief things in the picture which is to be called "Found" and for which my sister Maria has found me a most lovely motto from Jeremiah: "I remember thee; the kindness of thy youth, the love of thy espousals." Is not this happily applicable? "espousals" I feel confident, from knowledge of the two words in two or three languages, would probably be rightlier rendered "bethrothal", which is the word I want, and shall substitute as soon as I have consulted someone knowing Hebrew. The calf—a white one—will be a beautiful and suggestive part of the thing though I am far from having painted him as well as I hoped to do—perhaps through my having performed the feat, necessarily an open air one, in the time just preceding Christmas, and also through the great difficulty of the net drawn over him—the motion constantly throwing one out—me especially, quite new as I was to any animal painting. I wish that if anything suggests itself to you which you think would advantage this subject or any objection you would let me know of it, though otherwise than for such a purpose I cannot expect to hear from you before doing this duty at least once again. [(only Brown and Hughes told about it).] (Mrs. Burt.)

APPENDIX B

ROSSETTI AND BROWNING

From an article by Arthur A. Adrian in P.M.L.A., Vol. 73 (1958), based on letters from Rossetti in the Huntington Library, it appears that it was Read and not Allingham who introduced Rossetti to Browning. See letter to Deverell (HM 12910), page 220. The letters quoted show them to have been on easy terms of familiarity, moving from "My dear Sir" to "My dear Browning". Rossetti takes charge of sending a portrait of Browning by Page to the Royal Academy: (MH 12904) April 1, 1856. "Thither it shall wind, though it be to the *scena* of The Wolf's Glen;—owl, Sir C. Eastlake (his original character)." And on Sept. 21, 1859 (HM 12906) he sends an introduction for Burne-Jones, who is going to Florence, and ends "I wish most heartily that I were accompanying Jones and Princep (whom Jones will introduce to you, and who therefore needs this note no more than he does) and so could see you both at home (with Pennini (sic) too, double his size) sooner than I shall. But it cannot be just now I fear."

Other hitherto unpublished letters show that Rossetti's connection with the Brownings was closer than has been thought. In Mrs. Troxell's possession is the series of letters thanking Browning for the gift of each volume of his poems, extracts from which are quoted here.

Mrs. Troxell also has a letter from Browning to Bell Scott after Rossetti's death, 22nd Nov., 1882, which, after dealing with a missed appointment, continues "I want to talk to you on that particular subject very much—having myself been both misconceiving and—I now find—misconceived by poor Rossetti."

On Browning's connection with the Fleshly School controversy see also De Vane, *A Browning Handbook* (New York, 1955), and *The Harlot and the Thoughtful Young Man: Studies in Philology*, July 1932. In this Professor de Vane compares *Fifine at the Fair* with *Jenny*.

"In writing *Fifine* Browning chose a situation closely similar to Rossetti's. He has his young and thoughtful man of the world in Don Juan, and his harlot in Fifine. Don Juan walks through the fair at Pornic with his wife Elvire, his pale 'spiritual lady', beside him, and sees the gypsy-girl Fifine, who is the perfect representative of the flesh. Don Juan muses upon lust and love, much as Rossetti's young man does, only with more casuistry and sophistry than Rossetti was capable of, and he does not see why it is not possible to love Elvire in the spirit and Fifine in the flesh at the same time."

APPENDIX C

PROSPECTUS OF "THE FIRM"

MORRIS, MARSHALL, FAULKNER & CO.
Fine Art Workmen
In painting, carving, furniture, and the metals
8 RED LION SQUARE, HOLBORN, W.C.

Members of the Firm:

F. Madox Brown	P. Paul Marshall
C. J. Faulkner	W. Morris
Arthur Hughes	D. G. Rossetti
E. Burne-Jones	Philip Webb

The growth of Decorative Art in this Country, owing to the efforts of English architects, has now reached a point at which it seems desirable that Artists of reputation should devote their time to it. Although, no doubt, particular instances of success may be cited, still it must be generally felt that attempts of this kind hitherto have been crude and fragmentary. Up to this time, the want of that artistic supervision which can alone bring about harmony between the various parts of a successful work has been increased by the necessarily excessive outlay consequently on taking one individual artist from his pictorial labours.

The Artists whose names appear above hope, by association, to do away with this difficulty. Having among their number men of varied qualifications, they will be able to undertake any species of decoration, mural or otherwise, from pictures, properly so-called, down to the consideration of the smallest work susceptible of art beautiful. It is anticipated that by such co-operation the largest amount of what is essentially the artist's work, along with his constant supervision, will be secured at the smallest possible expense, while the work done must necessarily be of a much more complete order than if any single artist were incidentally employed in the usual manner.

These Artists having for many years been deeply attached to the study of the Decorative Arts of all times and countries, have felt more than most people the want of some one place where they could either obtain or get produced work of a genuine and beautiful character. They have therefore now established themselves as a firm for the production, by themselves and under their supervision, of—

I. Mural Decoration, either in Pictures or in Pattern Work, or merely in the arrangement of Colours, as applied to dwelling houses, churches, or public buildings.

II. Carving generally, as applied to Architecture.

III. Stained Glass, especially with reference to its harmony with Mural Decoration.

IV. Metal Work in all its branches, including Jewellery.

V. Furniture, either depending for its beauty on its own design, on the application of materials hitherto overlooked, or in its conjunction with Figure and Pattern Painting. Under this head is included Embroidery of all kinds, Stamped Leather and ornamental work in other such materials, besides every article necessary for domestic use.

It is only requisite to state further that work of all the above classes will be estimated for, and executed in a business-like manner: and it is believed that good decoration, involving rather the luxury of taste than the luxury of costliness, will be found to be much less expensive than is generally supposed.

APPENDIX D

OMAR KHAYYAM

At the Pierpont Morgan Library, New York, there is preserved the copy of the *Rubaiyát* that Whitley Stokes gave to Rossetti, dated July 10th, 1861. The Widener Library, Harvard, also has a copy given by Stokes to Sir Samuel Ferguson. Whitley Stokes (1830–1909) was a Celtic scholar. Born in Dublin he came over to London and then went to India to earn a livelihood, but returned without achieving much success and died with his talent largely unrecognised.

The facts are summarised by Carl Weber in *The Library Chronicle of the University of Texas*, Vol. VII, summer 1963. See also Swinburne's letter to A. C. Benson (pp. 108–109) in Benson's *Fitzgerald* in the *English Men of Letters* series and *Fitzgerald's Rubaiyát—Centennial Edition* (Colby College Press, 1959, Waterville, Maine).

For the story of Rossetti at Copsham I am indebted to Professor Lionel Stevenson, Duke University, who has allowed me to quote from his letter: "Meredith's description of the reading of the Rubaiyát at Copsham was given in a letter to *The Times* (15 April, 1909). An almost identical version had previously been recorded by Constantin Photiades in *George Meredith: His Life, Genius and Teaching* (pages 7–8). But in a letter written two or three days before (misdated in the *Letters* with W. M. Meredith's habitual inaccuracy, as July 12, 1862, but obviously written on June 12th), Meredith says 'Rossetti and Swinburne come on Saturday' . . . It doesn't seem to me that Rossetti was at that time so immobile that he would have been incapable of the short train trip to Esher and the walk from the station."

APPENDIX E

MEREDITH AT TUDOR HOUSE

To contradict the bleeding eggs story, Meredith wrote a letter to *The English Review*, 1909, p. 333. "Gossip is hard to deal with. Some years back a little book on Chelsea came to me, wherein I saw it stated that I had left Rossetti's house because of the appearance of ham and eggs on his breakfast plate: 'It was too much for one.' The publication was obscure, the instance given absurd, and I let it pass, as I do usually with newspaper tattle. These reviewers do not reflect on their chance of wounding. What I must have said to some friend was that Rossetti's habits were ominous for his health, and I mentioned the plate of thick ham and fried eggs, taken at once on the descent from his bedroom. I ventured to speak to him of the walk of at least a mile before this trying meal. But he disliked physical exercise, and he was wilful, though he could join in a laugh at his ways. The main point is that he came down with a head full of his work, and, not to be disturbed during the day, he chose a dish that would sustain him through it. The system could not continue for long, of which I had the sorrowful prognostic. Devotion to his work in contempt of our nature killed him. On no other subject have I spoken of the dear fellow—

sometimes playfully with regard to his peculiar habits, I daresay, never in the gossiper's manner."

For further explanation of this episode, see *Virginia Quarterly Review*, xxxii, Spring, 1956, for an article by Witter Bynner on an interview with Meredith at Box Hill in 1902. In this Meredith described his arrival at Tudor House after walking up from Surrey before he had accepted the offer of a room there. "There I found Gabriel in the dining-room, but hardly out of bed, and before him on the table a long slab of ham that had hung at the butcher's too long, been kissed too warmly by the all-kissing sun, and over the ham bled five great eggs. I sat down, looking at him in astonishment: 'Gabriel,' I asked, 'You will eat that?' He said he would. 'Gabriel,' I asked, 'You have exercised?' He said he had not. Wherewith he fell to and in a trice had consumed it all." . . . after working all day he would "walk to London, to one of those cellars where they sang madrigals and glees and loutish ballads. Thackeray put an end to the worst type of their songs by having Colonel Newcome rise up and walk out. I cannot bear the cellars. But some men can. Thackeray could. Gabriel could."

APPENDIX F

ROSSETTI AND WHISTLER

From hitherto unpublished material it appears that Whistler protested to Rossetti from Paris against his "friendship weak in faith" and Rossetti replied in a very carefully-worded letter. W. M. Rossetti drew up for submission to the Club Committee a form of explanation that was not to be an apology which ended: "The world is understood to contain some gentlemen besides English gentlemen: some codes of social honour besides the English and some communities in wh. practices such as that of duelling or the summary castigation of any form of personal insolence, are not yet obsolete. This may or may not be unfortunate or censurable, but a fact it is & it is also a fact that I happen to be a Virginian, a cadet of the military Academy of West Point, & for many years a resident in Paris [crossed out] France." (From the Library, Glasgow University.)

The Rossetti brothers resigned on a matter of principle, i.e. that a Club had no right to interfere in the private affairs of its members or to institute "inquisitional proceedings". Whistler's assaults (in these two cases) had not been committed on Club premises. It was in Paris that he pushed Seymour Haden through the plate glass window of a restaurant and at Luke Ionides' office that he knocked down Legros. Rossetti wrote to Bell Scott begging him not to vote against Whistler: "There will be plenty to do that and if never-theless he should come through with the friends he can muster, you will not be the man to regret that a brother artist should have been able to stand his grounds in spite of odds against him by amateurs and donkeys." (Mrs. Troxell.)

In the case of Legros, Rossetti considered there had been provocation but he tells Bell Scott that for the sake of peace he has had to give orders for neither to be admitted if they call.

Whistler is reputed on his deathbed to have declared that no one must say a word in disparagement of Rossetti. "He was a King." In a letter to W. M. Rossetti he apologises for not having been present at the opening of the Drink-ing Fountain memorial in Cheyne Gardens through the invitation going astray, and regrets that it should "have lost me an occasion of doing honour to a friend of your brother's rare calibre". (Glasgow.)

APPENDIX G

ROSSETTI'S DESIGNS FOR STAINED GLASS

Extracts from an article by A. C. Sewter in *The Journal of the British Society of Master Glass Painters*, 1961.

Of the group of artists upon whom William Morris called for designs when he set up his stained-glass studio in Red Lion Square in 1861, and in the sub-sequent twelve years or so, the most distinguished was Dante Gabriel Rossetti. Curiously enough, however, the voluminous literature on this artist does not include (so far as I am aware) any proper study, or even an adequate list, of his designs for this medium: and the subject remains full of difficulties and obscurities.

Marillier's List

1861	146	*Adam and Eve before the Fall* (cartoons). Two designs for St. Martin's, Scarborough.
	147	*Parable of the Vineyard* (cartoons). Seven designs for St. Martin's, Scarborough.
	148	*The Crucifixion* (cartoon). Design for St. Martin's, Scarborough.
	149	*The Last Judgment* (cartoon). Nine designs in circle executed for Morris and Co.
1862	160	*St. George and the Dragon* (cartoons). Six designs for Morris and Co.

161   *Tristram and Iseult drinking the love potion* (water colour on cartoon). One of the series done for windows in Birkett Foster's house.

162   *King Réné's Honeymoon* (Indian ink). Design for window in Birkett Foster's house.

163   *St. Margaret* (cartoon). Design for stained glass.

164   *Angel swinging a censer* (cartoon). Design for stained glass.

165   *The Annunciation* (cartoon).

166   *Joseph and Mary at the House of St. Elizabeth* (cartoon).

167   *Christ in Glory* (water colour).

272   *The Sermon on the Mount.*

Marillier's list is unfortunately not only very incomplete but also full of errors. The Scarborough *Adam and Eve* and *Crucifixion* are by Ford Madox Brown: neither the *Tristram and Iseult* series nor *King Réné's Honeymoon* have any connection with Birket Foster's house: and *The Sermon on the Mount* was designed in 1862, not 1869. Rather than attempting to proceed by adding to this list, it therefore seems desirable to essay a completely fresh one.

There is a scarcity of documents upon which full reliance might be placed, but the following notes are the results of my studies of Marillier's own MS. notes and indexes (now in the Library of the Birmingham City Art Gallery), checked against the windows themselves and against whatever other evidence I have succeeded in finding. Doubtless this list is still incomplete, but it includes everything of which I have sure information. Perhaps it is worth while to add that the *St. Peter*, in the centre of the chancel south window at Bradford Cathedral, was removed when the building of the new Lady Chapel was commenced (opened 1963) and is now in store. The original cartoon is at the William Morris Gallery, Walthamstow (A19), where it is attributed to Rossetti, but in my opinion is by Albert Moore, who designed the central figure for the Bradford east window.

Date	Title and description	When and where executed
1861	The Sermon on the Mount	1862. All Saints, Selsley, Gloucs.
		1864. Christ Church, Albany Street, London.
		1865. Christ Church, Sunderland (centre panel only).
1861	Minstrel Angel with double-pipe and crossed bands	1862. All Saints, Selsley.
1861	Censing Angel in circle, kneeling to right.	1861. All Saints, Selsley.
		1863. St. Michael and All Angels, Lyndhurst, Hants.
		1870. St. James, Brighouse, Yorks.

Date	*Title and description*	*When and where executed*
1861	*Censing Angel* in circle, kneeling to left	1861. All Saints, Selsley.
		1863. St. Michael and All Angels, Lyndhurst.
		1870. St. James, Brighouse.
1861	*The Visitation*	1862. All Saints, Selsley.
1861	*Christ on the Cross*	c. 1862. All Saints, Langton Green, Kent. Centre light of the east window. In a re-arrangement of the windows in 1910, this window was removed and is now the north aisle east window at St. Mary, Doddington, Cambs.
		1863. All Saints, Dedworth, Berks.
		1865–66. St. Olave, Gatcombe, I.o.W.
1861	*The Lady of Woodbank*, standing in a garden; a portrait of Mrs. Aldam Heaton, inscribed "AH EH / Woodbank / DGR AD 1861"; together with two small spandrels of Mrs. Heaton's daughters.	1861. These panels, which must be among the earliest made by the Morris firm, no doubt resulted from Rossetti's acquaintance with Aldam Heaton, who took "Woodbank", an old farmhouse at Harden, near Bingley, Yorks, in 1860. When the Heatons left "Woodbank" in 1876, they apparently took the glass with them; the three panels were returned to the house about 1952 by a grandson and have been fitted by the present owner, Mr. Geoffrey W. Wood, into the dining-room window.
1861	*The Parable of the Vineyard*, a series of seven panels.	The panels originally made for showing at the International Exhibition of 1862; subsequently incorporated in the east window of St. Martin's, Scarborough.
1861	*Last Judgment*, nine designs in circle.	Not identified.

Date	Title and description	When and where executed
	Bethlehem Gate.	Not identified.
1862	Abraham's Sacrifice	c. 1862. Peterborough Cathedral: south transept.
		1873. Holy Trinity, Bingley, Yorks.
1862	Joseph lifted from the Pit (attribution uncertain).	c. 1862. Peterborough Cathedral: south transept.
1862	Annunciation	c. 1862–3. Holy Rood, Rodbourne, Wilts.
1862	Christ in Majesty	1864. St. Peter's (now cathedral), Bradford.
		c. 1864. St. Paul, Manningham, Bradford, Yorks.
1862	The Story of St. George (series of six panels).	According to Marillier's notes, the glass was made for Harden Hall, Bingley, Yorks., but this is almost certainly a mistake. He notes that a second set was made for Sir Walter Armstrong in 1873 (still at Cragside, Rothbury, Northumberland) and a third set of five panels only in the same year for Pease. The full set in the V. and A. is almost certainly the original one of 1862.
1862	Two panels of the series and another illustrating The Story of Tristram and Yseult as told in Malory's "Morte d'Arthur".	1862. Commissioned by Walter Dunlop for the decoration of the entrance hall at Harden Grange, Bingley. The set is now at Bradford City Art Gallery.
1862	Music, or King Réné's Honeymoon	It is not known for what purpose the glass was made, but it may possibly have been for showing at the 1862 Exhibition. Now at the V. and A., London.
1862–3	St. Jude	1862–3. Christ Church, Sandgate, Middlesex.
		1869–70. St. Martin, Low Marple, Cheshire.
c. 1864	St. Mary Magdalene	1864. St. Peter's (now cathedral), Bradford.

Date	Title and description	When and where executed
c. 1864	*Martha*, carrying jug, saucepan and ladle.	1864. St. Peter's (now cathedral), Bradford.
		1865. St. Mary, Antingham, Norfolk.
	Joshua	Not identified. Similar to the *Joshua* by P. P. Marshall in the third window of the north aisle at St. Martin's, Scarborough, except that there he holds a lance with both hands.

APPENDIX H

ROSSETTI'S MEDICAL HISTORY

From a paper presented to the Royal Society of Medicine and published in "Proceedings LVI", December, 1963, by S. C. Dyke, D.M., F.R.C.P.

W. M. Rossetti noted the beginnings of ill-health in his brother in 1866, "when he became subject to a complaint (I do not care to define it) which requires medical treatment from time to time . . ." This was a hydrocele.

Towards the end of the summer of 1867 his eye-sight began to fail. He consulted Sir William Bowman, who assured him that the weakness of sight depended upon general overstrain and nervous upset. Sir William Bowman is one of the outstanding figures of Western medicine, who spread his name through the human body to an extent unequalled by any other anatomist. He was among the first to become expert in the use of the ophthalmoscope, invented in 1851 by Helmholtz.

In the year 1867 Rossetti also saw Sir William Gull (1816–1890), who appears to have been unable to find anything organically wrong. Gull was on the staff of Guys and was one of the most eminent physicians of his day. He is remembered mainly for his work with Sutton on sclerosis of the renal arterioles, which may be regarded as the commencement of present-day views on nephritis. Professor Paden, of Kansas, U.S.A., in his monograph on "La Pia", suggests that Rossetti's transient impairment of vision was due to arterial hypertension. Had this been the case Bowman and Gull of all practitioners of their day, would have been the most likely to identify it. His recovery provides abundant evidence of a psychological background to the episode.

W. M. Rossetti records that in 1867 at the onset of failure of vision, his brother began suffering from insomnia . . . "although his vision improved after 1869, the insomnia did not", and Rossetti embarked upon the use of chloral. Chloral was discovered by Liebig in 1832, but was not included in the British Pharmacopoeia until 1874. As with most things outside his poetry and his painting, Rossetti was very casual in his use of medicines. Hall Caine relates that he used to record with glee how, as a young man, he produced disastrous symptoms by taking three doses of a tonic containing *nux vomica* in quick succession to make them fit into his day. The initial dose of chloral, said to have been 10 grains, was washed down with neat whisky, then rapidly increased until Rossetti boasted to Hall Caine that he was taking 180 grains. Whether he did ever take this amount is doubtful, as John Marshall saw to it that the chemist diluted the prescription.

Dr. John Marshall attended all the P.-R.B. in the early days of the movement, apparently free of charge. Few readers of their biographies realise that he was one of the greatest surgeons of his day, at one time President of the Royal College of Surgeons and a Fellow of the Royal Society.

After the collapse on 7th June, 1872, when Rossetti was taken to Roehampton, Dr. Hake discovered an empty bottle of laudanum and initiated treatment by inhalations of *ammonia forte*. Fortunately, Dr. Marshall arrived soon after and at once started treatment by strong coffee, by what route is nowhere stated. On regaining consciousness Rossetti experienced some loss of power in the left leg, no doubt pressure palsy, which rapidly improved during convalescence in Scotland. He made an astonishing recovery and became active as ever at painting at Kelmscott. In 1874 he returned to London, where he became progressively more depressed. On 17th December, 1881, he experienced a paralysis of the left arm and leg which Marshall attributed to the chloral, and stated that "the time has come when the chloral must be decisively, instantly and entirely cut off". The agent chosen to bring this about was Henry (later Sir Henry) Carr Maudslay, described by W. M. Rossetti as a "young medical student" (actually he had qualified at University College Hospital in 1880), nephew of Henry Maudslay, founder of the hospital which now bears his name. He was then inveighing against the use of chloral in psychiatry. Sir Henry later migrated to Australia, where to him was attributed "the birth of neurology". In the 1914–18 war he was in command of the First Australian General Hospital at Heliopolis. He died in 1945.

Maudslay accompanied Rossetti to Birchington, where for the chloral he substituted laudanum, morphia by injection, and whisky in unlimited doses. W. M. Rossetti reported that on this régime his brother got "a fair amount of sleep but is perturbed by painful opium dreams and the same impression remains with him when awake. Maudslay says the real cause of these hallucinations is not the morphia but cessation of the chloral which seems to me odd." It also does to me.

The paresis of the left arm continued and the local practitioner, Dr. Harris, diagnosed some degree of softening of the brain. On 8th April Dr. Marshall and Dr. Harris agreed that the symptoms pointed to "uraemia (blood poisoning from uric acid)" and treatment was initiated by sweating and applying hot stupes to the loins.

The manner of death leaves no doubt that Rossetti was suffering from arterial degeneration. I believe that undue importance has been attached to the influence of the chloral addiction upon Rossetti's health, mental and physical: in spite of it he continued to do good work until within a short time of his death and its withdrawal can have had no effect upon the outcome of his last illness.

APPENDIX I

RELATIONS BETWEEN D. G. ROSSETTI AND JANE MORRIS

On the death of May Morris in 1939, her literary adviser, Dr. Robert Steele,* deposited at the British Museum a packet of letters from Rossetti to Mrs. Morris on reserve for fifty years from the date of her death in 1914. These letters therefore became free on the 27th January, 1964 (the 26th being a Sunday), and with three friends to help me to copy them, I was first at the British Museum to see them. I wrote a short article on them for the *Times Literary Supplement* of that week, 30th January. There are one hundred and seventeen letters: the first is dated 4th March, 1868 and the last 4th October, 1881. There must have been many others, now destroyed: e.g. the letter from Trowan about which Dr. Hake wrote is not preserved.

In my article I said that the letters provide no evidence to support the conjectures of contemporaries and those survivors of the period who could speak with authority—Sir Sydney Cockerell and Professor Mackail (see *A Victorian Romantic*, O. Doughty, O.U.P., 1960)—and further study of them has done nothing to change that opinion. In order not to interfere with the flow of narrative in the text I am giving the relationship fuller consideration here and have appended some little-known comments from contemporaries, together with a letter from Mrs. Morris referring to an article by Harry Quilter. As I concluded my article, what is important is that there remain Rossetti's pictures and poems for which she was the model:

"Let all men note
That in all years, (O Love, thy gift is this!)
They that would look on her must come to me."

*Dr Steele was a distinguished medievalist who admired Morris and remained a devoted friend to his widow and daughters. He edited Roger Bacon (*Opera hactenus inedita*) and translated, among other learned works, the *Love Poems* of Charles D'Orleans. He was also an expert on the history of printing on which he had several books published. An Honorary Doctor of Durham University, he was also a Corresponding Fellow of the Medieval Academy of America.

Reaction to the relationship goes through different stages for each of the protagonists. Although, according to Hall Caine, Rossetti declared that he had been in love with Janey from the time of the Oxford Union decoration, when he was already tied to Lizzie, the letters do not bear this out. In 1865 he was quite unsentimental over trading pictures of her with Boyce, whose *Diary* entry shows he bought a sketch of her for £10 which had been agreed upon in a letter to him from Rossetti referring to "Mrs. Topsy" and saying, "I'll send her on Monday with the rest." (University College.) The tone of the 1868–69 letters is purely friendly with no hint of emotion. It is in 1869–70 that they change, culminating in the Ems period. From these it would appear that he fell in love with Janey during her sittings in Tudor House, or, as I prefer to interpret it (not inconsistently with Hall Caine's version), Rossetti then came to realise that it was she he had loved all the time and should have tried to marry years earlier. His letters show him disappointed that he never had the opportunity to prove his love, whether by sexual intercourse or by setting up house together permanently is not clear.

Morris expressed to sympathetic women friends his sense of personal failure in marriage or in some other sexual relationship. That he was unhappy at this period his letters to Aglaia Coronio show, but it is possible that the allusions in them do not apply to Janey at all, but to some other woman—"a Female complication", for writing in 1881 to Georgie Burne-Jones he still refers to his depression and "troubles of which I wont speak". At this date Rossetti's relationship with Janey cannot have been the cause. When Mackail wrote to Mrs. Coronio (quoted by Philip Henderson, *T.L.S.*, 7th September, 1951) of his having been hampered by the need to use tact in his account of "all those stormy years of *The Earthly Paradise*" he may have been referring to suppression of evidence of the relations between Morris and Georgie Burne-Jones.

Jane's attitude is the most difficult to assess. It is essential to remember all through that she was not like her looks. She was not a goddess but a romp and a "little woman". Disconcertingly, she was also unexpectedly intelligent; capable of mastering foreign languages and absorbing serious books. That she could be on terms of intimacy with people like the liberal-intellectual Howards and the Scawen Blunts, with whom she travelled to Egypt in her widowhood, presents yet another puzzle, particularly in view of the fact that Mrs. Howard had invited Blunt specially to meet Janey in 1883 and it was not until six years later that he came to know Morris himself. Not only was Janey bored with Morris, but she grew tired of his sudden rages (a point very seldom emphasised, but what Bernard Shaw, an admirer, called his "not quite sane" displays of temper cannot have been easy to live with) and of his neglect of her; note that Rossetti expresses a hope that her daughters are worthy companions (B.M. letters). Towards Rossetti she seems to have been almost as much a *Dame Lointaine* as Elizabeth Siddal. She was not a Guinevere prepared to lose all for love, but a woman, intelligent and sympathetic, enjoying admiration and repaying it with tender but cautious solicitude. Professor

Doughty repeatedly implies that Janey caused Rossetti great suffering by her instability where he was concerned: "Was she temperamental, changeable, sentimental, tired of her 'romance' with Rossetti, growing afraid of him since his mental breakdown?" Even as early as 1874 he queries: "Was it accident or a revival of sentiment that led the Morrises at Bruges to occupy the rooms they had taken during their honeymoon some fifteen years before?" Actually Morris wrote one of his most depressed letters to Aglaia Coronio from the hotel at this time saying that *he* has the room now that he and Janey had on their wedding trip, and that he devoutly wishes he were at home. Again in 1877–78, when Janey is in Italy, Doughty writes: "Whatever the reason, Janey was certainly more elusive than of old." On the contrary Janey was writing to Rossetti from Italy for money; she was discouraging Morris from joining her; his stay when he came was made miserable, first by his illness and then by hers. There was nothing "elusive" about all this. Professor Doughty also says that there was more social life at Kelmscott and implies that Janey was thoroughly enjoying it. Again, turning to her own letters, she wrote Rossetti from Naworth Castle in August, 1879: "Kelmscott is out of the question for me this year. I was *too* ill to manage an extra house and entertain visitors." Of 1879, Professor Doughty writes: "Had that long sojourn in Italy of Janey's with the Howards and later with Morris, and again those weeks in August when she had been the Howards' guest at Naworth, had these combined with Gabriel's increasing age and illness to loosen the ties between them?" This stay with the Howards was at a time when she was so far from well that she ended one of her letters from Naworth to Rossetti: "I must finish. I have fainting fits still if I sit up for more than a few minutes."

Whether her ill-health was cause or effect of her withdrawals it is not possible to tell without medical evidence, and no doctors are mentioned in correspondence; even Marshall never appears. Fortunately for Rossetti's nerves, he did not only desire her physically (he was not always ill during the period of "regenerate rapture"), he also wanted her as a model for his pictures ("I loved thee 'ere I loved a woman, Art") and to a considerable extent in this— and in his poems—he was able to sublimate his sexual love for her. There are other forms of love and Rossetti was steeped in medieval forms of them. There were times when he asked nothing better than to sit and read to her. (19th February, 1870) "To be with you and wait on you and read to you is absolutely the only happiness I can find or conceive in this world, dearest Janey, and when this cannot be, I can hardly now exert myself to move hand or foot for anything." They found each other good company as their reading together, their jokes and gossip about friends, and their walks at Kelmscott show.

By the late 1870s, when his desire for her had subsided, her kindness towards him increases. She did not want to lose him. The letters quoted from Mrs. Troxell's Collection show her ready to call (indeed, it is he who insists on knowing beforehand, no doubt because of Fanny and, in the end, his family being there); she is as solicitious about his health as about her own, and on the subject of the weather they are in complete harmony. The correspondence, 1878–81, is like that between a long-married couple, or two people who have shared a love-affair in the past which, to their regret, was never consummated. In middle age love had turned to kindliness indeed.

Whatever reconciliation, or agreement to live together in outward amity, there may have been round 1875, it is clear that from the 1880's when Morris entered upon his socialist phase, Janey's withdrawal from him became a hostile aloofness. Bernard Shaw noted that she never spoke to her husband at all. He may then well have wished there had been another person ready to take the edge off her boredom and distaste! It is significant that when he travelled by rail third-class on principle she objected to being "scrowdged" by the proletariat and for going second he has to apologise to his new political friends. Perhaps the groom's daughter had been tamed all too well into a middle-class matron under the influence of the Burne-Jones' and their set, whom she met when she was only twenty, for she was certainly conventional in her insistence on respectability. Later she disapproved of her daughter May's marriage with one of Morris's workmen—Halliday Sparling—and discouraged the attentions of a penniless journalist like Bernard Shaw. There was a lot in Rossetti that seemed "mad" to her, but she did not break with him, no doubt because she enjoyed his admiration and wanted to retain it, and also because she felt sorry for him.

She seems to have mellowed with old age. She certainly became stronger in health: the invalid of the 1860's and 70's outlived both Rossetti and Morris, and died in 1914, aged seventy-five. Her letters to Sir Sydney Cockerell (Victoria and Albert Museum) show her as gentle—on the anniversary of Morris's death, 3rd October, 1898, she writes: "I perceive that I am really rich, but feel inexpressibly poor today". At the same time she is practical; with reference, for instance, to the sale of Rossetti's pictures of her. Her obituary referred to "the kindliness, good sense and the girlish love of fun which remained hers until the end of life".

Among those who met her, Sir Arthur Richmond has told me that as a boy he was terrified of her, as she never addressed him, but he knew that his mother got on well with her and saw a lot of her when they were neighbours on Hammersmith Mall. Probably the most illuminating description of her by a contemporary is that of the late Sir William Rothenstein in his *Men and Memories*, 1931. Here he says that he visited Mrs. Morris at her daughter's house in Hammersmith Terrace: "She had retained much of the beauty which Rossetti had immortalised . . . I had heard and read of her moving, a noble figure, among the great people about her husband and Rossetti—noble but silent. I found her serene indeed, but interested in a thousand things: an admirable talker, wholly without self-consciousness, always gracious, and in her person beautifully dignified . . ." Later on he recounts that Dr. Steele found she preferred Rothenstein's "concrete" mind to Shannon's poetical one.

After Rossetti's death, Janey wrote the following letter to Watts with its pathetic sentence, "I feel that I want to talk to someone about him."

Sunday Silverleigh
Lyme Regis
Dorset (Feb. 1883)

My dear Mr. Watts,

So many thanks for sending reviews. I suppose we must regard them as praising the works. But how it would have enraged the painter himself. Fancy his hearing it said that his greatest work was done about 1866! He would have gone raving mad on the spot, even though it had been but a remark of the pink pig's [Quilter]. The swinish tastes of the said creature are not to be wondered at, but it is a little surprise to me that Colvin and one or two others of the more decent art critics should have taken something of the same view of the works painted about that time. I agree heartily with those who consider the early work the best, but I think the same might be said of most of men's works. There is a freshness, an interest in everything, a wealth of invention which is seldom seen except in the productions of the first few years of manhood, and all this without questioning the sanity of a man. That Gabriel *was* mad was but too true. No one knows that better than myself, but that his work after 1868 was worthless (as Gosse has the impudence to assert) I deny.

I don't know why I'm writing all this to you but I feel that I want to talk to someone about him. I am not likely to be in town for a very long time to have any actual talk with you. Jenny is very ill still. I am almost in despair about her.

As to the copy of May's drawing, I would not for the world consent to having it copied for anyone else, but if you really wish it and Dunn can do it while on the matter of the Burlington, I say yes with pleasure, but I cannot let it go out of my keeping after the exhibition closes.

There is something written on the envelope of your letter I can't get at, it having all stuck together. Hope it was not important.

*Extract from article on Rossetti by Harry Quilter in "The Contemporary Review",
February, 1883*

". . . There is probably no record of a painter whose personality grew to be so submerged in the form and face of one woman as did that of him of whom we are writing. It is scarcely too much to say that for the last twenty-five years of his life everything he wrote and painted could be traced to her in one way or another.

But this is a personal matter upon which I have no right to dwell: it is only necessary that the man being what he was,—being 'out of suits with fortune', more or less from the beginning of his life, having suffered the great loss of his wife almost as soon as he had been united with her, and being subsequently possessed by the strange beauty of the face he has made so familiar to us,—it is not wonderful that towards the close of his life his painting grew to be little more than a desponding echo of itself, an oft repeated cry of grief or weariness."

Extract from a passage in Moncure D. Conway's Autobiography

"We comprehend the mystical meaning of that kiss of Eros (in Rossetti's painting 'Love leading Dante to Beatrice on the day of her death'), for the face of Love was that of the young wife he had lost, and the Beatrice on whom Love's lips were pressed was Mrs. William Morris. His wife . . . might well have leaned out of heaven to kiss Mrs. Morris for it was she who had lifted the soul of Rossetti out of the grave; I have not in my long life known any-thing more quasi-miraculous than this re-appearance in modern London of Dante and Beatrice . . . The superb lady, great-hearted, and sincere, recog-nised the fine spirit to which she was related, and responded to his visions and ideals . . . She was honoured by all who knew her and Dante Rossetti as one who thought for herself and was great enough to live in accordance with her own heart."

Unpublished extract from a letter written by F. S. Ellis to W. Bell Scott

(Torquay, July 7th, 1887) [following an account of a visit to Kelmscott where he managed to keep Morris off too much talk on his socialism] . . . "if I thought his opinions on the relations of the sexes in old days were the same as he professes to hold now—why then you might believe anything—as it is I am quite inclined to forget old histories—whatever fault, if any, attached to the poor lady in question I fear she has had and has ample room and cause for repentance & regret and has rather a sad time of it now all things considered." (Miss Courtney-Boyd.)

APPENDIX J

SOME POEMS BY ROSSETTI

THE END OF IT

Rossetti's first poem

His brows met, and his teeth were set,
    And his mouth seemed in pain,
And madness closed and grappled with him
    As they turned his bridle-rein
And albeit his eyes went everywhere,
    Yet they saw not anything:
And he drew the bit tightly, for he thought
    That his horse was stumbling.

There was a great shouting about him
    And the weight of a great din:
But what was the battle he had around
    To the battle he had within?
A pond in motion to the stress of the ocean,
    A lamp to a furnace-eye,
Or the wind's wild weeping-fits
To the voice of Austerlitz
    When it shook upon the sky.

Hark, hark, hark! through the spangled dark,
    To the left and to the right,
Hark, hark, hark! how the muskets bark
    Like ban-dogs heard at night;
While the trumpets, all day shrill for blood,
    Laugh with a cruel heave,
Ringing out fame and ringing in shame—
    A peal for a New Year's eve.

He stared right out, and he turned him about,
    And he knew that It must fall;
He knew the trodden ground for its bier
    And the cannon-smoke for its pall.
Spurring, he gazed not back, but sped
    As speedeth the speedy wind,
When, bound as far as St. Helena,
    It leaves Waterloo behind.

              18th June, 1845.

AFTER THE FRENCH LIBERATION OF ITALY

As when the last of the paid joys of love
    Has come and gone: and with a single kiss
    At length, and with one laugh of satiate bliss
The wearied man one minute rests above
The wearied woman, no more urged to move
    In those long throes of longing, till they glide,
    Now lightlier clasped, each to the other's side,
In joys past acting, not past dreaming of:
So Europe now beneath this paramour
    Lies for a little out of use,—full oft
Submissive to his lust, a loveless whore,
    He wakes, she sleeps, the breath falls slow and soft.
Wait: the bought body holds a birth within,
An harlot's child, to scourge her for her sin.

"This sonnet was written in 1859, after Napoleon III, seconded by the Piedmontese army, had expelled the Austrians from Lombardy, and had concluded the peace of Villafranca, whereby Venetia was left unenfranchised from the Austrian yoke, and all the rest of Italy had to shift for itself as best it might, while France secured Savoy and Nice, and garrisoned the Pope in Rome. Rossetti had, of course, no objection—quite the contrary—to Napoleon's action in liberating Lombardy: but he objected to the other features of his Italian policy, and wrote this sonnet to commemorate his forecast of bad times for Europe generally. The sonnet was printed in 1869, along with the privately-printed poems, but it was not published until 1904: the reason for withholding it being not anything involved in its real subject-matter, but the strong form of imagery and words in which this is clothed." W. M. Rossetti.

In the Berg Collection there is a corrected MS. with the last six words of the first line crossed through and pencilled at the side in substitute for them: "warm joy of hireling love".

NUPTIAL SLEEP

At length their long kiss severed, with sweet smart:
    And as the last slow sudden drops are shed
    From sparkling eaves when all the storm has fled,
So singly flagged the pulses of each heart.
Their bosoms sundered, with the opening start,
    Of married flowers to either side outspread
    From the knit stem; yet still their mouths, burnt red,
Fawned on each other where they lay apart.

Sleep sank them lower than the tide of dreams,
    And their dreams watched them sink, and slid away.
Slowly their souls swam up again, through gleams
    Of watered light and dull drowned waifs of day;
Till from some wonder of new woods and streams
    He woke, and wondered more, for there she lay.

APPENDIX K

CECIL SCHOTT

Some of the letters concerning the Schotts, bought by Samuel Bancroft and bequeathed to the Wilmington Art Centre, Delaware, U.S.A., were not used by Professor Paull Baum in his *Letters*, 1940. They deal with Cecil's progress in Shields' studio and what holidays he should be allowed.

A letter (Duke University Library) from Rossetti, only dated "Thursday", recommends Cecil Schott to Shields as an assistant. "This evening I named it to his mother, who said that it would be of all things what his father wd. most desire, she said the boy is perfectly tractable & wd. obey you in everything & I believe she is quite right. He has been well brought up. As for his talents, I believe he would profit by being with you to such an extent that he wd. soon do much of the subordinate work as well as you cd. do it yourself. . . . There was something said of paying *you* to take the boy, but I know they cannot afford it and I am sure his work wd. soon pay you." It is this letter which has the PS. on Schott's character.

Some light was thrown on Cecil Schott's later life by an article in *The Times* of 13 June, 1962, entitled "Victorian Village Worthies":

A series of sketches of local characters who were customers of The Darnley Arms in the village of Cobham was rescued by "an alert local historian from a heap of junk destined for the dustman". A Correspondent (author of the article) writes "I was told that the artist responsible for these caricatures was a young man who had come down from London and taken lodgings in the village . . . he had gone each evening to The Darnley Arms, where in return for a pint of beer he had been happy to draw anyone . . . But there was considerable element of doubt about his identity. I was variously assured that his name had been Cecil Scott, Cecil Schotte (a German) and Sir Cecil Shott (a Royal Academician) . . . The name Schott raised a faint echo in my memory and the pursuit of this echo led me to John Bernard Schott—the odd character Fanny Cornforth, Dante Gabriel Rossetti's model, mistress and housekeeper, married as her second husband in November, 1879. . . . J. B. Schott had had two sons by his first wife . . . The younger of these two boys whose early drawings Rossetti had praised and in whose artistic education Rossetti had taken a practical interest was called Cecil. I have little doubt that he was our man . . ." The writer goes on to say that the sketches show considerable artistic talent and had been considered to be "speaking likenesses" in the village.

APPENDIX L

LAST WILL AND TESTAMENT

This is the last will and Testament of me Gabriel Charles Dante Rossetti . . . of sixteen Cheyne Walk Chelsea I revoke all former wills I give and bequeath to my mother my sister Christina Georgina Rossetti and my brother William Michael Rossetti any such small drawing or other article as each of them may select as a memento of me and to my friends Ford Madox Brown late of thirty seven Fitzroy Square London William Bell Scott of ninety two Cheyne Walk Chelsea Edward Burne-Jones of The Grange West Kensington Walter Theodore Watts of The Pines Putney Hill London Algernon Charles Swinburne of The Pines Putney Hill aforesaid Frederick R. Leyland of one Princes Gate London Frederick I. Shields of seven Lodge Place St. John's Wood London and Thomas Hall Caine of sixteen Cheyne Walk Chelsea any such small drawing or other article as each of them may select as a memento of me subject to the approval of my executor hereinafter named I give and bequeath to my friend Mrs William Morris of Kelmscott House Hammersmith three of the largest and best of the chalk drawings for the subjects of which she sat that are now hanging in my studio at Cheyne Walk Chelsea aforesaid to be selected by her also the profile head of her in chalk now hanging over the mantelpiece in the studio And as to the remainder of my real and personal property I direct my executor hereinafter named as soon as may be found convenient after my decease to sell and convert it into money and out of the proceeds thereof after the payment of all my just debts and testamentary expenses to divide the entire sum between my said mother and my said brother William Michael Rossetti or their legal representatives in equal shares and proportions And I authorize and empower my said executor hereinafter named to act entirely as he thinks best as to the time and mode of realizing my estate more especially with regard to the copyrights of my pictures and writings I bequeath to my friends William Graham of Grosvenor Place London and L. R. Valpy late of London now of Bath any such small drawing or other article as each of them may select as a memento of me subject to the approval of my executor I appoint my said brother William Michael Rossetti of five Endsleigh Gardens sole Executor of this my will

Signed: April 8th 1882 at

Birchington

Kent

BOOK LIST

Allingham, H. (editor): *William Allingham: a Diary*, 1907.

Andrews, Keith: *The Nazarenes*, 1964.

Angeli, Helen Rossetti: *Dante Gabriel Rossetti, His friends and enemies*, 1949.

Angeli, Helen Rossetti: *Pre-Raphaelite Twilight: The story of C. A. Howell*, 1954.

Baldwin, Lord: *The Macdonald Sisters*, 1960.

Baum, Paull F.: *An analytical list of MSS in Duke University Library* (Duke, 1931).

Baum, Paull F.: *D. G. Rossetti's Letters to Fanny Cornforth* (Baltimore, 1940).

Bell, Quentin, *The Schools of Design*, 1963.

Belloc, B. R.: *A Passing World (Madame Bodichon)*, 1897.

Benson, A. C.: *Rossetti*, 1906.

Bickley, F.: *The Pre-Raphaelite Comedy*, 1932.

Blunt, W. Scawen: *My Diaries*, 1919 and 1920.

Bobbitt, Mary Reed: *With dearest love to all*, 1960.

Bottomley, Gordon: *Correspondence with Paul Nash*, 1955.

Bowra, C. M.: *The Romantic Imagination*, 1957.

Boyce, G. P.: *Diaries from The Old Water Colour Society's Nineteenth Annual Volume*, 1941.

Burne-Jones, Lady: *Memorials of Sir Edward Burne-Jones*, 1912.

Caine, T. Hall: *Recollections of D. G. Rossetti*, 1882 and 1928.

Caine, T. Hall: *My Story*, 1908.

Carr, J. Comyns, *Some Eminent Victorians*, 1908.

Cassidy, John A.: *Robert Buchanan and the Fleshly Controversy*, P.M.L.A., vol. lxvii, 1952.

Conway, Moncure D.: *Autobiography*, 1904.

Collins, Mortimer: *Two plunges for a pearl*, 1872.

Colvin, Sir S.: see Lucas, E. V.

Compton-Rickett, A.: *Portraits and Personalities*, 1937.

De Vane, W. C.: *A Browning Handbook* (New York, 1955).

Dickason, David H.: *The Daring Young Man* (American P.R.B.), Indiana University Press, 1953.

Doughty, Oswald: *A Victorian Romantic*, 1949 and 1960.

Doughty, Oswald: Letters to F. S. Ellis, 1928.

Dunn, H. T.: *Recollections of D. G. Rossetti and His Circle*, 1904.

Dupré, Henri: *Un Italien d'Angleterre*, Paris, 1921.

Falk, Bernard: *Five Years Dead*, 1938.

Forbes-Robertson, J.: *A Player under three Reigns*, 1925.

Ford Madox Ford: *Ford Madox Brown*, 1896.

Ford Madox Ford: *Ancient Lights*, 1911.

Ford Madox Ford: *Rossetti, a critical Essay*, 1902.

Ford Madox Ford: *The Pre-Raphaelite Brotherhood*, n.d.

G. Gaskell, Mrs.: see Whitehill, Jane.

Gilchrist, H. H.: *Ann Gilchrist*, 1887.

Gray, Nicolette: *Rossetti, Dante and Ourselves*, 1945.

Haight, Gordon: *Letters of George Eliot*, 1955.

Hake, T. Gordon: *Memoirs of Eighty Years*, 1892.

Henderson, Philip: *Letters of William Morris*, 1960.

Horner, Frances: *Time Remembered*, 1933.

Hough, Graham: *The Last Romantics*, 1949.

Howitt, Mary: *An Autobiography*, 1889.

Hunt, Diana Holman: *My Grandmothers and I*, 1961.

Hunt, W. Holman: *Pre-Raphaelitism and the Pre-Raphaelite Brotherhood*, 1905.

Hunt, Violet: *The Wife of Rossetti*, 1932.

Ionides, Luke: *Memories* (privately printed, Paris, 1925).

Knight, Joseph: *Life of D. G. Rossetti*, 1887.

Kretshner, Ernest: *The Psychology of Men of Genius*, 1931.

Litchfield, R. B.: *The beginnings of the Working Men's College.*

Lucas, E. V.: *The Colvins and their Friends*, 1928.

Mackail, J. W.: *Life of William Morris*, 1899.

Marillier, H. C.: *Dante Gabriel Rossetti*, 1901.

Maurer, Oscar: *Morris and Laxdoela Saga* (Texas Studies, Vol. V, No. 3, 1953).

Mégroz, R. L.: *Dante Gabriel Rossetti*, 1928.

Millais, J. G.: *The Life and Letters of Sir John Everett Millais*, 1899.

Mills, Ernestine: *Life of F. Shields*, 1891.

Minto, W. (editor): *Autobiographical Notes of the Life of W. Bell Scott*, 1892.

Morris, May (editor): *Collected Works of William Morris*, 1936.

Nash, Paul: see Bottomley, Gordon.

Packer, Lona M.: *Life of Christina Rossetti* (University of California Press, 1963).

Packer, Lona M.: *The Rossetti-Macmillan Letters* (C.U.P., 1964).

Paden, W. D.: *"La Pia"* (The Register, University of Kansas).

Patmore, Coventry: *Memoirs and Correspondence*, edited by Basil Champneys, 1900.

Pedrick, Gale: *Life with Rossetti*, 1964.

Pennell, E. R. and J.: *Life of Whistler*, 1909.

Quilter, H.: *Preferences in Art, Life and Literature*, 1892.

Reitlinger, Gerald: *The Economics of Taste*, 1961.

Robertson, W. Graham: *Time Was*, 1931.

Rosenberg, John D.: *The Darkening Glass, a portrait of Ruskin's genius*, 1963.

Rossetti, W. M.: *D. G. Rossetti's Family Letters, with a Memoir*, 1895.

Rossetti, W. M.: *Ruskin, Rossetti and Pre-Raphaelitism*, 1899.

Rossetti, W. M.: *Pre-Raphaelite Diaries*, 1900.

Rossetti, W. M.: *Rossetti Papers*, 1903.

Rossetti, W. M.: *Some Reminiscences*, 1906.

Rossetti, W. M. (editor): *Works of D. G. Rossetti*, 1911.

Rothenstein, W.: *Men and Memories*, 1931.

Sambrook, J.: *A Poet Hidden* (R. W. Dixon) 1962.

Savarit, Jacques: *Tendances mystiques et ésoteriques chez D. G. Rossetti*, Paris, 1961.

Scott, W. Bell: see Minto, W.

Sharp, W.: *D. G. Rossetti*, 1882.

Shields, F.: see Mills, E.

Skelton, J.: *Table talk of Shirley*, 1895.

Skottowe, Ian: *Clinical Psychiatry*, 1953.

Smetham, S.: *Letters of James Smetham*, 1891.

Stephens, F. G.: *Dante Gabriel Rossetti*, 1908.

Stevenson, Lionel: *The Ordeal of George Meredith*, 1954.

Stillman, W. J.: *The Autobiography of a Journalist*, 1901.

Swinburne, A. C.: *Letters, edited by Dr. Cecil Lang*, 1962.

Terry, Ellen: *Memoirs*, 1933.

Thompson, E. P.: *William Morris, Romantic to Revolutionary*, 1955.

Tillyard, E. M. W.: *Poetry and its background*, 1470–1870, 1955.

Troxell, J. C.: *Rossetti's Sister Helen* (Yale University Press, 1939).

Troxell, J. C.: *Three Rossettis* (Harvard University Press, 1937).

Tuckwell, Revd. W.: *Reminiscences*, 1907.

Vincent, E. R.: *Gabriele Rossetti in England*, 1936.

Waller, R. D.: *The Rossetti Family*, 1932.

Watts-Dunton, T.: *Old Familiar Faces*, 1916.

Whistler, J. M.: see Pennell, E. R. and J.

Whitehill, J.: *Letters of Mrs. Gaskell and C. E. Norton*, 1932.

Williamson, G. C.: *Murray Marks and his Friends*, 1919.

Woolner, Amy: *Thomas Woolner*, 1917.

INDEX